Robert Vaughn

ROBERT VAUGHN

A Critical Study

John B. Murray

THESSALY PRESS
London

First published in 1987 by:

Thessaly Press
PO Box 130
London
E11 1BP

ISBN 0 9511793 0 6

Printed in Great Britain by
The Chameleon Press Ltd., 5-25 Burr Road,
Wandsworth, London SW18 4SG.

Contents

	Acknowledgements	8
	Introduction	11
1.	Robert Vaughn — A Critical Approach	13
2.	The Screen Persona of Robert Vaughn	18
3.	The Politics of Misery	30
4.	Recurrent Motifs in Robert Vaughn's Screen Work	37
5.	The Thinking Man as Actor — An in-depth analysis of Robert Vaughn as Lee in *The Magnificent Seven*	54
6.	Robert Vaughn's Stylistic Techniques	71
7.	Robert Vaughn as Action Hero and Director — Aspects of *The Man from U.N.C.L.E.*, *The Protectors* and *Police Woman*	101
8.	The Actor as Moral Philosopher — Robert Vaughn as the Nazi Major Paul Kreuger in *The Bridge at Remagen*	118
9.	The Wages of Sin	127
10.	Trends to Resolution	136
	Conclusion	145
	Appendix: A Speech Delivered by Robert Vaughn at Harvard University, Cambridge, Massachusetts on Friday 5 May 1967	149
	Screen Credits	161
	Author's Note	178
	Stills	81-96

Acknowledgements

I wish to thank Robert Vaughn for taking an interest in this critical study while remaining completely independent of its judgements. After reading an early draft of this book, he commented: "In the critical analysis that you do of me, I'm not going to comment on that, because that's what you see. I mean, there's no way I'm going to *argue* about it, because that's what each man sees, each something else." Vaughn is pragmatic about the image people have of him, as he joked with me: "That's why when people say 'Aren't you worried about your image?', I say 'Thank God I have one!' If you don't have one, you don't work. Very often people will say 'Hey, we want a Robert Vaughn type. Is Robert Vaughn available?' That happened to me rather recently. 'And can we afford him?' or something like that."

Thanks also to those of his professional colleagues who contributed to this study and, especially, to John Sturges and Sam Rolfe who read relevant portions, to Susan Arnow for her kindness and to Jerry Pam for all his courtesy.

I would like to thank Mrs. Brenda Poland for the supply of Press clippings over the years, the distinguished critic David Quinlan for credits information, and the staffs of the British Film Institute in London, the Lincoln Center Library of the Performing Arts in New York City and the Screen Actors Guild in Hollywood for research assistance. Stills were located with the help of The Cinema Bookshop and The National Film Archive in London, The Memory Shop in New York City and Collectors Book Store and Larry Edmunds Cinema Bookshop in Hollywood, among others. All film stills in this book are reproduced with the kind permission of the copyright proprietors. I am most grateful to Miss Luciana Paluzzi and Sir John Gielgud for graciously permitting the reproduction of stills. Acknowlegement is also made to the copyright proprietors of all the works discussed in this book.

The greatest debt of all remains, of course, the public's debt to a unique performer, Robert Vaughn, for establishing a new bench-mark of excellence in screen acting and creating an extraordinarily impressive body of work over more than three decades of ceaseless artistic activity in front of and behind the camera, as well as on stage and in print. This critical study should be merely the first step towards a general re-evaluation of his striking artistic achievement.

John B. Murray
London, 1986.

"Robert Vaughn is not what you'd call the sexy star. Gary Cooper was never one. Clark Cable *was*, rightly so because he was an adequate actor. Not as good an actor as Robert Vaughn, but an adequate actor. I think primarily it's his performance that sold Vaughn initially. I do not think it was his great appearance. He wasn't the Gary Cooper type and wasn't a Cary Grant type or the so-called handsome leading man, six-foot-two tall, Robert Taylor pretty boy, nothing like that. It was his performance that was his basic quality . . . an intellectual performance."

Legendary Hollywood talent scout
Maxwell Arnow, who discovered
Robert Vaughn as well as Ronald
Reagan and an endless list of stars.

Introduction

This book comprises a series of critical essays dealing with the film performances of Robert Vaughn, who is not only one of the most powerful American film actors but also one of the most prolific. These essays cover only some of the areas of his work actually seen by the author. Indeed, it is doubtful if anyone can claim to have seen every Vaughn film performance. Even Robert Vaughn never saw all of them. But this book aims to analyse some of the more prominent or interesting performances in celebration of the creativity of his extensive career. Most of his television performances were filmed rather than taped, on occasion by the same directors as he worked for in the cinema, so this book does not limit itself to discussion of his cinema films, which is important as some of his finest work has been done for television.

A popular British critic, Philip Jenkinson, once called Vaughn's work in *The Magnificent Seven* "really underestimated", and perhaps Vaughn's overall achievement as an actor has been popularly underestimated (although his standing among film industry professionals has always been very high). Yet it takes only cursory scrutiny to see that the work shares a sensitivity welling from the artist himself that often achieves philosophical dimensions and occasionally exhibits the closely-knit organisation of poetry.

For Vaughn's best performances have a poetic incisiveness, even in the absence of gravity, which elevates him above such performers with comparable qualities as Robert Walker Snr., Brett Halsey and Pete Duel. That incisiveness is most readily apparent in his unflinching portrayals of the depths of human misery: this very political actor's examination of what shall be termed 'the politics of misery'. Vaughn's colleague John Hackett does not think it is possible to define where theatrical creativity comes from, but he is the first to detect in Vaughn's screen persona "this kind of edge of danger, contained, directed power that allows him to be believable as the cold head of a corporation".

In the first half of his career, Vaughn periodically unleashed an intensity that overwhelmed the spectator in the degree of its passion. It was an intensity that welled up from the quiet young actor in films like *The Magnificent Seven* so unexpectedly that there seemed to be no limit to the dimensions of his talent, to "the colours that were not readily apparent that you could kind of dig for" as Monte Hellman has described to me Vaughn's talent in 1958. But more . . . Vaughn was even then freezing all trace of that passion, to become in time the most cerebral film actor of his time — possibly of all time. Former long-time girlfriend Joyce Jameson has told me that this made him the most brilliant actor in the world, because his refusal to display emotion made the audience feel the emotion on the character's behalf, reading the deepest feeling into Vaughn's over-containment. This book of critical essays attempts, among other things, to highlight examples of how Vaughn refined film acting to the definition of emotion in purely cerebral terms. It also advances serious claims for Vaughn as the finest screen actor of his generation on the basis of an oeuvre that has both extended screen possibilities and enlarged our understanding of the dysthymic condition, thanks to this artist's remarkable ability to pare characters down to essentials, to rationalise away emotions into a series of icily intellectual profiles.

Artistically, this process has borne dividends, enabling Vaughn to render nothing inconsistent in the behaviour of a man like Major Kreuger in *The Bridge at Remagen*, even though depicting his dilemma as a conflict between head (duty) and heart (conscience). For the overriding intellectualism of Kreuger's conduct determines his consistent restraint of outward emotions. Close examination of Vaughn's most intellectual performances such as this and Lee in *The Magnificent Seven* may well lay bare possibilities of seeing the wellsprings of theatrical creativity at work — or, more simply, why Robert Vaughn acts the way he does.

1: Robert Vaughn — A Critical Approach

It is a matter of controversy among even Vaughn's admiring colleagues, but Vaughn's greatness as an actor does seem to reside in his unique approach, or rather in his unique screen *project* as an actor. Vaughn's original guru at Los Angeles City College, Tony Carbone, has elucidated it for me: "The capacity to bring everything down to an intellectual level *is* unique. And that's what he is." Of course, the *best* Vaughn performances have a *dynamism* that arises out of the mechanics of the fluctuation between intellectualism and emotionalism, e.g. Major Kreuger. Tony Carbone believes that fluctuation did come out of the dualisms in Vaughn's own private life, particularly the difficulties with his mother and his girlfriends; and, interestingly, the first phrase that Joyce Jameson used to describe Robert to me was "Jekyll and Hyde", a phrase that another girlfriend, Kathy Ceaton, had used years before. Because for Carbone, every actor is on a precipice. "There is a strain in acting, tremendous strain . . . When Robert gets up there, there's a strain. That strain brings out his self, that self that is conservative." For Carbone, the level of the material makes no difference to the fact that the actor's essential personality is drawn upon when he is "fighting with every part of his being" against that strain, and even *The Man from U.N.C.L.E.* exhibits an acting style that reveals a great deal of actor Robert Vaughn's essential personality.

But Vaughn's *project* as a screen actor covers not only his best performances. When we consider all his performances, one quality emerges paramount. His project as a screen actor almost deliberately seems to be the portrayal of intellectual presence. Engagement with characters' intellect rather than hearts. His later performances particularly (*Brass Target, Battle Beyond the Stars*) seem to present to a greater degree the process of thought. In *The Venetian Affair* he seems to be almost pure thought on celluloid and you can 'read his thoughts' with unusual clarity. It is not just a case of watching him thinking on screen. He seems to have moved into an area where the intellect unadorned by emotional or other factors is becoming his exclusive territory, to the exclusion of all else. This has brought the actor some negative reactions, from those who find themselves impressed but not moved by his performances — this was even true of his very popular performance in *Washington: Behind Closed Doors*.

Yet Joyce Jameson is the first to testify that beneath that degree of overt intellectualism, there is a mass of emotion. And once you understand that he's controlling that emotion (Tony Carbone describes Vaughn as "harbouring of his emotions and fearful of them": "As a human being, he is very warm. He is afraid of it because he can't control it. The reason that he appears to be controlled is that he *attempts* to control it. He desires to control because he's a little afraid of all that stuff within him that may . . . be considered sentimental") — that this wall of intellectualism or coldness is but a front, and can be breached — his performance becomes all the more moving.

Tony Carbone, now a teacher at the American Academy of Dramatic Art, has articulated this very well: "When you can sense continually that underneath this coldness is one who is checking their internal fire for whatever reason, then of course the moment when it approximates that fire driving *out* becomes a brilliant thing. Yes, if Vaughn has anything, it is that uniqueness that shines *through* that intellect. But when that intellect is by itself, it doesn't mean anything. When that intellect is driven with the total human being, that is to say, *body, mind* and *soul,* then it's brilliant. And he's done some brilliant work."

This is why Vaughn's performances have a power not to be found in any other actor. It gives Kreuger a greater sense of power being checked in the scene where at the end of his tether he nearly erupts and then checks it, *and a greater feeling for the character comes across.* This containment of great emotion, which Carbone and others have detected in Vaughn's own personality *in relation to people he did not know well,* is a valuable contribution to the enlargement of our understanding of screen possibilities. This is a very valuable, specific, stylistic advance Vaughn has proferred. Of course, his career as a whole has made a wider contribution. In the delineation of the typical homo Vaughnianus, he made a contribution to our understanding of the human condition under stress. His exploration of the less joyful sides of human personality enriches our understanding of ourselves in the experience of intellectual and emotional crises (whether reacting against the brutality of Edward Campbell in *Good Day for a Hanging* or sympathising with the plight of Luke Martin in *The Way Station* episode of *Bonanza*).

Of course, the reasons for Vaughn's arriving at such a unique screen project need not be in themselves admirable. Tony Carbone thinks that his career has suffered from a "fear of failure", with the result that Vaughn has also done some work that is "dreadful" by comparison with what Carbone knows Vaughn is capable of. While Carbone acknowledges that Vaughn operates with "much more conscious deliberation" than Ralph Bellamy attributes to the acting style of his father Walter Vaughn, he has a reservation about Robert's style that goes right back to the days when he first directed him at Los Angeles City College in *Mr. Roberts,* a reservation that was also behind Monte Hellman's disagreement with his admittedly superb performance in the play *The Great God Brown.* Carbone explains: "I don't mean to imply he didn't search, but a lot of actors rely on what they know about themselves that works. Robert does that. In spite of the fact that he can search until he comes to the moment of truth, he relies on what he knows. And *perfects* what he knows. If there *is* a problem, it is that if I intend to search out through improvisation its significance to me, I must then involve myself not just here (head) but here (heart). Now I could go through a process of improvisation with my mind and be able to establish its meaning but its meaning is *abstract*. When I commit myself to improvisation not knowing where I'm going, then I'm going to experience revelation. If there is a problem, it is that Robert would invest himself intellectually and from that intellectual investment, what can you arrive at? It's an axiom that cannot be denied: if you invest that (head), then you're going to get that from it. If you invest this (heart), you're going to get this from it . . . If I invest myself in *every* way, I don't know what I'm going to get. You see, not knowing is lack of control. Lack of control is not what Robert ever wanted."

Yet the very heart of Carbone's disagreement with Vaughn's style — also the reason that fellow actor Jonathan Haze has criticised Vaughn's performance in *Teenage Caveman* — rests on the assumption that the creation of *abstract* values is a project that doesn't "arrive" at anything or that does not by itself "mean anything". The prime thrust of this book is that the abstract values that Vaughn *distils* through a highly analytical screen process in such movies as *The Magnificent Seven* and *The Bridge at Remagen* are the very essence of his greatness. To distil moral heroism and existential freedom from stock characters such as the gunsmith Lee and the Nazi Major Kreuger as written (and Sam Rolfe, creator of *The Man from U.N.C.L.E.*, once joked with me that it was a toss-up between Robert Vaughn and James Mason to be cast as the next stock German General, this being a little while before the death of James Mason and the casting of Vaughn in precisely such a stock role in the television film *Inside the Third Reich*), to the degree that the values become abstract ones — that the values are *abstracted* from the mundane surroundings of the fictional film, dignifying these values with the purity of cold logic — is surely to universalise the problems these particular characters face. And by that universalisation to give them relevance to an ever wider audience, to whom they come to symbolise and clarify problems in their own lives. Certainly Vaughn's very best work does this, although much of his work never approaches that level. But enough of it is at that level of broader relevance for the importance of the construction of *abstract* values to be demonstrated. Herein lies the ultimate value of Vaughn's unique screen project. Vaughn is no less on a precipice than Carbone's emotionally free actor: it is just a different precipice. Vaughn risks falling into pools of abstraction from which he can distil no values (*Brass Target, Last Salute to the Commodore*) but can at other times dignify an almost impossible task, to give life to an abstraction such as cowardice, even when the part itself is only being written the night before shooting, as was the case when Vaughn had to prepare for playing Lee in *The Magnificent Seven* without benefit of a script.

While Lee is the definitive example of Vaughn giving life to an abstraction such as cowardice, the process was already at work even in his very first featured role in the cinema as Bob Ford, the man who shot Jesse James, who was played by Henry Brandon, in the Republic Pictures Western *Hell's Crossroads*. Henry Brandon told me of his surprise at seeing Vaughn's performance on screen, particularly the scene where he is shot by Vaughn: "When he shot me, I was up on a chair trimming the Christmas tree. We had quite a long scene, during which he was preparing to kill me, of which I was totally unaware because we were the best of friends (in the film). So it was shot, printed, and I had no idea what he was doing while I was up there with my back turned. When I went to see the picture, he'd done what was probably the most effective thing in the film. His indecision and his cowardice were very vivid. He took the gun out covertly and then it took him most of the scene to get up the courage to pull the trigger, and his hands were shaking violently as he did it. And it was tremendously effective on the screen. I had had no idea what was going on, but it *was* the best thing in the picture. The best *moment* was his fear and indecision. I'm *sure* that he had no instructions to do that. I'm sure that was his preparation." Brandon put Vaughn's playing on a par with Porter Hall shooting Gary Cooper in *The Plainsman*! Brandon was also impressed that Vaughn walked off with the best review in *Variety*: "They loved his performance. I think this is significant, to make your first movie and get the best review. Says something for the future."

Of course, some audiences might be tempted to think that there are *two* Robert Vaughns: the television artisan and the cinema artist of *The Young Philadelphians, The Magnificent Seven, The Venetian Affair, The Bridge at Remagen,* etc. While this distinction has some superficial validity, it is not an accurate representation. It is closer to the truth, while not yet the whole truth, to say that there is only *one* Vaughn and the apparent dichotomy in the quality of *his* work (as distinct from the quality of the finished article, which is out of his control) *is* only apparent. For the actor's performance simply breathes life into the materials presented to him as that day's work. Marc Daniels, who directed such superior *U.N.C.L.E.* episodes as *The Finny Foot Affair* and *The Love Affair*, has told me that Vaughn on set was "imaginative, conscientious, and willing to go to any lengths to 'get it right'". Where those materials will accommodate such qualities as intellectual complexity and passionate feeling, Vaughn will prove outstanding. Note particularly producer Douglas Benton's comment on Vaughn's soured idealist Simms in *Police Woman — Blast*: "What makes Vaughn such a superior actor is that he can understand that type of personality and project it."

Where the material allows no scope for excellence, which is the case of some of his television work in his mature years playing villains and corrupt power figures, Vaughn simply does what is required of him. Or so it seems to critics of the likes of the less effective episodes of *The Protectors*. Yet the whole truth is something different. Because, for those alerted by the performances of obvious quality, the apparently routine performances become almost equally rich on close scrutiny. The richness may well be *periodically* equal but the difference in the routine appearances is that it is not sustained. It breaks through the stock written characterisation, cliched dialogue and dull direction with rewarding glimpses of power, but is soon again submerged. One of the clearest examples of this occurs in the television film *The Woman Hunter*.

The point, though, remains that there is an almost equal degree of value among both quality and routine Vaughn performances. Almost equal, at any rate, for those alerted by the likes of *The Bridge at Remagen* and *Police Woman — Blast* and prepared to recognise the more secret signs of Vaughn's power, as *momentarily* unleashed in the likes of *Kiss Me, Kill Me* or *Nightmare at*

Pendragon's Castle. While it is obviously essential to apply a wholly different set of criteria in critically approaching a film like *The Bridge at Remagen* and an episode of a lightweight series like *The Feather and Father Gang*, there is enough equality of accomplishment in terms of *pure* screen acting for the proposition that there are two Robert Vaughns to be proved false. There are simply two modes in which the same actor's gifts find expression, the one obvious, the other oblique. Given the exceptional dynamism of the former in the classic films he has made, it is all too easy to overlook or underestimate the latter. In Vaughn's case, this is a very dangerous practice, as for every routine *Police Woman — Generation of Evil* episode, there may be an outstanding *Police Woman — Blast* episode, and those were two episodes of the same television series! And, in the light of *Blast*, new values can be detected in *Generation of Evil*. Robert Vaughn simply demands expansion not only of critical categories and methodologies but also of audience expectations *and* responses to what they may only *think* they are watching.

2: The Screen Persona Of Robert Vaughn

Robert Vaughn is a prime contender for what André Bazin called an aesthetic cult of personality. This one time 'Most Popular Actor in America' is to some extent another axiom of the cinema: at least to the extent that writers like Pauline Kael have used his name as a form of journalistic shorthand for a certain cinematic type. This appreciation examines the uniqueness of Vaughn's achievement, particularly in terms of his technique and its effect, and more generally in terms of his axiomatic contribution to the repertoire of cinematic types by coherently elaborating an identifiable homo Vaughnianus, the protagonist of Vaughnian values in whatever setting (e.g. *Modern Screen* referring to Vaughn's Bill Fenner in *The Venetian Affair* as "a bitter man — more like the roles Bob played before *U.N.C.L.E.*"). This does involve consideration of the actor as auteur (and Douglas Benton has told me of Vaughn's power virtually to create a character as he interprets it) but we are more interested here in attempting to delineate the extraordinary qualities in his work, to try and set its cinematic and social relevance in perspective.

For as the work of a great American screen actor should, Vaughn's oeuvre can be readily seen to embrace some of the classic themes of the American cinema: the difficulties of the individual's integration with the collective (*The Loner*), caught (*Moral Dilemma*) between fear of death (*Existential Terror*) and the longing for security (*The Yearning for Affection*), willing to use all his gifts (*The Omnipotence of Charm*) to avoid isolation (*Rejection in Love*) and even prepared to risk all (*Qualifying Test of Manhood*), even if it involves betrayal of those most dear (*Test of Loyalty*), rather than submit to the inevitable (*Tragic Fate*). But his valiant efforts avail him little (*The Loser*). If he is not effectively destroyed (Root in *No Time to Be Young*, Lee, Kreuger), his very efforts to win have taken their toll and are a constant reminder of his precarious individualism: the bitterness of Harry Rule or Bill Fenner is typical.

Vaughn's dualism (even if only the dichotomy between the effect of his melancholy eyes and the effect of his readily smiling mouth) brings an ambiguity to the characters he plays: if heroes they can be remote, bitter or cold-hearted, and if villains they can be sympathetic or attractively sinister. Many of Vaughn's characters are highly ambivalent because in the sensitivity of his portrayals he has not flinched from portraying the complex set of oppositions at work within one man (Kreuger, Lee, Rule, Solo, etc.): heart vs. head, good vs. evil, action vs. passivity, will vs. nature, courage vs. fear, failure vs. success, friendship vs. loneliness, life vs. death, etc. Because Vaughn either makes moral judgement of his characters virtually impossible (Kreuger, Solo) or, if it is clear-cut, manages to cajole the viewer into voluntarily suspending it (Chalmers, Simms), sometimes shocking him into doing so (the finales of *The Protectors — Chase* and *Clay Pigeon*), he sets up a series of antinomies between the charm of virtue and the charisma of evil.

Those characters who are Vaughn heroes imbued with the omnipotence of charm (Napoleon Solo par excellence) represent a set of values directly in opposition to those of characters who are Vaughn villains and losers besides: this basic opposition neatly divides into two screen syndromes, in which the respective polarities of human behaviour are clearly delineated in Vaughn's tender mercy as on the one hand the charm of virtue and on the other the charisma of evil. Loosely, these may be dubbed 'the icon syndrome' (exponents of which must be at least heroic, debonair or tongue-in-cheek, though not necessarily more than one of these things) and 'the eminence grise syndrome' (exponents of which must be at least villainous, depressive or excessively brusque, though not necessarily more than one).

The amazing thing about Vaughn is the ease with which, in a performance like his Andrew Simms in *Police Woman — Blast*, the charm of virtue and the charisma of evil become quite indistinguishable. Simms' childlike belief in the almost spiritual value of affluence (he thinks his life to have been worthwhile because he is dying in a room with a carpet), reflected in his appearance and property-owning pipedreams, is maintained by viciousness and murder: innocence vies with guilt and debonair Simms, a highly compelling figure, is as much an exponent of the icon syndrome as of the eminence grise syndrome. Walter Chalmers in *Bullitt* is a vital example of Vaughn's dialectic between the two. Even as early as *Good Day for a Hanging*, Vaughn presented in Edward "The Kid" Campbell a character whose latent viciousness qualified him for the eminence grise syndrome but whose baby-faced charm also afforded him good standing in the icon syndrome.

There is no need to mention how easily Vaughn has gone from an extreme example of one syndrome in one film to an extreme example of the other in his next: what is most astonishing is his ability to effect such transitions so smoothly *within* one dramatically coherent screen performance.

To pick on a rapid fluctuation (made very obvious for the purpose of comedy) from one syndrome to the other and back again, let us take the television interview with Whiteley (Vaughn) and Bolt (David Niven) in *The Statue*. When they go on the air, Whiteley is well-groomed, well-heeled, smiling charmingly and referring to "my friend Alex Bolt". Once they go off the air for a commercial break, the angered Whiteley assumes full eminence grise proportions, becoming suddenly egotistical, excessively brusque, with a severe expression and rude language: "Forget about the sculpture crap. What the hell are you trying to do Alex, make me out to be schmuck?. . . Will you quit talking about yourself for a moment, we're dealing with something important, ME!. . . now will you butt out. . ."

Then the moment they go back on the air again, Whiteley immediately reassumes iconic stature, angelically addressing the viewers: "Gee, Alex, it's good to talk to you again. Now this is a man that I'm proud to call friend. . ."

Of course, Vaughnian fluctuations are rarely as readily detectable as this, which only arose out of the technology governing the situation (the on/off nature of television transmission). More usual in Vaughnian characters is the momentary flare-up of annoyance (e.g. Rule with Ilona when he learns she has made a telephone call from the airport in *The Protectors — Border Line*, thereby possibly jeopardising their mission) that confirms even the nicest and most iconic of Vaughnian heroes to have proclivities towards the eminence grise syndrome (e.g. Solo's threat to perform "a very messy frontal lobotomy" on a prisoner in *The Arabian Affair*). A counterbalancing tenderness after such a moment of anger (e.g. when Rule counterbalances his definition of Ilona as "a great actress" with the addition "And a good person") often completes the fluctuation.

Even this is rather too demonstrative an example, however, to portray accurately those extremely subtle fluctuations between the syndromes that Vaughn's style at its most elliptical effects when a character begins to merge the charm of virtue with the charisma of evil. These extremely fleeting and usually impossible to pinpoint — given rise to perhaps by a typically elliptical action such as a momentary narrowing of the eyes — but successive and numerically endless fluctuations may well be the prime source of the dynamism of Vaughn's basic screen presence. Certainly they account for the mysterious ambiguity of so many of his characters.

Vaughn's basic screen presence, then, is an endless fluctuation between the two syndromes he has thoroughly mastered. Only with very limiting, one-dimensional scripts has he remained entirely within one syndrome. Not even as cursory a role as Senator Gary Parker in *The Towering Inferno* is entirely within the icon syndrome in that Vaughn instils a natural pomposity and insincerity, possibly even loneliness, into the obviously ambitious character that edges him towards the eminence grise syndrome. The main effects of this fluctuation are to add complexity, an air of mystery and, above all, ambivalence to the characters Vaughn depicts.

Any attempt to define Vaughn's screen persona must, when analysing resonances in Vaughn's career, take account of which syndrome they represent and how much (or how little) they are an admixture of the two. If Vaughn's basic screen presence can be summarised as the dialectic between the icon and eminence grise syndromes, specific moments in his work will either typify or vary this dialectic, enlarging our understanding of Vaughn's screen persona. On one memorable occasion, a certain resonance first typified and then varied Vaughn's screen presence, though Vaughn was not aware of this until I asked him how conscious he had been of it. It involved actress Luciana Paluzzi, to whom he points out he was attracted.

In *To Trap a Spy*, the luscious Angela (Luciana Paluzzi) takes Solo home, so that he can meet agent Lancer. He wryly asks: "So I'm not to get any ideas about you bringing me here?" She amusedly replies: "I didn't say that!" Once inside, she asks what she should change into, he replies "Oh . . . anything . . .

but a boy" and the seduction commences. This sexual resonance firmly belongs to the icon syndrome. Yet, moments later as the lovers get dressed, Solo's discovery of Lancer's papers and immediate recognition of her treachery — indeed, of the necessity of her death if he is to save himself — cause him to become cold, hard and brutal ("I enjoyed you in return . . . so we're equal . . . we don't owe each other anything . . . do we?"). His behaviour puzzles and alienates Angela, who then prepares to have him killed: alienation of feeling is a prime condition for a Vaughnian character (Chet Gwynne in *The Young Philadelphians*, Chalmers, Simms when he slaps Pepper's face in anger) coming to represent the eminence grise syndrome. In this brief sequence, Solo thus makes the transition right from one syndrome to the other. Its resonance as a whole typifies Vaughn's screen presence.

But later in Vaughn's career that resonance is recalled to provide a variation on Vaughn's screen presence. The performers of the above, Robert Vaughn and Luciana Paluzzi, find themselves in *The Venetian Affair* in a (so it seems) deliberate inversion of the earlier resonance. (Amazingly, though, director Jerry Thorpe told me he had never seen *To Trap a Spy*!) Just as Solo had already been established as a debonair charmer (notably in his flirtation with Gracie on the plane) prior to the above scene of transition, so *The Venetian Affair* had already established Fenner as its eminence grise: a failure at his job, an alcoholic, unable to look after himself, despised by both current and former employer, and incapable of happiness. Solo was taken to her bedroom by Angela; Fenner has Giulia come up to his room with the file. Angela dropped hints to Solo and let herself be seduced; Fenner drops hints to Giulia who rejects him. For Solo the politics of ecstasy, for Fenner the politics of misery. Certainly this scene is significant, not only in the light of Vaughn's previous cinematic success with Luciana Paluzzi, but also by contrast with all the other smooth successes of his large and small screen career. Not for that reason, however, is its resonance a variation on Vaughn's screen presence, but rather because Fenner, who will eventually regain a certain pride when reunited with his wife, does in the graciousness of his smile at Giulia's ability to stand up for herself negate the hangdog air of melancholy that alienates his colleagues. This alienation diminished, Fenner takes leave of the eminence grise syndrome but is still too scarred a man for Vaughn to let him pass into the icon syndrome. And, sure enough, by the end of the film Fenner's bitterness over his wife's death has him alienating his colleagues once again ("Go to hell, Rosie" he tells Rosenfeld) and wandering back alone in the final seconds to the dominion of the eminence grise syndrome.

For the middle section of the film, then, Vaughn's characterisation of Fenner belongs to one syndrome no more comfortably than to the other. Nor is it accountable as an admixture. Rather Fenner inhabits a twilight zone in which the character's very nobility *is* sensitivity to defeat. The former negates the alienation of the eminence grise syndrome and the latter negates the charm of the icon syndrome. Here is not a case of the charm of virtue lapsing into the charisma of evil (or vice versa) and resulting in an ambivalent character. Here the very syndromes they represent have themselves become indistinguishable within a very depressing nobility.

Misery, not ambivalence, is Fenner's hallmark. Yet this misery is not without its heroic aspect. Such Vaughn characters as are adept at steering a course between the two syndromes are politicians of misery whose nobility consists in making themselves more adequate by recognising as personal inadequacies what in others less sensitive would be virtues. The very depressing aspect comes in the subsequent need to fend off that feeling of inadequacy with various local anaesthetics such as alcohol (Chet Gwynne, Lee, Fenner, Bergen in *The Mind of Mr. Soames* and Senator Stratton in *The Islander*) or total dedication to work (Harry Rule).

The politics of misery are thus occasioned when Vaughn's perpetual fluctuation between the two syndromes is allayed by the two cancelling each other out. Vaughn can thus render indistinguishable the polarities of human conduct themselves within one of his performances. Naturally, the resonances that fall within neither syndrome but within their cancellation of each other which is the domain of the politics of misery are not in a state of fluctuation but one of stasis: for this reason Lee's first and final leap into action at the end comes as such a shock (firmly within the eminence grise syndrome at the start, Lee goes through his night of fear which is nothing other than the transition via the politics of misery towards the heroic status of the opposite syndrome which his final action achieves). Vaughn's elliptical style of film acting makes him the perfect actor for rendering this stasis.

So far we have noted that the fluctuation between the two syndromes typifies Vaughn's screen presence. The politics of misery (exemplified by Fenner's highly depressing nobility) end that fluctuation inasmuch as they are the mutual cancellation of the syndromes and are therefore a variation on Vaughn's screen presence. Here it must also be noted that in some cases (Lee as mentioned above) the politics of misery are not simply a limbo into which characters pass when they leave one syndrome and are not qualified to enter another, and from which they return to their own syndrome after a while (as Fenner notably does). They can also be the intermediate stage of *transition* from one syndrome to the other. Below are examples of transitions each way:

THE YOUNG PHILADELPHIANS

FROM	VIA	TO
Icon Syndrome	Politics of Misery	Eminence Grise Syndrome
Chet in his tuxedo at the party	Loss of his arm in Korea	Disgusting spectacle of the figure in jail

THE MAGNIFICENT SEVEN

FROM	VIA	TO
Eminence Grise Syndrome	Politics of Misery	Icon Syndrome
Lee's past villainy, his remoteness, cowardice, alcoholism	Cold sweat of his terrifying dream and subsequent self-disgust	Heroic status of his return to Ixcatlan and honour-bound behaviour

The two Luciana Paluzzi resonances adduced above have shown how moments from Vaughn's career can either typify or vary his basic screen presence. It would be tedious to make an extensive list of moments here and demonstrate how far they each typify or vary his screen presence and hence accord each a relative significance for Vaughn's screen persona. So if the reader will trust this critic's choice of the most significant moments from Vaughn's career, we may proceed to a quite arbitrary synthesis of significant Vaughnian resonances. Thence will emerge a more general view of the homo Vaughnianus than from our analysis of the fluctuating Vaughnian screen presence and its periodic cessation into the politics of misery. This more general view in fact constitutes Vaughn's screen persona.

The homo Vaughnianus is painfully aware of inhabiting a world where the relationship between cause and effect is, if not mysterious, at best rather tenuous. Fenner finds he is not in Venice for the reasons he thought and is caught in a maze of perplexing events (such as the hanging of two of Vaugiroud's men) because of his past with Sandra: and why should she give him new life only to die herself? Lee goes to Ixcatlan to escape death, only finally to accept it there: an absurd causal nexus. Kreuger's premonition of his fate in the roadside execution scene betrays a universe of implacable determinism that no amount of diligence can deter and which is mysteriously beyond his ken: the failure of the explosive is one example. Bergen's humanitarianism does not prove the salvation of John Soames (even if Dr. Maitland's disciplinarianism certainly could not be) and only results in Soames injuring him badly (the pitchfork in his arm). Caesar will not die at Casca's first blow. Harry Rule lives in a world of perpetual deception and mistrust, peopled by characters who are not what they seem.

Faced with a cruel, mystifying universe all the harder to bear for a man of his acute sensitivity and lucid rationality, the homo Vaughnianus either retreats into himself like Lee or tackles it head on in seemingly suicidal fashion (Vaughn once said of Napoleon Solo: "Sometimes I think he's insane"). Occasionally the means he adopts are even more cruel than the world in which he is trying to assert himself: in *Clay Pigeon*, Neilson beats young Tracy and has her given a massive overdose of heroin. But be he introverted and dubious of his own personal value (Chet Gwynne, Lee) or extroverted and exultant either in his corruption (Chalmers, Neilson) or in his refusal to be corrupted (Solo in such scenes as his refusal to become the 'eighth wonder' for Kingsley in *How to Steal the World*), the homo Vaughnianus will ever evoke an admiration, however grudging, of his courageous — frequently tragic — refusal to compromise. The boldness of his individualism goes way past foolhardiness, but it is precisely its often costly (see the tragic fate motif) extremism that ordinary men must admire.

And it is precisely this refusal to compromise (in Rule's case by remarrying, in Fenner's by pretending to be engaged in life, in Simms' by admitting the futility of his ambitions and abandoning them) that makes the homo Vaughnianus slightly irrational, indeed slightly dangerous, by the mediocre standards of a well-integrated citizenship. This accounts for Vaughn's so often having portrayed those at odds with society either legally (villains) or socially (loners). Vaughn's dislike of playing Chet Gwynne may be traced to the fact that Chet is not, in this one crucial regard, a typical example of the homo Vaughnianus: he is too weak to resist compromise (already decimated by the failure of his marriage, upon losing his arm he reverts to total emotional dependency and lets himself be manipulated by his family).

One cannot pardon this mediocrity as cowardice. That splendid example of the homo Vaughnianus, Lee, was himself more deeply in the grip of cowardice yet refused to let it compromise his life, even if death was the only definitive way of avoiding such mediocrity: a self-sacrifice it would take a homo Vaughnianus not to see as in any way irrational. As André Breton put it: "the man who, forewarned that all others before him have failed, refuses to admit defeat, sets off from whatever point he chooses, along any other path save a reasonable one, and arrives wherever he can". Vaughn's most magnificent loser, Kreuger, would have won Breton's approbation on account of his 'unreasonable' humanitarianism and catastrophically individualistic flouting of orders.

In any event, it is the threat this individualism poses that makes the Vaughn villain an exponent of the eminence grise syndrome and edges the Vaughn hero closer thereto, even if he be too admirable to pass beyond the politics of misery (as is the case with Fenner). To put this point in different terms, if Vaughn's portrayals have a convincing complexity, it is in no small degree due to the fact that even in the good men he has played he has insinuated — through the gravity of his presence — with Wellesian flourish that 'touch of evil' which offsets their virtue enough to delineate it more clearly (e.g. the ruthless authoritarianism of Kreuger or of Crawford in *City in Fear*); while his bad men have in the ineradicable charisma of his playing always elicited a certain sympathy even if only on behalf of the cruelty of their not undeserved fate. Vaughn has told me that this has always been his intention, to show other aspects of the characters he plays on the basis that "Hitler and Stalin loved children and animals."

The precariousness of his lifestyle lends to the homo Vaughnianus an aura of romanticism that proves highly alluring to the opposite sex. Hence Solo's seductive skill, Rule's casually gliding Susan (played by cultish continental film actress Margaret Lee) into his bedroom at the end of *The Numbers Game*, etc. Yet, in the long run, women sense the self-destructiveness of his life and their instinct tells them to fly. Sandra left Fenner without even saying goodbye. Harry Rule's wife Laura took his son and put 5,000 miles between them, changing her name and trying to forget him (as she explained in *With a Little Help from My Friends*). His talent for one-night stands (the early episodes of *The Man from U.N.C.L.E.*) is at the expense of an ability to cultivate a deep relationship (Stratton's marriage has broken up in *The Islander*; Crawford's is undergoing great strain in *City in Fear*). Too intelligent not to recognise this deficiency, he experiences, as we have seen, a permanent yearning for affection which — and this is his tragedy — his basic instability will forever deny him. And in the crucible of his own isolation, he becomes soluble in thought (e.g. Fenner's poetic recitation, Neilson's bizarre poetic composition).

Engaging less and less with the real world, more and more with his own psyche, frequently with the aid of alcohol (*The Young Philadelphians, The Magnificent Seven, The Venetian Affair, The Mind of Mr. Soames, The Islander*), the homo Vaughnianus lives his life increasingly according to the mandates of the politics of misery by scorning conventional value judgements (good and evil, the polar syndromes) to live a life closer to the actualisation of his heart's desires (be it the humanitarianism of Kreuger or Bergen, the promiscuity of Solo, the lust for power of Chalmers, etc.).

Hence, Vaughn's screen persona is one of commitment to values natural to a man sensitive to the vagaries of fate. The homo Vaughnianus is conscious of the incomprehensibility of events, particularly the mysteries of love, and eternally baffled by the nature of his isolation from other men (which is precisely this self-consciousness). Baffled also by the reasons for his romantic failure (which are precisely his inability to *accept* love without questioning it: witness Fenner's mistrust of Sandra in the moments before her death), he responds with a wild despair (Lee's suicide; Kreuger's shooting the deserters) in an irrational attempt to outdo the strangehold of loveless rationality by extreme adherence to respectable social codes: the above mentioned humanitarianism of Kreuger and Bergen, Jim Melford's fears for his marriage in *The Caretakers*, the materialistic Charles Clay's fears for the reputation of his business in *Last Salute to the Commodore*, Klaus Everard's desire to win his father's love and esteem in *The Big Show* etc. If the values themselves are very conservative ones (love, security, respectability, the assertion of personal value), 'conservative' is the last word one could apply to the homo Vaughnianus' passionately intense, often wildly inappropriate devotion to realising them. One recalls Andrew Simms' totally unreal ambitions to begin with.

Unsurprisingly, the homo Vaughnianus becomes an axiom of the stylishness which refusal to surrender one's individualism accords, and accords quite indiscriminately to well-meaning straights (Solo) and sinister villains (Neilson in *Clay Pigeon*). Through the dignity of all his characters, including the villains and failures, Vaughn has tellingly depicted, with frequent insight into tragedy, the ineffable value of every individual's life. In his great performances (Lee, Fenner, Kreuger, to name only three) the questions Vaughn raises about the meaning of an individual's life take on all the greater urgency for his action being pitted against the stark backdrop of a hostile, seemingly meaningless order of events. Not even the quite understandable lapses into the politics of misery can diminish this stylishness, being only the price the homo Vaughnianus must pay for protecting his own raison d'etre. That the homo Vaughnianus, even in the depths of the politics of misery, is of far greater fascination than his contemporaries is a proposition requiring no further proof.

In interview, Vaughn has emphasised to me his tremendous vulnerability to humour and silliness. His close friend and colleague John Hackett has also told me of the jaunty, eccentric humour Vaughn has manifested on stage, though rarely on film. It is worth briefly commenting that on a few occasions Vaughn has presented this persona on film, notably in *Clay Pigeon*, where he greatly embellished the scripted character Neilson.

This tendency also arises in more normal scripts, where Vaughn does not seem able to take a role too seriously, e.g. his King Darius in the cheap-looking *Daniel in the Lions Den*, where he exhibited a campness in the scenes where he had to embrace his beloved Daniel before sending him into the den of lions, mainly by means of a manic gleam in the eye. It was also apparent in the sexually rampant Pendragon in *Nightmare in Pendragon's Castle*, pilot for *The Eddie Capra Mysteries*. Pendragon's death was played by Vaughn in a comically exaggerated fashion (it also aped Lee's death posture, which had earlier been aped in *The Spy With My Face* where Vaughn slid unconscious down the frontage of masseuse Donna Michelle; later, he revamped Lee himself, comically, for *Battle Beyond the Stars*). "One day", said Max Arnow, who discovered Vaughn, "they'll discover Robert Vaughn as a comedian". In the meantime, a couple of scenes in *One Spy Too Many* highlight the comedic potential of the mobility of Vaughn's facial expression: his grimacing and eye-popping when being throttled by Ingo's bar, and his distasteful expression when Tracy kisses Illya at the end.

Indeed, in one of his very few film comedies to make use of his comic talents (though he appeared in drag in the black comedy *S.O.B.* he remained serious), *The Statue*, Vaughn was most effective, even if the film was not. A 'penis' comedy, *The Statue* features Vaughn as the second male lead in a role only notable for being another political one, as the U.S. Ambassador to the Court of St. James's, Ray Whiteley. Thanks to Watergate, *The Statue* has in retrospect assumed a special irony, particularly in the first scene at Whiteley's office at the Embassy where the camera frames Whiteley, who is using Alex Bolt's invention Unispeak as a way to get to the White House and with mock humility claims "If called, I shall serve", on the right of a large portrait of President Richard Nixon hanging in the background. Not only does Whiteley's cynicism (he refers to "this Unispeak crap", has Chuck arrange a hotel room so he can seduce a married woman and kisses the American eagle plaque in counterpoint to Chuck's criticism of his lustful desire to "serve") contrast with such obvious displays of patriotism as the American flag by his desk and the Nixon portrait, an object that would now represent a greater cynicism in its owner than Whiteley's, but Nixon's orders to Whiteley to do a cover-up job on the statue (literally, with a fig leaf) amusingly foreshadow the most famous cover-up that came a couple of years later.

Vaughn agreed with me that *The Statue* was one of his lesser-known pictures: "Yeah. Well, I thought it was a funny idea, albeit dirty, that they had done, and David Niven did also, and Rodney Amateau was a well-known comedy director. It didn't *work*, that's all. Everybody goes into almost every picture, *if not* every picture, with the highest expectations of making it work. We all did that, and it didn't work. It was awful. I only saw it once in a screening room and it never appeared again anywhere." Vaughn laughed at the thought.

Although *The Statue* offers Vaughn a poorer role than did *The Mind of Mr. Soames*, he manages to make it a more satisfying appearance. There is an idiosyncratic touch in the character's feverish use of 'worry beads' when faced by a problem, foreshadowing the eccentricity Vaughn would display in *Clay Pigeon*. It is a sexier and more forthright appearance than is usual for Vaughn, e.g. the bedroom scene with Mrs. Southwick at the Hilton, the close-up of his buttocks at the steam bath, the sprawling on the couch with Rhonda and much coarse language ("ass", "crap"). The screenplay often descends to a crude level: in reply to "If you were to put it to her. . .", Whiteley, who has tried unsuccessfully to seduce Rhonda, remarks "I tried and she put it back".

Although Vaughn is not as well used in the film as he might have been, still the Vaughn student finds several interesting moments, e.g. the Japanese restaurant scene with Whiteley trying to charm Rhonda (a scene reminiscent of the geisha house scene in *The Karate Killers*), comic moments of discomfort when he sits awkwardly on his ankle after passing food to Rhonda by mouth and when she later collapses in hilarity with her full weight onto his leg as he lounges on the couch (scenes comparable to Charles Clay's discomfort in Mac's sports car and beneath Columbo's telephone wire in *Last Salute to the Commodore*), his final appearance in a top hat and morning dress at the unveiling ceremony (morning dress is rare in Vaughn's career: one thinks only of Rule's top hatted impersonation of Van the rich American gambler at Ascot in *King Con*, and Charles Desmond's top hatted riding scenes with Joseph Armagh in *Captains and the Kings — Part Three*). Whiteley is undoubtedly what we will term a 'wages of sin' character in that he has benefitted through corruption (the nude statue of him at the end being his final comeuppance), though a light and comic one, with a ruthlessness and nastiness only hinted at, and typical of Vaughn's post-Chalmers performances, with the added fillip of Vaughn's eccentric humour, which is seen to best advantage in *Clay Pigeon*.

Laced with prurient sex, strong language and vicious violence, *Clay Pigeon* had moments of pure cinema dotted around Vaughn's strangely humorous performance as speed merchant McCoy, cover name Henry Neilson, whom Margaret Hinxman (London's *Sunday Telegraph*) called "a comic strip Genghis Khan". Vaughn's ironic, tongue-in-cheek interpretation is beguiling, for he makes little attempt to have the audience take him seriously, even though the film is no comedy. So he camps up the character with eccentric clothes (funny caps worn indoors, bermuda shorts, track suit, a parrot on his shoulder a la Long John Silver, etc.) and strange behaviour.

This approach leads to two genuinely amusing scenes, one in which he insists that his subordinate Simon (played by Ivan Dixon, later a director of shows like *The Rockford Files*) play pool according to his rules, stressing that he can take as long as he likes to count to three because it is his pool table; the other in which he composes pretentious poetry in a mini-jungle he keeps in an indoor greenhouse because twenty minutes a day is good "for the mental energies", a sentiment Vaughn delivers with great seriousness and with a great parrot on his shoulder!

Perhaps this amusing eccentricity does defuse the tasteless viciousness of the role, involving the nasty deaths of the girls Tracy, Saddle and Angeline. In mock self-concern, he puts in ear-plugs before the shotgun is used and after Angeline's back is blown off comments to gunman Simon, rather callously, "Well-bowled!"; all of which contrasts oddly with Neilson's initially gentle conversation with Tracy before her death (a paternalism reflecting the fact that he has a 14 year old daughter named Denise, of whom Tracy reminded him) and his love of birds, plants and poetry. The latter interest, of course, conflicts amusingly with the character's foul mouth, which produces the coarsest language Vaughn had ever spoken on screen ("How the Christ do I know?". . . ". . . and you stand round here with a pool cue up your ass" . . . "Get him, you dumb bastards") which, incidentally, reflects the increase in the dominance of Vaughn's screen authority (note the viciousness with which he shouts "Move!"), reaching its culmination in the days of *Washington: Behind Closed Doors*.

If Neilson does not gell, it is still a striking appearance by the former Napoleon Solo (and may well reflect a difficulty for Vaughn at that time in getting more mainstream Hollywood film work through overfamiliarity from the *U.N.C.L.E.* series) and certain scenes are very memorable, notably the savage climax, with Vaughn blasted by a shotgun in the chest, his back blown off, lifted bodily by the impact to drown in the pool and with fountains coming on as Ryan leaps onto him flailing with his fists in vengeance.

Clay Pigeon, unjustly, did Vaughn's career little good and his publicist Jerry Pam later told me he had never even heard of it! Even Vaughn told me: "I never saw it, frankly, and I don't even remember doing it, the reason being that I was in the midst of chaos with Kathy Ceaton (Vaughn's former girlfriend who brought a paternity suit against him) at the time, and I just wanted to get away from it all and work, and I did it so I wouldn't have to hear her haranguing me! You work for various reasons in life! Tom Stern, Samantha Eggar's ex-husband (Stern would later become Executive Producer of the disastrous Vaughn production *Next Week Rio/Three Way Split*), came to me and I read the script. It fitted into my time schedule and he paid me whatever I was getting at the time salary-wise. I guess I thought it was such a weird character that it was interesting, and then I embellished it with the hats and parrots and everything." Vaughn agreed that he camped up the character with these embellishments, though it was "just out of boredom and something to do" than out of derision for the script: "I don't think I was consciously recognising the material for being inadequate." Vaughn recalls that director/star Stern did not mind this decision to parody, even though all the other characters play it straight: "I think he was delighted that I was coming up with all these hats and odd costumes and everything, because it wasn't in the script and he was happy to have a contribution to an otherwise fairly weird character going in, but embellished by wardrobe and so on."

After four years in *The Man from U.N.C.L.E.*, Vaughn was not perturbed by the overt violence and explained when I queried him on this point: "I've never been one to subscribe to the fact that either violence on television or violence in motion pictures creates violence in the viewers. I'm opposed to the whole psychological concept that you go out and kill somebody because you saw somebody kill on screen. It may be that if somebody sees *The Deer Hunter* and he's inclined toward doing something strange like shooting either himself or somebody else, he would use Russian roulette, but that person's inclined anyway. It wasn't *The Deer Hunter* that did it: it gave him a device." Vaughn's performance as Neilson, who keeps on the wall of his office numerous photographs of Robert Kennedy, to whom Vaughn was close in private life, may not have qualified as art in the way that other performances of his obviously do, but it still proved an interesting development in Vaughn's screen persona in the area of humour.

Yet, regrettably, one cannot claim that humour forms an important part of Vaughn's screen persona, devoted as it is to other concerns: in his work, Vaughn has shown common sense to be not incompatible with emotional honesty (Kreuger, after all, was in every way unlucky) so that the restraint one senses in Vaughn's screen persona is not something tragic but something admirable. The dictates of reason and the dictates of feeling, even if they are antithetical, need not confuse the man who knows himself (well enough to master himself, one might add).

Many of Vaughn's directors have told me of the basic dualisms in Vaughn's personality, which almost symbolises the truth of Fitzgerald's remark "the test of a first-rate intelligence is the ability to hold two opposed ideas in the mind at the same time, and still retain the ability to function". This remark has much in common with a remark once made by Vaughn concerning "the ability to adapt to change, which according to a professor I once had, is the barometer of a man's intelligence" (Vaughn has told me that he was a professor of International Relations at the University of Minnesota). For, on the one hand, if one can assess the merits of an action prompted by reason and an opposing action dictated by instinct yet come to a decision consistent with choices successfully made in past; and, on the other hand, if one can refuse to permit unstable conditions to alter the necessity of that choice being a pure one, while still taking stock of the exigencies of the moment; then, come what may, that choice is an expression of the most capable sensibility.

Accordingly, in Vaughn's work, a reasonable consistency of conduct has been underpinned but not upset by an undiminished emotional honesty.

3: The Politics Of Misery

Only within one set of cinematic co-ordinates is the fluctuating Vaughnian screen presence nullified, i.e. divested of its internal dynamic. The circumstances are those of wretched despondency, to which Vaughn has a uniquely sensitive response. Those circumstances in conjunction with Vaughn's response to them map out the co-ordinates of an area of cinematic experience best called the politics of misery.

The politics of misery *is* the government of the condition of utter despair for artistic purposes. That state may be depicted in a style that is a continuous emotional outburst (Chet Gwynne) or a wallowing in stasis (Harry Rule). But in any event it steers a course right between the polar syndromes and owes nothing to them: being itself a negation of life, the politics of misery has nothing to do with the extremes of human behaviour that make up life itself. In the politics of misery, the charm of virtue and the charisma of evil are not only absent, but the syndromes they represent cancel each other out, as we have seen in the case of Fenner, whose nobility *is* sensitivity to defeat.

It was, indeed, probably in *The Venetian Affair* that Vaughn's mask of tragedy gave the politics of misery its most exhaustive cinematic treatment. For *The Venetian Affair* contains screen acting by Robert Vaughn of such intellectual precision that it is one of the fullest displays of his unique talent.

Helen MacInnes' novel *The Venetian Affair* was not purchased by M-G-M with Vaughn in mind and, in fact, writer and producer E. Jack Neuman and producer Jerry Thorpe, who also directed, were the third writer/producer team assigned to the project. Vaughn did not audition for the role of Bill Fenner and, when I put it to Jerry Thorpe that the allusion in the script to Fenner's eyes flashing in anger, made by the villain Wahl, played by Karl (*Peeping Tom*) Boehm, suggests that the script was tailored to match Vaughn's personal screen qualities, he observed: "This was a relatively unusual example of original material coincidentally coinciding with the performer's essential quality." Thorpe discussed the film with Vaughn before shooting began and recalls: "We concurred that espionage, or counter espionage if you like, is a lonely, unfulfilling hum-drum way of life." Vaughn had evidently not been affected by the glossy fantasy life of secret agent Napoleon Solo. So they had been aware that in presenting Bill Fenner as a sexual failure, notably in the "What's your hurry?" . . . "What's yours?" scene with Luciana Paluzzi, they were significantly undermining the sex symbol image M-G-M had constructed for

Vaughn in the likes of *To Trap a Spy* and *The Spy With My Face*? Thorpe affirmed this: "We were trying to depict a member of the 'intelligence microcosm' as somebody far short of an heroic figure."

There remains, however, the problem for film criticism of who was responsible for Vaughn's finished performance which is exceptionally introspective and sorrowful even for Vaughn, who naturally inclines towards these qualities. Jerry Thorpe offers some evidence when he states: "Most of Fenner's characteristics were inherent in Neuman's script. Of course, in a healthy working relationship final choices are usually the result of a collaboration between writer, director and performer. Spying is an introspective, sorrowful way of life." Yet Thorpe does hint that Vaughn did try to stick to his own conception of Fenner, for when I asked Thorpe to describe how Vaughn took direction, he said that he found Vaughn "receptive, articulate and malleable whenever he could justify behaviour within the parameters of his concept of Bill Fenner". Given Vaughn's mastery of the mechanics of screen acting, it is difficult to believe he was unaware that his conception would lead to such a searing portrayal. Certainly Jerry Thorpe admired Vaughn's work from a technical standpoint: "He is a total professional. Far better versed in film grammar than most actors. . . I've always been aware of his talent. I enjoyed his work in *Bullitt* as well as *The Venetian Affair* and many other films . . . There's no doubt in my mind that given the right 'break through' role, Vaughn could have become a big star."

On the other hand, I did discover that Vaughn had not been aware of the significant element of melancholia in his portrayal of detective Harry Rule in *The Protectors* and he expressed surprise at this reading of his interpretation, suggesting ironically that it may have been a reflection of his dissatisfaction with the making of the series: "That may have had to do with the fact I was doing the show! I don't consciously remember attempting that, so it may have been just my . . . I mean, I recall days where I just went in and had to get it over with, to get back to Belgravia!" It is possible, therefore, that in addition to the conscious collaborative decision to portray Fenner as a deeply sorrowful character, there may have been an unconscious artistic contribution by Vaughn that deepened Fenner's characteristics beyond what Neuman and Thorpe would have regarded as sufficient.

The allegorical overtones of this "mystifying" (as *The Observer* found it) attempt at myth-variation (i.e. "the usually immaculate Vaughn" — as British film reviewer Norman Woodman once described him — being presented as '*The Spy Who Came in from the Canal*') are ironically pitched against the sunny splendour of the world's loveliest city as well as the more predictable dark alleys and cellars. The spy thriller genre is uniquely accommodating to such overtones: it exploits the clandestine, criminal situation of the secret agent with a naturalness that portrays the alienation of modern man to be possible in even the most beautiful or everyday places. In director Jerry Thorpe's universe, or at any rate in the universe of actor Robert Vaughn, love is the last straw to cling to and if that is plucked away, the world becomes a maze of perplexing events mysteriously executed by alien, hostile forces: e.g. Fenner's — and the audience's — genuine shock at Sandra being shot as he held her in his hands. Wahl's action is illogical insofar as she was in the act of persuading Fenner to give up the Vaugiroud report. Thorpe, in contravening audience expectations, pulled off a master stroke and provided Vaughn with one of his most memorable moments. "Such incidents have the very greatest effect on the mind when they occur unexpectedly and at the same time in consequence of one another; there is more of the marvellous in them then than if they happened of themselves or by mere chance": Aristotle. The sadistic insanity of Wahl was revealed (his enjoyment of cat-and-mouse toying with his victims was in the subsequent scene made literal when the cat savages the mouse) in this brutal cold-blooded killing (Austrian actor Boehm's neo-Nazi connotations in the film never acknowledged but detectable), the greatest impact of which was the shattering of Fenner's prospects of future happiness. Its unexpectedness, followed by the entire sequence until Wahl's death, conforms perfectly to the Aristotelian formula. Sandra's death is a tragedy arousing pity for Fenner, fear of Wahl and is only the start of a marvellous chain of images from the cat savaging the mouse through Fenner's drug-induced fear of a mouse (in a scene almost consciously a reprise of Lee's night of fear in *The Magnificent Seven*) — the irony of which, on the basis of Vaughn's tough Solo image, critics remarked upon — to the body of Wahl floating up to the canal steps.

Vaughn's wholly successful performance is pitched at a heart-felt level, engaging both our sympathy (drinking deeply from the hip flask until he coughs; sexually rejected by beautiful Giulia; sensitively reciting poetry; agonised that he will see Sandra involved in all this to the point of striking Rosenfeld) and our affection (his shyness with women, even with Sandra when he sees her for the first time). When he observes the effect of the injection upon the cat before being injected himself, Vaughn well conveys consternation: he swallows, sniffs, puts his tongue against the roof of his mouth, closes his eyes and shakes his head. The film features many beautiful close-ups of Vaughn's face, often with the most soulful expression in his eyes, and one stunning profile at night that is a silhouette of agony, as well as a turning of his head round to a profile of the left side of his face when he first sees Sandra (the turn to a profile in his first moments in *Bullitt* being of the right side).

Sandra's disguise as a nun at one point allows *The Venetian Affair* to be admitted to that select genre, what *Variety* called the "gun-and-nun flick" (others in the genre being *Madron* and *Two Mules for Sister Sara*). But *The Venetian Affair* bears comparison with better films than those, and not just the likes of *The Spy Who Came in from the Cold*: in its way, Vaughn's performance is as moving and as charming as that of Maurice Ronet in *Le Feu Follet*. Indeed, Ronet's final human contact is with a maid with whom there is a near-flirtation (rendered impossible by his despair: as also with Vaughn) in a scene very similar in effect to Fenner's token attempt at Giulia's seduction. Moments such as these bring the dysthymic condition alive.

For *The Venetian Affair* operates within an elegiac set of co-ordinates, connoting images of evil (Wahl's sadism), of experience (Fenner's cynicism) and of mistrust (Sandra dies unbelieved). It is therefore entirely fitting that Vaughn should wear the mask of tragedy: "Tragedy, however, is an imitation. . . of incidents arousing pity and fear" (Aristotle). The plot serves as a series of not-quite-logical operators upon the perfect equation of Vaughn's features to result in the logical truth of his expressions. The new heights of aesthetic rapture engendered by Vaughn's work in this picture are the outcome of the politics of misery, that twilight zone of cinema where the icon syndrome and the eminence grise syndrome are irrelevant and where Vaughn's only worthy antecedent was probably the Bette Davis of films like *Beyond the Forest*.

Although when I put it to Vincent Sherman (who, of course, also directed Davis at her peak) that Vaughn had always seemed to me in his more emotional roles such as *The Young Philadelphians* and *The Venetian Affair* to be as affecting a representative of male misery as Davis was of female misery, he replied: "I'm not sure I agree with your premise. He was certainly an example of male misery in the *Philadelphians* but he has not made this a trade mark. In fact I don't know if any of his roles were similar to that."

Yet Vaughn's charm now *is* his pain (hence the number of occasions when Fenner breaks into a smile at the moment of greatest imposition and despair). In Vaughn's politics of misery, sensitivity is a candidate for Cynicism. Adding fuel to the fire, Jerry Thorpe modifies the (avuncular) Vaughnian saga by inverting the Paluzzi resonance of *To Trap a Spy.* Giulia's rejection denies Fenner the active life, making *The Venetian Affair* a sophisticated modulation on the myth of masculinity as firmly established in Vaughn's career, namely man as metaphor for motion (Solo, Rule). This defeatist modulation well accords with Vaughn's stylistic ability to render stasis, one of Vaughn's unique features being to have continually instilled into the man of action a subversive intellectual stillness. In its way, the unrelieved pessimism of *The Venetian Affair* is a negation of the will to live. Fenner can only tell his compatriots to go to hell and leave alone, slowly and with a backward glance because, as Thorpe has made clear, he has nowhere to go, no reason to live any more. Lee faced his problem and died: Fenner is more tragic. He faced his problem (like Kreuger), solved it (unlike Kreuger) and had the solution removed, leaving him worse off than before. His suicidal streak, hinted at in the symbolic death of his alcoholism and self-deprecation to his boss Penneyman (and in the latent masochism of the torture scene), can now only gain full control: it is even articulated in his readiness to die for the Vaugiroud report. No wonder Thorpe ends the film so abruptly: few audiences could accept anything bleaker or more despairing than what has gone before and beside which Thorpe's few comic touches are completely overshadowed.

There are some visual clues, however, to what might have become of Bill Fenner in later years in the three episodes of *The Protectors* shot on location in Venice, *Lena*, *Decoy* and, especially, *Fighting Fund*. For Vaughn's portrayal of Harry Rule also conveys an alienated man, even in unemotional scenes, simply by way of Vaughn's earnest screen acting approach. Six years on from *The Venetian Affair*, Bill Fenner could well have gone into Harry Rule's line of work and perhaps gained the greater self-assurance Vaughn lends to Harry Rule in *Fighting Fund* as he leads the police launch along the canals. Certainly the crisp photography of Brendan J. Stafford and elegant framings of Vaughn amid flurries of pigeons against fine architecture by director Jeremy Summers offer a more hopeful universe to the homo Vaughnianus than the shadowy universe of Bill Fenner, leading one to the supposition that in the course of six years Fenner may have learnt to live with the death of Sandra just as Harry Rule has learnt to live with his divorce from Laura. Vaughn's contained performance in *Fighting Fund* makes this supposition reasonably tenable.

The misery of Vaughn's situation in *The Caretakers* elicited a performance many feel to be the closest Vaughn ever came to the screen quality of one of his early idols, Montgomery Clift. He played Jim Melford, the husband of the mentally disturbed Lorna (Polly Bergen), who lashes out at his approach. It is worth considering how Vaughn's approach to the part creates dramatic focus upon Melford's exposition of misery.

Vaughn's performance is aided by very poignant dialogue, extremely well-suited to this actor's particular strengths, which he renders all the more effective a display of a distraught mind by constant pausing and re-phrasing to collect his thoughts. The scenes in which he relates in close-up his distress to the doctor, MacLeod, are among the best evidence available to illustrate the extreme sensitivity of feeling Vaughn had the ability to convey in those days: it is as if the briefness of his role allowed him to concentrate all his effort, emotion and control into one finely focused representation of a deeply wracked husband. Note the phrasing in the following expressions of his pain: "Well, she's . . . she's always been . . . well, you know . . . a little . . . different. At times she . . . Then our little boy was killed and after that we . . . we never seemed to have anything together. I tried everything but . . . but she just . . . she was always in her world . . . she had her own feelings and her own thoughts and I . . . I couldn't seem to get through to her. I felt that . . . that she blamed me for what had happened. You understand what I mean, Doctor?" . . . "She'd come into a room, you see . . . er . . . like I wasn't even there and she'd . . . stare right through me . . . er . . . as though I were nothing."

Vaughn's phrasing also conveys his embarrassment over his wife's condition when he faces her. Note the awkwardness of his stilted delivery in their exchange: ("How have you missed me?") "What do you mean, how? I mean. . . in every way. There's nothing the same at home now. You see, when you . . . I mean . . . I think that you look much better . . . er . . . I can tell . . ."

After Lorna Melford's irrational and violent rejection of her husband's concern, we again encounter the typical homo Vaughnianus' sensitivity to rejection in love, prevailing rationalism and emotional bewilderment, as his distress pours out to MacLeod: "Could you love someone who looked at you half the time as if she was going to kill you? Or was terrified if you even tried to touch her? That day I came here to see her . . . I wanted to see something . . . a flicker that reminded me of the woman that . . . I loved. Instead, there was some sort of . . . stranger in my wife's face and body. My wife is gone, Doctor!" . . . "It's not my fault!" "I've always loved her. There was never any other woman. There was never any reason for . . . What have I done to her, Doctor? I mean, why does she hate me so?"

In similar vein, Sam Rolfe has told me of Vaughn's performance as a father in a 1962 episode of *Eleventh Hour*, which Rolfe produced. In *The Blues My Baby Gave to Me*, Vaughn and Inger Stevens, an actress of great sensitivity with whom Vaughn had a rapport that extended into their personal lives, played Peter and Christine Warren whose marital happiness is threatened when she suffers severe post-natal depression and tries to kill him as well as their daughter. Rolfe found Vaughn's performance one of the most touching he had ever seen and nearly twenty years later recalled vividly a scene where Vaughn tries to communicate with Inger, who is distressed, and cannot think what to say, so simply hesitates and reaches out his hand silently. For Rolfe, it remains his favourite Vaughn performance ever. While Rolfe was not responsible for casting Vaughn in *The Man from U.N.C.L.E.*, he was consulted once the choice was made and approved the decision, partly because he felt Vaughn "had dash" and partly because he remembered how effective he was in *The Blues My Baby Gave to Me*, something of a precursor of the screen quality he then exhibited in *The Caretakers*.

Jerry Pam, who was Vaughn's publicist for twenty-five years, was as strongly affected by Vaughn's work in *The Caretakers* as Sam Rolfe was by its precursor, despite the fact that he thought the film itself was terrible. To this day, Pam considers that Vaughn gave his best performance in the film: "I thought that could have changed his screen career. I thought he could have become a Monty Clift. He was very soft. I thought there was an interesting quality there, but somehow the roles never came along."

As a screen actor, Robert Vaughn is a master of interior deliberation; like the mature Alain Delon of films like *Someone is Bleeding* or *Blood on the Streets*, a poet of interiority on screen. This is but one of the reasons why, when watching Vaughn on screen, one never detects the slightest hint of his being aware of the presence of the camera, so natural seems his behaviour before the lens. Another reason may be, as John Hackett opined to me, that Vaughn has the charmingly rare quality among Hollywood leading men of being slightly self-effacing, which is often translated into a generosity towards his fellow actors on screen.

The politics of misery canvass support for the protagonist's dramatic credibility: Chet Gwynne's horrified gulp at his revelation to Tony that he has lost his arm is alone capable of rendering alive the role of a one-armed drunk, of establishing pathos as opposed to grotesquerie. Sympathy is, of course, dependent upon dramatic credibility. The politics of misery might be characterised as the eminence grise syndrome without the alienation: that is, the protagonist is too alienated to be able to alienate the audience from him and he evokes a deep sympathy for all that his presence is rather depressing. Misery pardons all, even brusqueness. Fenner is caught in a vicious circle, symbolised by the padded walls that enclose him in the drug scene, objectifying his own interior prison of grief. Sandra's death is the shattering of the first life-hope Fenner had had in years. In Vaughn's "Oh my God!", the audience witnesses the death not only of Sandra but also, symbolically, of Fenner. The courage Vaughn has shown on screen in the face of misery has ennobled the status of politicians of misery, whose affliction becomes no longer something shameful

(Chet Gwynne) but something to be borne with pride (Harry Rule) as evidence of emotional awareness. Furthermore, the politician of misery *is* miserable *because* he faces the opposition (Lee, Kreuger) instead of ignoring it for his own ends (Chalmers). Sensitive yet forthright, the politician of misery is not miserable enough to diminish all admiration of his sterling qualities.

How poetic that, of all actors, this should be the highly political Robert Vaughn's most individual contribution to the cinematic art. For the politics of misery *is* 'political cinema' since it is committed, in a humanism expressed through the humanity of Vaughn's portrayals, to ameliorating man's place in society. The commitment is none the less deep for all that the politics of misery is concerned with establishing the well-being of the individual rather than of the state — the antithesis of Communist ideology. It attempts the latter by focusing upon personal ills as a microcosm of ideological ills, specifically the dysthymic condition as opposed to — but also as metaphor for — social unrest.

If the art of Robert Vaughn is a cinematic intoxication, it is because his politics of misery employs the humanity of the dysthymic condition in the service of a humanism that is, in the widest sense of the word, political.

4: Recurrent Motifs In Robert Vaughn's Screen Work

The loner motif has been prevalent in Vaughn's screen work from the very beginning. Indeed, the very originality of *Good Day for a Hanging* came from the explicit breaking of the implicit Hollywood social code that the law-breaker is an outcast, a loner. For the Kid is more popular than the town Marshal! Later Vaughn films such as *Bullitt* would implicitly break this code by emphasising the sordidness of the hero's life (Frank Bullitt's callousness at the scene of strangulation, and his symbolic washing of his hands at the end), in contrast to the charmingly serene lifestyle of the villain (the highly sophisticated Chalmers). Although even in those films where the villainy of Vaughn baddies has failed to make them social outcasts (e.g. the affluent Neilson in *Clay Pigeon*, the materially ambitious Andrew Simms in *Blast*, the well-to-do Gerry Hunter in *The Woman Hunter*), there have at least been scenes to indicate the loner nature of these men: Simms' slapping of Sgt. Anderson at her rejection of him only manifests his need for her and leaves him worse off than before, while Hunter's false relationship with his wife would culminate in his cold-blooded acceptance of the need to kill her. Non-villains such as the U.S. Ambassador Ray Whiteley in *The Statue* even admit to being lonely: "It's not easy for either of us . . . when two people are lonely . . . two Scorpios", he argues to Rhonda.

The poster of *No Time to Be Young*, a film pseudonymously written by the distinguished Philip Yordan, featured Vaughn in a pose remarkably similar to that of James Dean on the poster of *Rebel Without a Cause*, accompanied by the question "Will he prove to be the successor to James Dean?" I asked Vaughn if this really *was* deliberate and he confirmed it: "I'm sure it was. I mean, I'm sure I didn't look at a Dean-type picture and do it, but I'm sure that in my head I was slouching and whatever he did . . . wore windbreakers!" According to the film's Press Book, the "sensational new star" was already "considered by many to be the successor to the late James Dean". London's *Monthly Film Bulletin* indeed conceded: "Robert Vaughn's performance, in the James Dean style, is quite interesting." Another British magazine, *Picturegoer*, a few years later judged Vaughn the most successful of those trying to succeed Dean: "Robert Vaughn, the newest threat to the Dean boys . . . has the lean and haunted look you love. And for scores of Reader Service writers he scores more heavily as a successor to James Dean than most of the current Dean-type favourites – Dean Stockwell, Dean Jones and Dennis Hopper."

Vaughn was not at all comfortable with this kind of image and admits: "I wanted to do Noel Coward!" And in fact he was not even aware that he was being publicised and received as a successor to James Dean, although he agrees that that was what he was trying to be in this picture. Vaughn commented when I asked him about his reaction to being presented as Dean's successor: "That I didn't know about, but everybody my age wanted to be the successor to James Dean. Saxon, Hopper, Nick Adams, you name it, everybody wanted to be James Dean. He just died September 30 1955 and we all wanted to *be* him. At least, I don't know we all wanted to *act* like him, which I didn't think I could do. I tried. I tried a little bit, but it was really rather hard. I am not inarticulate, so it was hard for me to be that person. I tried it to some extent in *No Time to Be Young*, and at the time I was seeing Natalie Wood, who had just done *Rebel Without a Cause* and talked a great deal about Jimmy, and I had known Jimmy very briefly. I had seen him a couple of times around town, couple of times in an acting class, and I think *every* young actor in his early 20's was trying to get his Jimmy Dean 'shock' on the screen. But I wasn't aware that anybody was aware of me trying to do it." In retrospect, however, Vaughn's portrayal of 'Buddy Root' is less important as an attempt to recreate the James Dean persona than as the first elaboration of a major facet of Robert Vaughn's screen persona, the motif of the independent, socially self-sufficient loner.

David Lowell Rich recalls the genesis of Vaughn's first leading role: "You ask me to think back a long time, but *No Time to Be Young* having been my first effort as a motion picture director, the memory is quite clear. The late Harry Cohn, having seen a live television show I directed in New York starring the young Audrey Hepburn, asked me to come out and make a film at Columbia. This was, I believe, the year before he died. He put me together with a well-known writer-producer named Philip Yordan. Mr. Yordan apparently had sold a paperback novel to Mr. Cohn and Columbia for motion picture development. Mr. Cohn then assigned Mr. Yordan as the writer of the screenplay, as well as being the producer of the film, and I was introduced to him as the director. Mr. Yordan, somewhat weary of labouring in the Hollywood vineyards, offered me a choice. I remember he said, 'Look, kid, you want to work, I'll work. You don't want to work, neither will I.' I took this to mean that we could make a significant film or a melodramatic potboiler, which in effect the paperback was. Young, enthusiastic, full of energy, I, of course, replied I wanted to work. Mr. Yordan, a man of considerable talents – you may remember him as the author of the play 'Anna Lucasta' – and I set to work. Out of our mutual efforts and his typewriter came a screenplay which was tough, emotional, and highly reflective of the charged atmosphere in which we lived at the end of the 1950's. It was a screenplay designed to illustrate in highly dramatic form and action the quandry which peacetime civilians – young men with their lives and careers about to begin – faced when unwillingly drafted into a peacetime army. It was a real problem, and one which I think the screenplay faced honestly. I was pleased beyond measure to have as my first motion picture assignment a screenplay with such substance. When Mr. Cohn read it, however, he was enraged as only Harry Cohn could be enraged. 'This is not what I bought', he stormed at me and Philip Yordan. I remember he looked at me and said, 'You want to direct this?' And I said, 'Yes, Mr. Cohn, I do. I think it's good.' He left nothing to my imagination when he told me how wrong he thought I was. In retrospect, I realise his pride was enormously piqued. You see, I hadn't consulted him about this major change in emphasis. After the meeting was over, Philip Yordan, I believe almost overnight, complied with Mr. Cohn's last edict, which was to 'put it back the way it should be'. This was the genesis of the final screenplay for *No Time to Be Young*. The picture was shot in ten days, and, almost as a postscript, I must add that as soon as the screenplay was delivered – now faithful to the paperback copy which Mr. Cohn had purchased – Mr. Yordan left Columbia for far greener pastures."

Rich enjoyed working with Vaughn: "We cast three unknowns, and Robert Vaughn was the leading player. He was a young man of much promise with an interesting, brooding, intellectual sense which I thought the character needed to help make more dimensional what was essentially a thinly-drawn characterisation. To the extent that the material allowed, I believe Mr. Vaughn did as much with it as anybody could, as did I. I am somewhat surprised that you write that he tried 'to emulate James Dean in terms of screen attitudes'. It never occurred to me at the time that he was doing so. I don't recall that he ever discussed it with me. Had he done so, I feel I would have attempted to steer him away from this kind of emulation, and perhaps that's why he over the years now thinks of that attempt as an uncomfortable one. I found Bob to be enormously intelligent and responsive to direction, though keeping a core of himself interestingly shielded from public view."

No Time to Be Young's Buddy Root prefigures the future homo Vaughnianus very accurately, embracing most of the major motifs of Vaughn's career. A semiological reading of Vaughn's attitude on the film poster — a still used in all the film publicity material — reveals the symbolic density of the Vaughnian presence. Root's matchstick protrudes from his lip in minor but defiant slobbishness as an individualistic counterpoint to the sober conformism of his attire. His car, clothes and general appearance place him firmly within a precisely defined socio-cultural background (W.A.S.P. and prospering mid-Fifties America), but Root's dissatisfaction with his circumstances (rather than rejection of them — his attempt to ameliorate them through crime, rather than drop out of them, reveals a tacit approbation of his particular socio-cultural milieu) is conveyed both by the deeply sorrowful aspect of Vaughn's eyes and this deliberate 'toughening-up' of his otherwise highly respectable appearance.

These subtle signs of Root's malaise are, to be sure, only noticeable as details of the effect of the pose as a whole, an effect that was itself deeply entrenched in mid-Fifties' American socio-cultural awareness: the Dean phenomenon. For as Levi-Strauss writes, "particular actions of individuals are never symbolic in themselves". Because Vaughn's pose *is* an unashamed imitation of James Dean's pose, we are alerted to symbolism, and instantly we 'read' Root to be a Dean successor, and thus, though better groomed than Dean, to be full of pent-up frustration, bitterness and explosive anger. Thus alerted, we also 'read' the melancholy of Vaughn's eyes as a sign of Root's capacity for the desperate action that costs him his life. Buddy Root's loner qualifications are thus impeccable. As are those of the Boy, who alone dares break the Law in Vaughn's following film, *Teenage Caveman,* which deserves greater attention than its title indicates.

Teenage Caveman is a very weird film that has polarised critics as few films of its type have done. For some it is the epitome of Corman's early flair, while others have nominated it one of the worst films ever made. All would probably agree with those French critics who have remarked on how strange it is in the light of Vaughn's future screen image. While it is all too tempting to regard *Teenage Caveman* as a cut-price though more intelligent *Man and His Mate*, with Vaughn in the Victor Mature role, for those of us who regard Roger Corman as what Chris Wicking has labelled "one of the most important directors of his generation" the film has greater importance. In his book *Science Fiction in the Cinema*, John Baxter has lauded the film as a good example of Corman's "genius" and, alas, of Vaughn's "ineptitude". At the time of release, *Variety* was equally laudatory but kinder about Vaughn: "Vaughn is satisfactory as the questing caveman although there is a tendency, on occasion, to give the role a little too much 'method'." Critic Wheeler Dixon later observed (*The Velvet Light Trap*, Autumn 1976) that the brilliant framing of each shot disguises the fakeness of the physical realities of the location, so that this fakeness then becomes an acceptable low-budget economy. Much, one might say, as the emotional significance of the dialogue about Rule's inaccessible son, shared by Vaughn and Nigel Green, relegated to insignificance the poor quality of the back projection of the Thames from Hungerford Bridge in the *Balance of Terror* episode of *The Protectors*. Reflecting the imagery of Plato's allegory of the cave in Chapter XXV of *The Republic, Teenage Caveman* involves the same test of a loner's loyalties as would recur in *The Protectors*. Corman indeed once claimed: "All of my films have been concerned simply with man as social animal." In his recognition of choices, the Boy's social behaviour defines him as a typical Vaughn loner, however untypical his environment in terms of Vaughn's sophisticated protagonists.

Vaughn had wanted to do the role because he thought the script was an argument for disarmament, as he once commented: "I couldn't wait to do it. It was a magnificent script written in blank verse." However, upon his acceptance, Corman hired, in Vaughn's opinion, "the worst actors in the world". Worse yet, although the working title was *Prehistoric World* (and it *was* released in Italy as *Mondo Preistorico*), American International Pictures, hoping to cash in on the success of their recent film *I Was a Teenage Werewolf* starring Michael Landon, released it as *Teenage Caveman*, to the considerable chagrin of both Vaughn and Corman, who still regards the film fondly.

Vaughn has told me that he was young enough then to agonise about getting his interpretation of the Boy as natural as possible and commented ruefully: "O yes, I tried to be very real with my sarong! I tried to make this guy in a bear suit, whatever it was I was wearing, believable. That's a very hard job. By keeping it low-keyed and sensitive and gentle and being aware that the picture, because it had such bad actors, was probably going to be shot down, I was trying to give the best performance I could under the circumstances with the tremendous pressure of Roger Corman's insistence on everything getting done yesterday. It was really a ten-day shooting schedule. And I gave a lot of thought to it because the writer, R. Wright Campbell, of the picture had just been nominated for the Academy Award the prior year for *Man of a Thousand Faces* and also had dated Joyce Jameson for several years prior to the time that I met Joyce, and I wanted to impress Joyce that I was doing her ex-boyfriend's language well. I remember that was a very important thing in my head." Vaughn, who like all the cast drove to the Bronson Canyon location each day from home, never met Campbell during the making of the film.

Contrary to popular legend, Corman, who had already directed nineteen low-budget features in the previous three years, did do retakes. This was just as well, for as cast member Jonathan Haze has told me: "Everyone lost patience, concentration, and forgot lines. Vaughn always kept a straight face both on and off screen." Yet Vaughn's working relationship with Corman was reportedly cordial, perhaps because Corman did not involve himself much in Vaughn's interpretation. "As long as the production remained on schedule and on budget, Roger was satisfied", comments Haze, who today argues that the picture was totally miscast: "How can a group of clean-shaven, neatly-coiffed, well-spoken, soft-bodied in most cases, actors be in any way believable playing prehistoric cave dwellers? Robert in particular was soft, untanned, sophisticated and mannered. An actor with more gut-animalism might have helped the film but I doubt it." It is certainly true that the casting of Robert Vaughn of all people does add to the film's quintessential surrealism.

Corman, who has referred to Vaughn as "a very fine young actor" (in Ed Naha's *The Films of Roger Corman*), has told me: "In regard to Vaughn's performance in the film, it is true that he was on his own for the most part. He and I discussed the role before we began shooting, as I do with all the lead actors in my films. Once we began the film, it was clear that he had prepared his role in great depth. Since he created his character with such detail, I did not feel the need to get too involved with his performance, outside of a few comments now and again. I confined my directing to the other less experienced actors, since we had only a ten day schedule. When thinking about *Teenage Caveman*, I believe that Vaughn held the picture together, and its success was largely due to his intelligent and emotional performance."

Jonathan Haze is virtually unique in my experience of Vaughn's colleagues in finding fault with Vaughn's talent itself while bearing the actor no malice at all, so it is interesting to hear his summation: "As I recall, Vaughn was more of a poseur than he was an actor and his acting was more studied behaviour than it was visceral organic acting, so that the range and depth of his emotional instrument was far exceeded by his intellect. His craft as an actor was intellectual and cerebral, rather than organic and emotional. In my opinion, Robert always played Robert. It didn't matter if he wore grey flannel trousers and a blue blazer or an animal skin, the characterisation was the same." One can only attribute this reaction to opposing conceptions of acting held by the two men, the one towards containment of emotion (Walter Doniger has remarked that he thinks Vaughn has controlled "too much" inside himself and wishes the actor could "break free"), the other towards what he himself terms "visceral organic acting", which certainly sounds like the antithesis of Vaughn's approach, with the possible exception of his work in *The Young Philadelphians*. I discussed Haze's viewpoint with Vaughn and he accepted it philosophically: "I think his observations are what he saw. So that's what he saw, internalising, technical, kind of aloof and sophisticated . . . well, his whole idea was everyone should have had a beard, shouldn't be Hollywood actors playing cavemen!" Corman, however, went on to employ Vaughn in his future productions *Battle Beyond the Stars* and *Hour of the Assassin*, although he had by then sadly relinquished the reins of direction. Gelt in *Battle Beyond the Stars* is an extreme example of the Vaughn loner, although the performance does not carry the punch of Lee in *The Magnificent Seven*, so I asked Corman if he was satisfied with Vaughn's reworking of the original mercenary: "I *was* satisfied with his performance in *Battle Beyond the Stars*. In comparison to *The Magnificent Seven*, our picture was shot on a much lower budget, with less time to spend with the actors. Jimmy T. Murakami was a first time director who had little experience working with actors. Bob and I have recently worked on a new film together. The film is now called *Hour of the Assassin*, formerly *Licence to Kill*. The director of this new film is Luis Llosa, the leading Peruvian television director in Peru. This is his first feature and I think he will shortly become recognised as a major talent in the international film arena."

As Chester or 'Chet' Gwynne in *The Young Philadelphians*, Vaughn is aided in maintaining a powerful impact by the fact that he appears in a number of sequences throughout the rather long film which are punctuated by long scenes of occasionally tawdry melodramatics. So he acts in short spurts which enable him to dominate the scenes he is in, as in the memorably amusing drunken scene with Paul Newman in the telephone booth, or his movingly performed revelation of the loss of his arm. Newman asks "How's the arm?" Chet's answer is "We parted company". Chet Gwynne is a Vaughn loner par excellence, but through weakness rather than strength (independent men like Solo, Kreuger and Rule). His weakness is apparent in his reliance on alcohol in his first scene, at the party which he tells Tony (Newman) is as "dry as crossing the Sahara", whereupon he advises them to "head for the nearest oasis", namely the bar. Later, in the scene where he discusses Tony with Joan, Chet confesses that he has taken to the bottle because his marriage only lasted two days: "You don't think I actually like this stuff?" That same weakness reached pathetic proportions in his horrified collapse upon being charged with murder and his whining to Tony, who is trying to help him: "I must know first . . . what's going to happen to me?"

Vaughn's performance is *uncomfortably* brilliant in that he makes Chet's self-pity so disgusting (after the amputation of his arm, Chet refers to an old girlfriend, cruelly and with self-pity, with just the right note of throwaway despair as he intones: "what a picture that would make . . . two-headed Zelda and a one-armed drunk") that, although by no means a Vaughn villain, Chet has a little of the terrible compulsion of Lee, Chalmers or Andrew Simms and thereby creeps into the eminence grise syndrome. Chet's physical handicap is, of course, not only a reason for, but an outward manifestation of, being a loner, a physical symbol of spiritual impotence.

It is thus unsurprising that Vaughn said of this golden opportunity: "I didn't enjoy that role at all. It was a personality that I don't care to play — a very weak, ineffectual guy who was an alcoholic. That's something very unattractive to me." And, indeed, when playing future ostensible weaklings such as Lee, Vaughn would employ a restraint in performing not in evidence here which would suggest a certain inner strength that made those men more admirable than the whining Gwynne.

Director Vincent Sherman had never seen Vaughn before this film, either on screen or in person. Vaughn's agent brought him to Sherman's office and he read for the part of Gwynne. Sherman recalls: "While readings are not always a perfect indication of an actor's ability, they do convey his approach to the role, his listening, his emotional responses. He was excellent, that's why I cast him." Vaughn has told me: "I did a screen test for *The Young Philadelphians* in addition to reading for it. I did the test with Paul Newman, which is how I finally got the role. Jack Warner had to 'ok' the casting. I did not know Paul prior to the time I met him to do the first screen test for the film." Newman and Vaughn, fortunately, were very friendly, which made Sherman's work easier.

When Vaughn read for the part of Don Bigelow in *Unwed Mother*, it was a special quality the actor possessed, rather than good looks or acting talent, that persuaded director Walter Doniger, who had heard about him but not seen his previous work, to cast him. Doniger has tried to define this quality for me: "The quality was the inner duality of his nature. The feeling he transmitted that it was a corrupt world and so was he, but he, unlike the rest of the world, perceived the corruptness of both." (It must be recounted that Vaughn laughed when I quoted this to him.) This is intriguingly close to Sherman's impression of Vaughn at the reading for *The Young Philadelphians:* "I was most favourably impressed with a kind of intensity that he possessed and an indication of hidden reserves of bitterness which the part needed. He had a brooding personal quality but not sullen or aggressive." Sherman consciously tried to make use of Vaughn's intensity and found him "most responsive". He detected in Vaughn a very slight nervousness at the beginning "but then his concentration took over and there was no problem. He was as I recall relatively inexperienced with the technical problems, which I think is good. When an actor becomes too conscious of technical problems, I feel it can interfere with the depth of his performance. I recall that during the shooting of the scene in the prison when he tells Paul what happened, we changed the lines considerably, which I thought diminished his performance. Nevertheless the audience was not aware, since they had nothing to compare it with. He picked up the changes quickly. In fact, the total scene became almost completely improvised. There is no question that his performance was most effective."

Pressed to elucidate the creative process at work in Vaughn that gave birth to the extraordinary passion of this performance, John Hackett opines: "I don't think that he probably gives a great deal of thought to these things. He just does it. There's no rule about this. For instance, he told the story one time of how he and Paul Newman went over to Paul's house on a couple of nights to work on the scenes they had together. Newman was a very hard-working, precise guy, who broke the script down in all kinds of ways and had notes, just intensely, intensely figuring it all out to get the most out of it. Newman told Bob: 'I just worked my ass off trying to get this thing down, I spent hours and hours and hours studying and working, and my wife, who has the Oscar on the mantelpiece, gives it not a thought. She just goes in and does it.' So Joanne Woodward doesn't approach her role like Paul Newman does. She goes on her instinct, which she trusts, and does wonders with it. I think Bob is closer to that, in a sense, than to Paul Newman, even though Bob, as a director, did a lot of homework. He was capable of doing that kind of detailed work that Paul Newman did but I think Bob left on his own devices goes on his instinct, rather than burning a lot of midnight oil trying to figure out the best ways to go." Perhaps, but he certainly did make marginal notes in the case of the more prestigious roles. Sadly, his annotated copy of the script of *The Young Philadelphians* is not in his possession. He explains: "I'd love to have kept the script from *The Magnificent Seven* and *The Young Philadelphians* but I just didn't do it, because I didn't think about it at the time. I'd like to have kept mine because I probably had marginal notes, things like that, because when I hoped that something would be good, I always put a little more effort into it and made notes."

The most engaging of all Vaughn's early loners was possibly his gunman in *Bonanza*, which therefore deserves closer attention in terms of performance. As guest star of the 1962 *Bonanza* episode *The Way Station*, Vaughn played desperate killer Luke Martin who holds Adam Cartwright (Pernell Roberts) as a hostage to escape a posse: Vaughn might be said to have had it in for the Cartwrights since it was because Little Joe Cartwright (actor Michael Landon) became a highly lucrative 'teenage werewolf' for A.I.P. in 1957 that Vaughn was forced to become a 'teenage caveman' in 1958. *The Way Station* is another of Vaughn's early works to celebrate. It illustrates all the more clearly our contention that Vaughn's early television work was often richer than his cinema work, because the role of killer Luke Martin, beloved by a girl he cruelly uses to try to save his life from those denizens of the law who would execute him, is indistinguishable from the part of Edward 'The Kid' Campbell in the film *Good Day for a Hanging*. The results, however, partly because of television's greater use of close-up, are altogether more rewarding. *The Way Station* is, in fact, a superior (if simple) *Bonanza* show, with effective performances also from Pernell Roberts and especially from the very beautiful Dawn Wells as Marty, whose brief but fine screen flirtation with Vaughn is very memorable.

Luke Martin is an epitome of the young Vaughn's screen persona and so is worth remarking upon. The performance also offers splendid examples of Vaughn's range at the period, seen throughout so many television performances of those years that it became very likely that Vaughn can assume the mantle he himself told me he would confer on the late David Janssen: that of the best dramatic actor to have emerged from a sequence of television series.

Luke Martin is an epitome of the young Vaughn's screen persona *because* the performance contains all the motifs prevalent in Vaughn's best work. Luke is a classic loner: to the girl Marty he explains that his plea of self-defence will be ignored "and that's why I'm runnin' . . . and that's why I have to travel alone." Vaughn actually accentuates the word "alone", pathetically breaking it into two syllables, with a long 'o'. He is an obvious loser (is eventually hanged), himself rejects the possibility of love with Marty as impractical (he refuses to kill Adam to win Marty because "it ain't that important to me": Vaughn delivers this line with a tortuous grimace), is fearful of capture and death, has a natural charm that enslaves Marty, etc. All reminiscent of *Good Day for a Hanging* — but also, here and there, strongly reminiscent of Lee. Certainly Martin shares the same slightly pathetic personality as Lee. At the moment of his greatest peril, Martin explodes in violent self-pity: "If you figure I've got to worry about everybody else's problems and never my own . . . well this time it's gonna be different." This element is a natural outgrowth of Martin's status as a victim as great as Lee. For Martin's crime is killing in self-defence (but doubting whether this justification will save him).

As in all his most impressive performances — and given the level of the material, Vaughn's performance here is one of his more impressive — Vaughn instils redemptive qualities into this villain. Mercy (in refraining from two opportunities to kill). Romantic tenderness (in graciously accepting Marty's sketch of him). Rationality (when Adam points out "But he's not you", Vaughn looks very thoughtful, underlining Luke's acceptance of the point that he does not *have* to be a killer: the young Vaughn had a great and ready capacity for facial reactions to dialogue at this time). Humour (a twinkle enters his eyes after his expression has been very grave, as he says he is the only one who *can* take Marty away from the Way Station).

Martin's lack of inherent 'badness' (his situation, like Lee, is not one of brute aggression but of simple self-preservation) allows the sympathetic side to predominate, so that his horrified reaction when Adam points out that the posse won't jail him but will hang him (a reaction accompanied by dramatic chords on the soundtrack that accentuate his horror) is all the more striking.

Still, though the redemptive quality of Martin is very strong (his last action being to ask that the 5,000 dollars for his death be given to Marty as a gift), the performance carries weight primarily as an example of the dominating side of the young Vaughn's personality, demonstrated in a steely expression (as when he says "Well that kinda makes me feel like you're asking me to kill you"), in gruffly delivered orders ("Shut up old man . . . back that stage up . . . Get it in the barn!"), in desperate tones ("I'm fightin' for my life, friend") and angry, accusatory facial expression ("Well, what do you know about it, you weren't there when the kid came across the table with a knife in his hand"). This early experience qualified the actor for portrayals of such dominant personalities as Napoleon Solo. Perhaps one's most abiding impression of Vaughn's performance, however, remains the young actor's highly expressive frowns which vary a basically highly candid facial appearance (note the frowns as he talks about Paris as he eats, as compared with the facial candour of his pronouncement "I don't think there's gonna be a need for any gun"). Sensitive use of close-up highlights Vaughn's unique abilities here in ways his films often failed to accomplish. Luke Martin is a brief but excellent early Vaughn creation. Though filmed in five days, this show and others like it proved good exposure for Vaughn: *Bonanza* attracted 400 million viewers in 80 countries when first aired.

Actor John Hackett, a friend and colleague of Vaughn's since their days of studying Theater Arts together at Los Angeles City College, who researched and drafted most of Vaughn's political speeches on the topic of the Vietnam war because Vaughn, himself immersed in the research material, was too busy filming *The Man from U.N.C.L.E.* other than to make revisions and additional flourishes, has given me an illuminating characterisation of Vaughn's early, pre-*U.N.C.L.E.* screen persona as witnessed in shows like *The Way Station*. For Hackett, the key to Vaughn's early non-heroic persona was "that kind of cold edge that he brings to characters": "When he first started doing leads, some people thought that what he was best at was doing heavies, not the protagonist of the piece. This was still the era of the good-looking young leading man, the Rock Hudson, Tab Hunter and so forth kind of pretty, handsome young men. Bob didn't really fit that. So, while a good deal of handsome young men were going to the unemployment office, this fellow that wasn't quite the type was suddenly working a lot. The non-Rock Hudson part of his image was more prone to that kind of role for a young man. In other words, he wasn't initially getting cast as the heroic young soldier leading the cast over the hill. His style was lending itself more to an 'off' type character. Some of that 'coolness' or 'remoteness' or 'brooding', or what have you, worked playing a psychotic young killer or whatever, where a Rock Hudson type wouldn't get that role because he wouldn't have had the theatrical *style* for it. Bob had a theatrical *style* and could get into those kinds of roles."

Some of that 'remoteness' in these roles seems to have been detectable in Vaughn's own personality, in his early years as an actor especially. Richard L. Bare directed Vaughn in *If You Have Tears*, a 1963 episode of *The Virginian* in which Nancy Sinatra and the beautiful Dana Wynter also appeared, and has told me: "Robert Vaughn was an actor that didn't 'open up' much to a director personally. All I recall was that he was competent, knew his lines, hit his marks, and, I assume, was promptly at the pay window for his cheque. He always seemed somewhat aloof. Perhaps it was because he was acting only in television and not in a major motion picture." Not all Vaughn's early directors share this opinion of Vaughn, especially if they worked with him on a number of occasions, as did John Brahm.

Looking at Vaughn's enormous list of credits, one has to remark on how few directors of *genius* Vaughn has worked for: Roger Corman, Robert Altman, Monte Hellman (on stage only) and Patrick McGoohan. Even then, he has appeared in the lesser works of these artists. So it was fortunate that he worked a number of times for one director of undeniable genius, John Brahm. Brahm's genius is apparent not only in Hollywood masterpieces such as the atmospheric film *Hangover Square* but even in his masterly orchestration of such television shows as *The Twilight Zone*, *The Outer Limits*, *The Naked City* and, happily, *The Man from U.N.C.L.E.* I spoke to John Brahm when he was 87 and not in good health physically but mentally as alert as anyone, and he could vividly remember the impact the young Robert Vaughn had made upon him. Of the occasions that he worked with Vaughn prior to *The Man from U.N.C.L.E.*, he recalled especially an episode of *The Alfred Hitchcock Hour* in 1961. Brahm was working for the Hitchcock show and came from New York and found the cast in Los Angeles: "I thought Vaughn was suitable for the part and I suggested him. I had seen him and liked him extremely well. I thought he came through extremely well. I thought the show helped him extremely well." I asked Brahm to compare Vaughn's early screen persona with that of *The Man from U.N.C.L.E.* but he felt that the *U.N.C.L.E.* material did not really permit him to gauge how the actor had developed since the *Hitchcock* days: "My God, the part I gave him for *Hitchcock* was just the part of a young person where he just for the very first time had a chance just to be himself, where in *The Man from U.N.C.L.E.* he just had the chance to be in the situation. At the time, he became in this show a great, great star!" It is slightly to be regretted that Brahm never had the opportunity to direct Vaughn in a feature film. *Hangover Square* is, of course, one of George Sanders' best films and Tony Carbone thinks that the mature Vaughn is best summed up as a George Sanders without the English accent, a description that John Hackett and Jerry Pam have also offered as an approximation of the mature Vaughn's image. Brahm did actually direct Sanders and Vaughn in *Screen Directors Playhouse — The Bitter Waters*, and Sanders later played the villain in an *U.N.C.L.E.* episode, *The Gazebo in the Maze Affair*. Television producer Douglas Benton was a friend of John Brahm and first met Vaughn when he was playing the villain in a television pilot for Brahm: "He was just getting started. Brahm later told me that he was not only the best thing in the film but the only good thing. John raved about him as a performer."

This loner element in Vaughn's charismatic presentation of evil creates sympathy for the losers he portrays: and not only the likes of Klaus Everard in *The Big Show* or Andrew Simms in *Police Woman — Blast*. Such stalwart heroes as Harry Rule can even be classified as losers. The pain of his divorce is still alive, bringing sadness even to the admission that he has a son and evidently the reason for his remaining single. Occasionally grief may overcome him, as when a good friend found again is senselessly killed, leaving Rule sadder than before his return (the finale of *Zeke's Blues*) or when what seems to be a victory becomes only a premonition of defeat (finale of *Shadbolt*). The definitive example is Bill Fenner.

The unscripted quality Vaughn imparts is an air of quiet but grave acceptance of defeat, created by Vaughn's furtiveness of glance. *The Venetian Affair* bristles with such moments, with Fenner's defeat explicity represented by Giulia's rejection. Andrew Simms' introduction to Sgt. Anderson has him lower his dark glasses and peer tentatively over the top of them; the character has been all his life striving after things he knew he would never have and is satisfied to die in a room that has a carpet ("I guess I made a little progress"). The rather melancholy scene in which he tells Pepper that he is "making good contacts" has an air of muffled hopelessness which conveys that neither Pepper nor he really believe he is not deluding himself. Herein lies the sympathy which even Pepper, at his death, cannot help feeling for this murdering ex-convict: loner credentials allied to a fervent will to be somebody even in dream, a resolute conviction in the supremacy of fantasy over unattainable realities, and a quixotic romanticism (offering her the casinos on the French Riviera, asking her name before he dies) he cannot in any sense afford. In their own ways, men as different as Harry Rule, Bill Fenner and Andrew Simms have all responded to the conditions of their lives with courageous individualism (whatever the morality of their deeds) and are thus all worthy representatives of the *homo Vaughnianus*.

Any scripted situation of conflict suffices for Vaughn's brooding presence to contribute a moral dimension. Thus the moment of shock between realising Angela means to kill him after their lovemaking and the decision to let her die instead is one of great moral refraction (*To Trap a Spy*). This quality is even noticeable in routine scenes of *The Protectors*, arising from the camera's deliberate emphasis on the highly suggestive immobility of Vaughn's features. The finest example of this is the finale of *The Last Frontier*.

For the homo Vaughnianus is engaged in defining a set of moral co-ordinates within which he can act decently: thus Harry Rule overcomes his bitterness and honours the necessity of helping his ex-wife Laura in her distress (*With a Little Help from My Friends*). In *It Was All Over in Leipzig*, Rule was momentarily pulled between his strong suspicion of Palmer's guilt and Caroline's lingering affection for the man. The tension that arises out of moments of indecision or moral conflict constitutes a test of the protagonist's loyalty, e.g. when Rule has to shoot Caroline or be shot himself in *Quin*.

As a theme, the loyalty test focuses attention upon the moral consciousness of the homo Vaughnianus and permits much delicious introspective musing on the actor's part. Furthermore, its very nature reflects the extreme seriousness of Vaughn's persona, even in amusing dramatic settings (*Teenage Caveman*, *Unwed Mother*, and sometimes *The Man from U.N.C.L.E.* and *The Protectors*). It even seems to be responsible for determining which characters achieve iconic stature. The heroic loyalty (and hence the iconic stature) of a Vaughnian character is to a large degree dependent upon whether the issues that constitute the test are clear-cut (*The Protectors*) or highly complicated (*The Bridge at Remagen*).

The homo Vaughnianus also attempts to be loyal to his own image of himself, a loyalty test that is in fact a qualifying test of manhood: there is the Boy's initiation into the tribe upon becoming a man (*Teenage Caveman*), Lee's option to return to Ixcatlan and thus at last be a man among men, and young acting-marshal Dan's attempt to prove himself by riling a gang of rowdy cowhands in *The Rifleman — The Apprentice Sheriff*. Buddy Root first showed this concern in *No Time to Be Young*, and it is still detectable in a mature performance such as *Police Woman — Blast*, in Simms' recollection of how he has tried to live by his mother's advice to "suffer pain with pride, live with pride, do good things", i.e. to live up to a manly image.

Not that the masculinity of Vaughn characters is in any doubt. As an actor,

Vaughn has capitalised on his natural charm in dramatic situations that reveal its omnipotence, particularly with women. A villainous Vaughn has constantly won good women over to his lawless side: outstanding examples are Laurie in *Good Day for a Hanging*, Marty in *The Way Station*, Betty in *Unwed Mother* and Pepper Anderson in *Blast*. So non-villainous Vaughn characters met no resistance at all in their indiscriminate seductions: Sandy *and* Serena in *The Spy With My Face*, Mrs. Southwick in *The Statue*, Susan in *The Protectors — The Numbers Game*, etc. Social and political advantages were also gained this way: Chalmers' affability puts the press in his pocket, and Desmond's social ease at the party in *Captains and the Kings — Part Three* prefigures his appointment as Ambassador to the Court of St. James's.

Many of Vaughn's losers have a compelling charisma of evil, but *are* losers precisely because people are only taken in by a charm that they associate with virtue, rightly or wrongly (wrongly as in the case of The Kid in *Good Day for a Hanging*). Hence their frequent rejection in love. In *Blast*, before she is won over by him, Pepper shatters Simms' romanticism with a brutal rejection that causes him to slap her in the face. She leaves with the words: "I've done a lot of things and I will probably go to Hell, but it will not be by your hands." In *Generation of Evil*, Lou Malik puts his hands round Pepper and she rebuffs him ("Cool down, Lou"). *Columbo — Troubled Waters* has Danziger's mistress Rosanna threatening him with blackmail; *Columbo — Last Salute to the Commodore* has Charles Clay abused and coldly treated by his alcoholic wife. *With a Little Help from My Friends* contains the sad scene of Rule's ex-wife telling him how she has put 5000 miles between them, changed her name, tried to forget him and yet thought often of the moment of his death. In *Riverboat — About Roger Mowbray*, Jeanette had doubts that Vaughn's Roger married her for her money; and in *Empire — No Small Wars* an impossible situation developed between Connie and Vaughn's crippled Paul Terman that could have no future.

The homo Vaughnianus, then, embodies a problem searching for a solution in love. This yearning for affection is often not verbally expressed at all, but unmistakably apparent in poignant close-ups of Vaughn's eyes, e.g. Lee in his "Insults swallowed — none" dialogue or Klaus Everard and Jim Melford in certain close-ups.

Commercial guidelines have conditioned his characters to exposure to danger and yet Vaughn, able to reconcile commerce and art, has gone beyond the call of duty in instilling in them a reaction to danger that is frequently nothing less than existential terror. Lee is an obvious prototype. The hazards of being an U.N.C.L.E. agent only very rarely caused Solo's nonchalance to subside into existential terror (his panicky flight from the plant guards in *To Trap a Spy* being atypical) but trained Vaughn for the more serious reaction of Rule. For writers of *The Protectors* consistently played up this element, as if with malice aforethought.

Brian Clemens' script for *Chase* was entirely built around the unrelieved existential terror of Rule when forced to undergo what Richard Connell termed 'the most dangerous game' (films of which include *The Hounds of Zaroff*, *A Game of Death*, *Run for the Sun*, *Devil's Garden* and *Open Season*) and, upon

Rule's eventual inability to bear up any longer, the tension of the episode rapidly climaxed in bloody violence, unpleasant but contextually suitable (it was, as in *Straw Dogs*, what the script had been leading one to expect right from the start).

Talkdown put Rule in control of a plane he could not fly. His occasionally grim personality was very susceptible to existential terror, even if the detective was disciplined enough to keep it in check. In *The Big Hit*, Rule kept his cool while trapped inside a packing case being slammed against a wall by a crane but when apprised of his deliverance collapsed not only from physical exhaustion, one felt, but also from his sudden release from existential terror, well conveyed by Vaughn's acting: Vaughn closes his eyes and opens his mouth wide to breathe in deeply, his chin held high, his forehead creased and his body collapsed against the interior of the packing case. Akin to *Chase*, *Shadbolt* had Rule hunted across waste ground by an armed assassin paid to kill him, and Vaughn suggested Rule's terror as he rested by a shack momentarily by means of very heavy intakes of breath.

Aware of this susceptibility, directors also contributed to it by emphasising the very slight flinching Vaughn's face revealed in peril. Don Chaffey economically exploited Vaughn's adeptness in conveying nervous introspection escalating to panic at the end of *The Numbers Game* wherein Giocovetti (Peter Arne) points his gun at Rule's back and, his drug smuggling exposed by Rule, says he has nothing left to lose as he prepares to fire. Chaffey's camera focuses on the back of Vaughn's head as Arne speaks, intensifying the dramatic tension by not showing what the expression on Vaughn's face is, a lesson that might well have been drawn from Boris Karloff, thrice Vaughn's co-star, who once spoke of his work in *The Criminal Code*. "There was a moment of deathly silence; then the stool-pigeon turned. Before he could do a thing I had plunged a knife into him. He flopped to the floor. The audience still couldn't see my face. But they were imagining the most terrifying expression on it — far more spine-chilling expressions than I could possibly have achieved. I had simply provided the frame; they had filled in the picture." Karloff talked Hawks out of inserting close-ups of his face into the sequence: "I knew that a single shot showing my face would have spoilt the effect. Imagination alone provided those thrills. Imagination is the quality most needed in screen thrillers."

It is in the light of these remarks that Chaffey's subsequent cut to a close-up of Vaughn's face, an insertion that actually accentuates the suspense rather than diminishing it, is a tribute to Vaughn's ability to convey existential terror. His look of worry bordering on despair is all the more interesting for being resigned worry, his panic contained and accepted as a legitimate business risk. With all the luck of a television series hero, Rule was no more perturbed about Giocovetti's decision to turn the gun on himself than if his controlled existential terror had had more substantial cause. Existential terror was also in evidence at the climax of the *Balance of Terror* episode wherein Rule lets a test tube full of deadly toxin slip and wedge between two planks over a vast reservoir: with millions of lives in the balance, he manages to extract it before it falls and expresses relief from existential terror with characteristically Vaughnian conviction, much more heartfelt than Solo's perfunctory collapse in relief from anxiety in *The Karate Killers* after saving Illya from the ice-hacking machine.

Whatever the setting, the motif recurs. The existential terror manifested by Vaughn in *The Magnificent Seven* as the gunman's immobilising fear of death is examined in the next chapter. Kreuger's terror is effectively brought to light in Vaughn's expression of contained panic at the roadside execution which ominously foreshadows his own destiny. This terror is well-founded, as so many of Vaughn's characters do suffer a tragic fate.

Vaughn is a *magnificent* tragedian: only his charm can excel his efficacy in this department. So many of his characters being losers, he has thankfully been given the opportunity to exercise this talent, particularly in the depiction of the tragic fate most of them suffer, whether by their own fault or bad luck. Root dies in a smash-up, The Kid dies in a shoot-out, Chet loses an arm, Lee is shot, Klaus Everard is mauled to death, Paul Terman is a cripple, Kreuger is executed for treason, Neilson is blasted with a shotgun into a pool and then forcefully beaten and drowned, Senator Parker is jettisoned to the pavement from 135 stories, Hunter is caught in a petrol tank explosion, Simms is shot, Clay is murdered, Gelt in *Battle Beyond the Stars* is vaporised and Ryland in *Black Moon Rising* is hit by the rocket car. The only common significance of these gruesome fates is, of course, thespian: i.e. Vaughn's ability to capture every sympathetic nuance and make these fates, even the deserved ones, more than token climaxes to the characters' screen lives but often memorable and moving (particularly Lee and Kreuger).

One of Vaughn's most notable enactments of a dying character occurs in the film *Virus*, with Vaughn gasping painfully for breath. As Senator Barkley, Vaughn early in the film is at his most serious, especially in his angry confrontation with General Garld played by Henry Silva, in which he goes beyond facial attitudes of ferocity and points his finger at him aggressively, a demonstrative gesture of rage unusual among Vaughn's generally contained characters. Of course, in *Virus* it is the imminent destruction of the world that Barkley is getting steamed up about! This display of strength contrasts with the vulnerability of Barkley dying from the super Italian 'flu, with Vaughn rocking back and forth, coughing and groaning, his eyes creased in pain, giving a characteristic Vaughnian sniff to signal distress before he says hopefully "Maybe it will snow". Vaughn very convincingly represents the character's debilitation, moving from chair to chair all hunched over. Vaughn's breathing control, punctuating his dialogue emotionally with intakes of breath, allows a lilt to the delivery of Barkley's lament that is very reminiscent of Lee's manner of speech in *The Magnificent Seven*: "God, how many civilisations have *sputtered* out with those words! As our speechwriters were so *fond* of having us say about history, 'Those who can't remember the past (cough, cough) are condemned to repeat it (cough, cough).'"

The loyalty test is one of the most interesting of these motifs, and the fluctuations in Vaughn's image are reflected by its outcome. These loyalty tests permeate the Vaughnian canon, so let us list only some of the more obvious tests and then list the respective outcomes.

1. Bob Ford's loyalty to Jesse James, who saved his life (*Hell's Crossroads*)
2. Buddy Root's loyalty to Doris Dexter when their affair is broken up by his mother (*No Time to Be Young*)
3. The Boy's loyalty to his tribe when tempted to break The Law and cross the river (*Teenage Caveman*)
4. Don Bigelow's loyalty to Betty whom he has made pregnant (*Unwed Mother*)
5. Edward Campbell's loyalty to Laura (*Good Day for a Hanging*)
6. Tony's loyalty to Chet Gwynne when he is in need of defence (*The Young Philadelphians*)
7. Lee's loyalty to the other six and to his own expectations of himself (*The Magnificent Seven*)
8. Klaus' loyalty to his family (*The Big Show*)
9. Jim Melford's loyalty to his disturbed wife (*The Caretakers*)
10. Solo's loyalty to U.N.C.L.E. (refusing to join Kingsley in *How to Steal the World*), to his colleagues (*The Spy in the Green Hat*), to old flames (*The Terbuf Affair*), to new loves (when he realises what the lethal Angela plans for him in *To Trap a Spy*)
11. Bill Fenner's loyalty to the wire service re. not revealing the whereabouts of the Vaugiroud report, loyalty to Sandra (*The Venetian Affair*)
12. Kreuger's loyalty to his countrymen, to his superiors (*The Bridge at Remagen*)
13. Casca's loyalty to Caesar (*Julius Caesar*)
14. Bergen's loyalty to the difficult Soames (*The Mind of Mr. Soames*)
15. Harry Rule's loyalty to his estranged wife and son (*The Protectors — With a Little Help from My Friends*), to old friends (*Zeke's Blues*), to colleagues (Caroline at the finale of *Quin*)
16. Charles Desmond's loyalty to Joseph when he overhears Rory's plans (*Captains and the Kings*)

The results of these tests are as follows:

1. Totally disloyal
2. Not entirely loyal (the affair *was* broken up)
3. Repeatedly disloyal (the Boy makes two trips over the river)
4. Apparently loyal but only for his own purposes (he proposed in order to get out of prison)
5. Totally disloyal (deceptive but unrepentant)
6. Chet is worthy of loyalty and the recipient of it
7. Admirably loyal
8. Disloyal (Klaus turns out his father and tries to kill his brother)
9. Touchingly loyal and concerned
10. Entirely loyal, unless it would be suicidal (Angela's trap)
11. Almost masochistically loyal
12. Too loyal for everyone's good (Kreuger's actions end in catastrophe for his own side and himself)

13. Most disloyal (Casca strikes the first blow against Caesar)
14. Selflessly loyal (even to the injury of his professional standing and his own person)
15. Very loyal in all instances (as one might expect of a *protector*)
16. Predictably, ruthlessly disloyal

The loyalty test is either a general tension arising in the Vaughnian canon out of the overall dramatic conflict, as in *The Bridge at Remagen*, or else a specific moment of indecision or moral dilemma, such as many of the examples above. There are an almost endless number of other examples that could be cited.

Of course, the cinematic image is always in the present tense, so it is by small mannerisms and embellishments that Vaughn establishes certain motifs, as the next chapter argues is apparent in his attention to detail for Lee. Now there is little point in noting all the different times Vaughn has narrowed his eyes to suggest a character's feeling of vulnerability. The important thing is that Vaughn has introduced such an element where another actor would never have thought of doing so. In doing this in a given dramatic context, Vaughn thus enlarges the characterisation. Perhaps the best example comes in the final frames of the memorable *Protectors* episode *With a Little Help from My Friends*.

Vaughn's soulful look of longing for his wife may be another instance of the Yearning for Affection motif, but it contributes to our sense of Rule's essential humanity by associating the detective with certain archetypal human situations, feelings and modes of conduct. In this case, Vaughn's deliberate screen action draws on our collective memory of poignant movie partings, instantly establishing that Rule's pain is a type best exemplified by Rick watching the plane depart at the end of *Casablanca* (and Vaughn found *The Protectors* "more Humphrey Bogart than James Bond"). Or Dirk Bogarde turning away when Julie Christie notices him watching her board the plane at the end of *Darling*: a film Vaughn had seen and admired. Perhaps the ending of *Darling* lingered in his sub-conscious until the filming of *With a Little Help from My Friends* (certainly Dirk Bogarde is one of the few screen stars to have shown something of Vaughn's overt intellectualism). So Vaughn's embellishment not only creates a motif, it also gives Harry Rule's reaction to his wife's departure an emotional (not simply critical) significance.

At one point in *With a Little Help from My Friends*, Vaughn appears to assassinate actor Martin Benson, which might be construed as an ironic act of revenge by Vaughn on Benson for being the screen's first 'Mr. Solo' in the James Bond film *Goldfinger*, a minor baddie role. Because of this minor character in the Ian Fleming novel, M-G-M had to shelve their plans for a series titled *Solo* and opted instead for the title *The Man from U.N.C.L.E.*

5: The Thinking Man As Actor —An in-depth analysis of Robert Vaughn as Lee in *The Magnificent Seven* (1960)

LEE, THE VENGEFUL ONE

Nous ne sommes rien, ce que nous cherchons est tout. Aragon

Men shouldn't be admired: they are all alike, all equal.
The important thing is what they do. Sartre

(You don't owe anything to anybody . . .)
Except to myself. Lee

Succeeding a performance of cowardly weakness in *The Young Philadelphians* that was appallingly convincing, Robert Vaughn gave in this film a performance of real cowardice that was sympathetically convincing. Our sympathy is incurred both because Lee's own cowardice worries him greatly and is only for him the lesser of two evils ("this emotion by which a man is so disposed as not to will the thing he wills, and to will that which he does not will, is called 'fear', which may therefore be defined as that 'apprehension' which leads a man to avoid an evil in the future by incurring a lesser evil": Spinoza) and because of the understanding nature of Vaughn's portrayal (his gravity, remoteness and grimacing all conveying the aura of a man "so disposed as not to will *the thing he wills*", i.e. to deserve his place in the Seven, "and to will *that which he does not will*", i.e. to let the others do the fighting; an aura of cool but desperate frustration). Death is the evil Lee most fears, and it is the overcoming of his cowardice (but not his fear) that makes Lee by this redemption a moral hero.

In examination of Vaughn's creation let us adopt as our motif the following remarks by Wittgenstein, the two clauses of which here italicised span both Lee's entire screen life and Vaughn's stylistic interpretation: "It is possible to say 'I read timidity in this face' but at all events the timidity does not seem to be merely associated, outwardly connected, with the face; but *fear is there, alive, in the features*. If the features change slightly, we can speak of a corresponding change in the fear. If we were asked 'Can you think of this face as an expression of courage too?' — we should, as it were, not know how to lodge courage in these features . . . Perhaps one says: 'Yes, now I understand: the face as it were shews indifference to the outer world.' So we have somehow read courage into the face. Now once more, one might say, *courage fits this face*."

Insofar as Lee's sympathetic stature derives from both the style and the content of Vaughn's creation and as these relevant remarks by Wittgenstein (relevant since the example of Lee reveals, under Vaughn's handling, how courage of an existential kind *can* be lodged in features expressive of fear) span both style and content, a clearer perspective can be gained from examining style and content separately. Since it is by the style of playing that an actor achieves a performance of worthwhile content, style is logically prior (truth is the essence of Vaughn's style, artistically speaking, and as truth operates on many levels, his style is responsible for establishing the material that makes up the character on many levels of interpretation: one might note too that, as for Plato 'beauty is the splendour of truth', Vaughn's style is accordingly very beautiful) and examining it first should provide the perspective in which to see that Vaughn's style is not only perfectly attuned to the character's demands but also responsible for giving it mythic qualities of universal significance.

Céline writes "when one has no imagination, dying is a small matter, but for the imaginative man, dying is too much". And so fear, for all that it 'eats the soul', is a phenomenon of mind. Matching style to content, the performance of Robert Vaughn as Lee in *The Magnificent Seven* is an example of the thinking man as actor: by which I mean that given the standard Hollywood Western fare of pounding hooves, blazing barrels and taciturn tough-as-nails he-men, Vaughn has taken all this, subsumed it and turned in a performance that while in tune with the film and Western myth in general is yet truly cerebral.

Examining the content of the performance reveals that Vaughn makes Lee a complex intellectual gunslinger by suiting his performance to that which is cerebral in the scripted character: but here we are concerned with how he manages to do so. It is by the apparently effortless accumulation of fine points of detail that serves to create whole moods, as well as by the actual authorship of scenes (e.g. Lee's death). A few particular examples of Vaughn's cerebral style of film acting follow.

The subtlety and intelligence of Vaughn's characterisation of Lee through care for suggestive detail (as opposed to the scriptwriter's art) are only highlighted by the fact that *The Magnificent Seven* is otherwise a film of generally showy performances. For example, Chris' code of personal honour *is* owed to the scriptwriter and is conveyed in solely verbal fashion: the contract, formed on trust and not legally binding, he deems "just the kind you have to keep". Denied a part as verbal as Brynner's, though in ways it is more articulate, Vaughn benefits as an actor, however, from his having to convey Lee's code of personal honour by careful attention to his physical behaviour, since the results are both subtler and far more graphic. For a picture is worth a thousand words, and the succession of moving pictures composing the scene in which Lee (who, about to burst into a room full of enemies gun in hand, suddenly pauses, replaces the gun in his holster and, at heightened personal risk, bursts in and only draws when his enemies have had a fair chance at beating him to it) deliberately chooses to obey his own ethic of fair play regardless of fear or risk, is a classic sequence that bespeaks volumes about his code of personal honour that thousands of words in the script would have made no more convincing. Director John Sturges, who, incidentally, cannot recall who originated this action "except it was obviously the thing to do", gives a slightly different interpretation to this action, which is undoubtedly the more correct one and for which I am most grateful, yet it does not invalidate this essay's remarks about Lee's code of personal honour. Sturges remarks: "He didn't do it to give his foes a fair chance but to face up totally to his own capability — to go for broke."

Such a minor detail on Vaughn's part is thus pure cinema, for, as Godard has pointed out, the cinema is interested in men's actions, not their thoughts. Yet it is also an example of the thinking man as actor and in this role, as in others, Vaughn's screen actions require the audience's thoughts in order to be fully understood. Only by paying attention and asking oneself *why* Lee replaces the gun in his holster, for example, does one fully appreciate the depth of Vaughn's characterisation.

Seen often in camera close-up, Vaughn's performance as Lee is faultless. His face is a mask of varying moods that reveals more each time one sees the film and at all times we feel we are in the presence of a very cultured, sensitive and intelligent gunslinger. Vaughn proves himself particularly adept at creating a strong sense of Lee's charisma, both by close attention to detail and by imbuing him with some of his own personal charm in an expert and carefully-calculated performance of a difficult and intellectual role. Moreover, it is a non-heroic role that in Vaughn's playing ultimately proves to be heroic in a sense much more profound than the others' schoolboy bravery. Vaughn seems to have intuitively realised these implications and carefully honed his performance to the refined but suggestive facial and physical mannerisms actually on the celluloid. These mannerisms constitute clues to the character of Lee that Vaughn subtly details. For example, his continual slight grimacing well conveys the grip fear has upon Lee, particularly in the cautious squinting (e.g. at his moment's hesitation before he bursts into action) that is one of Vaughn's screen idiosyncrasies.

Subtler examples of the thinking man as actor are to be found in the brisk, business-like way he has Lee pulling on his gloves when leaving with Britt to check on some spies, or the almost mock-heroic way he soon after prepares for danger by releasing the holster-loop on his gun, a useless gesture since we know Lee's nerve to be too shaky to use it. Both of these thoughtful embellishments are ironic in their bluff eagerness for action, in their discrepancy between appearance and reality. Such simple gestures in character building are powerfully suggestive of Lee's general shame at his cowardice, his isolation within the charade he must maintain and, above all, the truly serious nature of his fear that he should think such cover-ups necessary.

Further examples of Vaughn's cerebral style of adducing fine points of suggestive detail to create a complex living portrait of Lee can be found in discussion of the performance's content, but now let us notice that Vaughn's stylistic approach not only gives us details that cohere into a film portrait but also reveals an overall conception of the role that is characteristically personal. This being so, the cerebral element here lies both in the truth of that conception and in the fact that Vaughn has the intellectual courage of his convictions (in the realm of the cinema as well as in the literary and political realms where the forthrightness of his book *Only Victims* is a splendid example): in the action Western framework he does not flinch from giving a performance of great pathos unique in facing up to the full horror and degradation implicit in the unpopular topic of cowardice. For the cinema, either through fear of not entertaining or of not seeming to condemn cowardice, which is the antithesis of everything the American cinema and especially the Western have traditionally affirmed (virility, patriotism, self-sacrifice etc.), has on the whole maintained an unsympathetic attitude toward the coward and so remained tacit on these vital implications as if cowardice were something one *chose*. Vaughn's conception of Lee is the exact opposite, so that he portrays him in a highly sympathetic manner in order to *emphasise* the horror and degradation he undergoes. This emphasis is fully justified by the fact that Lee's experience of them is terrible enough to make him choose certain death instead. In analysing this role with intellectual rigour, Vaughn the actor arrived at its most fraught implications, which he boldly did not fail to portray in a récit of images of great power.

If fear 'eats the soul', it does so both directly and indirectly: directly by filling us with sheer horror of the object of our fear and indirectly by gnawing away self-pride and courage with the feelings of degradation that are the likely consequence of horrified behaviour. Neither of these unpleasant psychological processes escape this actor's uncompromising delineation. Real horror is apparent in the facial close-ups of certain scenes: "fear is there, alive, in the features." It is remarkable how committed the actor is to communicate such horror. In the scene of Lee's night of fear, Vaughn acts with such intensity that sometimes one can almost literally see his soul in his eyes. The actor manages to portray the cerebral by means of strong emotion, so that a redolence of horror surrounds his near-delirious enactment of the fearful nightmares besetting Lee. In the final melancholic seconds of the scene, as Lee comes to realise his only avenue of escape ("Only the dead are without fear"), Vaughn looks into the camera and his head almost involuntarily sways in stunned awareness bordering on disbelief, excellently conveying how the reality to which he has awoken, more nightmarish than his dreams, has rendered him almost senseless with an endless vista of horror.

Latent horror presides in many other scenes. It is evidenced in the rigid immobility of Vaughn's whole body as Lee hides from the gunfire, literally frozen with fear; in Lee's heavy drinking alone, suggestive of the need to quell the horror within; in his verbalised conviction that one day the next gun will be faster than his; in his eventual effort to summon up nerve; and even in the pain Vaughn does not spare us seeing on Lee's dying face.

Even the most faithful adherence to the innate principles of self-preservation cannot diminish Lee's permanent horror of violent death; meanwhile, pitiful degradation is the cost of such adherence. This element might easily have predominated in Vaughn's representation of Lee but that he counters it with a recognisable nobility that demands respect for the character. Thus safeguarded, Vaughn is unequivocal about the perpetual degradation Lee undergoes. The degradation of being a renowned gunslinger on the run (and thereby easily exploited) is evoked by the bitterness Vaughn injects into Lee's voice as he says "I've got the most stylish corner of the filthy storeroom out back, that and one plate of beans — ten dollars a day". The degradation Lee feels at having to hide as before his terrified eyes people who hired him to defend them are slaughtered is apparent in Vaughn's having him glance cautiously around to ensure nobody sees his emergence from his coward's hiding place. As Lee's professional ability deserts him as his nerve shatters, Vaughn suggests a man beyond consolation as he intones the fly-catching scene; and how degrading not even to have the respect of his colleagues, who rarely speak to him, even round the dinner table, and genuinely expect nothing from him after their expulsion from the village by Calvera.

With Vaughn the undeniable eminence grise of the film flashing unmistakable expressions of terror, shame and regret continually upon the screen, the appalling psychological suffering involved in cowardice is fully realised, specifically in the constituent horror and degradation, in a performance of remarkable intensity and sensitivity. A truly poetic performance.

There is a particular example of the poetry of Vaughn's performance being owed directly to one of those subtle details that, even if intuitive in origin, exemplify the cerebral style in which Vaughn communicates his personal conception of the character. The example is of Lee's poignant death scene, which was of Robert Vaughn's own creation. On his own 1973 account: "We were all very competitive. Steve McQueen competed against Yul Brynner and the other five of us competed against one another. We were also all trying to think up effective ways to die. 'How would this be for an effective death?' I asked the director, John Sturges, one day at rehearsal. I fell against the wall and let my face be distorted by dragging against the wall as I slipped slowly down. On film it looked memorable. People still ask me if I hurt my face doing it, but of course I didn't." Here I am indebted to John Sturges for pointing out one very interesting psychological aspect of Vaughn's contribution, which could have significant ramifications for the arguments concerning Lee's death wish: "He did devise the mechanics of his death, i.e. the face slide and (surprised you didn't comment on it in your very detailed analysis) his reversion to the foetal position."

It is to be contended below that the underlying pathos of Vaughn's interpretation of Lee is reinforced by this scene to the extent that the scene becomes just one more blow, the final blow, of a tragic destiny; but for now let us note that the scene of this coward's demise draws from Vaughn's authorship of it peculiar dramatic force. For Vaughn here contributed, intuitively it seems, a scene of which the imagery is resonant of poetic justice. As Lee's failure to survive might be seen as paying a penalty for his former cowardice, so the physical context of his death is a stone wall just like the one he used for cowardly shelter. We see, to Gilbert and Sullivan's delight, 'the punishment fit the crime' insofar as the former takes place in the same physical context as the latter, thereby complementing it, and Lee dies as he lived, flat against a wall. Vaughn here thus rounded out the destiny of Lee poetically.

At this point it is imperative to stress that whatever thought Vaughn has put into his portrayal of Lee is not at the expense of the character's ability to register in the audience's *gut*. An intellectual appreciation of the character is the result of reflection upon the role *after* seeing the film, but as Lee's tragic destiny unfolds on screen before one's eyes, as Lee takes that first hesitant leap into action that (whether one has seen the film before or not) one *knows* will cost him his life, it is primarily a gut level reaction one experiences. And it is because Lee has the latter effect that he is a successfully acted screen character as opposed to an uninvolving abstract, for the cinema, as Godard summed it up in one word, is emotion. It is not difficult to trace, behind the premeditation and intuitive poeticising that elevate Lee to a level of universal significance (as regards his motivation), the unifying factor that enables him to succeed on the basic level of sheer credibility (as to whether his behaviour is consistently characterised): Robert Vaughn himself. For Vaughn owes his achievement in the very first place to drawing on his inner resources and living out the role with relentless intensity. Vaughn gets inside the skin of the role to such an extent that it becomes impossible to separate him from it, to delineate the acting from the fear and to tell where the one begins and the other leaves off (this thanks to an artistic restraint in the playing which was less in evidence in his Chet Gwynne performance). It is in this sense, regarding his face as he hides by the wall or in the fly-catching scene, that " the timidity does not seem to be merely associated, outwardly connected, with the face": it wells from deep within and Vaughn is not so much acting the part as living it. This shows in his face for "fear is there, alive, in the features" and, as noted elsewhere, not only in some scenes can one almost literally see his soul in his eyes but also, alone among the film's protagonists, Lee almost comes alive from the celluloid, a human symbol of rational cowardice.

Wittgenstein proposes that one possible description of how we could say of a face that constitutes an expression of fear that it could also constitute an expression of courage is that "the face as it were shews indifference to the outer world". One of the cinema's most fleeting but fullest illustrations of this is Lee's last moments in the film. With slit-eyed caution, Lee has burst into a room full of enemies and emerged the victor; then, for a few seconds before the fatal shot rings out, he holds his head high and surveys the violent action. Being only a few out of Lee's screen life of thousands of seconds, the sequence is too brief for Vaughn to express any emotion and his face is blank, but this is all the more effective, since it is the first time in the film his face has not been dominated by fearful caution. The very contrast of its inexpressiveness all the more "shews indifference to the outer world" and constitutes a courageous expression with no use of acting technique on Vaughn's part: here above all he can be said to live the part and not merely act it. His performance progresses from fear to courage and illustrates how courage automatically "fits" a face when the reasons for fear remain but the fear itself, although not overcome, is disregarded: when fear no longer features in one's acts, it no longer acts in one's features. Vaughn thus stylistically spans the transition from "fear is there, alive, in the features" to "courage fits this face" by simply relaxing his face muscles. The actor and the part are here indivisible. This unity is perhaps the source of the rapture this performance presents on an aesthetic level.

The details of Lee's character noted later (mode of speech, dress etc) are all examples of how Vaughn's attention to suggestive detail effects a generally stylish and charismatic portrait that makes Lee sympathetic to the audience. This then permits Vaughn not to alienate the audience in actualising the full extent of Lee's suffering and to delineate his situation in an acceptable light of tragedy. Furthermore, this aspect makes Lee a credible human being instead of The Vengeful One, adding complex, even contradictory, elements to his psychological make-up (e.g. his outwardly noble, proud and detached bearing contrasts with the fact that he is inwardly gnawed and consumed by self-disgust at his cowardice). Vaughn's performance is thus well-balanced. Lee's stylishness and charisma complement his gravity and remoteness, just as the bitterness of the voice in his introductory scene is tempered by the softness of the voice that says "Except to myself".

To conclude, Vaughn plays Lee in a style that is cerebral as well in its conception of the part as in its imaginative accumulation of subtle details; unflinching in realising with unprecedented intensity the full horrific and degrading implications in the nature of the overwhelming fear that goes with cowardice; poetic in its sensitive rendering of the coward's dilemma and in shaping his tragic destiny; totally convincing as Vaughn lives the part out; and complex enough to accommodate a number of conflicting traits. If Lee almost comes alive from the celluloid as a human symbol of rational cowardice, it is because Vaughn has, in adding some of the complexity of his own personality to his artistic attention to subtle details, made Lee a multi-dimensional character transcending his Western bonds in the universality of his dilemma.

In the cinema of affliction, where is the *Lost Weekend* of cowardice? Only in this gripping footage of Robert Vaughn do we find the rushes of what such a film would be like. Heroes of Western dramas are not often plagued with cowardice as crippling as that of Lee, whose own character is unusually downbeat for this type of film. The content of this performance can be roughly divided into the personal character of Vaughn's Lee and its particular import. Now Lee's personal character constitutes the direct results of Vaughn's acting style (e.g. his premeditation, intuitive poeticising and intense self-identification), but it is the particular import of that personal character that constitutes the *achievement* of that style. After all, a protagonist's character can very well constitute the results of an inappropriate style but such a style would be no achievement since such character would be of no import.

What, one might ask, does such import depend on? Well, an actor is always concerned with motivation and the import of Lee's personal character depends on how convincingly that character as Vaughn portrays it enables us to grasp the motivation behind Lee's behaviour. It is to be contended below that, thanks to Vaughn's cerebral style being perfectly attuned to such demands, the personal character of Lee magnificently fulfils such demands, to the extent that Lee seems the only fully rational member of the Seven, and as a result takes on an import of great significance, but to investigate the import of Lee's personal character as Vaughn portrays it requires first an investigation of that personal character. Then we shall be enabled to see that Vaughn's style is 'not only perfectly attuned to the character's demands but also responsible for giving it mythic qualities of universal significance' and in this latter formulation of the import of Lee's personal character lies the achievement of Vaughn's style. As regards his character, Lee is first and foremost . . . *a loner*.

Throughout this film Lee is an archetypal Vaughn loner, instinctively imbued with the same gravity Vaughn has employed in all his serious characterisations. It is this gravity tinged with bitterness, as in his complaint over the rent, that makes his self-sufficiency credible: a notorious gunslinger on the run, his instinctive caution is hardly likely to allow him to develop friendships with his new allies. And thus a sense of detachment, of Lee's difference and isolation from the rest in terms of both motivation and behaviour, is struck from the very beginning: even on recruitment Vin expresses unhappiness as to Lee's suitability. Sturges stresses Lee's remoteness by excluding him, and *only* him, from most of the scenes in which the group shows a spirit of kinship or community. He does not socialise. In one scene he rolls in after drinking, alone, all evening, while in the earlier campfire scene he stands alone by the tree, unlike the others sprawled together round the fire in camaraderie.

Although the sixth accepted member, Lee was in fact last of all to be introduced, and thus the emerging identity of the group was fixed and determined before he could have even attempted to characterise it differently. In this regard, Lee remains almost an afterthought, an *addition* to the group rather than a critical constituent; a fact confirmed by Vin's early reservations and by Chris' exhortation to him to leave shortly before the climax, which reveal the general feeling of Lee's dispensability. Moreover, whenever he must act as a member of the group, e.g. when Calvera disarms them all, Sturges keeps him insignificantly in the background. Critics Warman and Vallance once noted of Sturges that "one of his characteristic tricks is to place one man very close to the camera and to have the rest of the action in the far distance". In such group action scenes, Lee is too often in that 'far distance' for those of us fascinated by the character. John Sturges, however, disagrees: "Your essay notes and understands the way Lee is isolated in staging (except possibly to realise this is partly to make the audience attach importance to Lee — what's with *him*?) but on one page you say he is "too often in that 'far distance'". It's not too often if it worked."

And, of course, Lee's most memorable scenes (the fly-catching on his night of fear, and even his death) are played out alone, isolated from the others not only morally but physically. For their part, the rest of the Seven express their sense of his alienation from them less by verbalised doubts about his loyalty (Vin, Chris and Harry) than by their general silence towards him, as when he walks out to search for spies, passing right by Chris who merely looks at him.

No scene better illustrates Lee's non-belonging with the others than the juxtaposition of his cowardly sheltering with the heroics of the others. This striking image, in which Vaughn wears a look of haughty (albeit fearful) disdain on his face, comes as such a surprise, since it is the first real evidence in the film of Lee's cowardice, especially after seeing the brave actions of formerly timid villagers, that it remains one of the film's most effective and haunting compositions.

Vaughn's aloofness as Lee permeates every aspect of the performance. For example, Vaughn's general bearing is distinct from the other six. In contrast to the blasé superior stride of Brynner as Chris the leader or the nervous jerky movement of Buchholz as the immature youth Chico, Vaughn's demeanour as Lee is one of diffidence, of calm and almost philosophical resolution. Note the calmness with which he pulls on his gloves when going to hunt spies, the look not only of fear but also of aloofness when hiding from the gunfire, his unprotesting compliance when he has to surrender his gunbelt and his wry and understated reaction at finding himself a gunfighter with an empty holster. John Baxter has even singled Vaughn's movement out for comment, noting how graceful it is: "Sturges gives balletic grace to the battles . . . Vaughn . . . leaping into a room crowded with bandits and shooting them all in a motion as superbly choreographed as any dance routine." French critics Astre and Hoarau have also singled out "le sixième mercenaire", describing him as "ce dandy aux allures désinvoltes". This unhurried and undemonstrative attitude is set from the very beginning. Lee's entrance in the film is not even an entrance, for a door is opened on a hotel room and the light outside reveals him lying on a bed.

Dandyism has always been an assertion of individuality, of difference. As one *Observer* critic has written: "Preoccupied by what Beerbohm called 'the great art of self-embellishment', the dandy hardly has much talent for friendship." Again it is a way in which Lee marks himself off from the others. Vaughn characterises Lee's aloofness by making him easily the most stylish of the Seven, not only moving in an unhurried graceful manner but looking smartly attired all the time in well-cut suits, resplendent waistcoat, shirt and bow, black gloves and hat.

Lee's loner stance is not only explicable but completely logical when seen in perspective. This aristocratic coward has little in common with his comrades (not even professional ability): yet why should he? He is hardly among these men by choice; it is a last resort. Only the need to survive forces him to compromise. In many ways, being forced to band together with the other six is itself a compromise for an inveterate loner like Lee, a compromise he is partly railing against by ducking out of combat. The loner is not unsympathetic however, for, Vaughn's style of presenting him apart, the very qualities that form the essence of Lee are those we can only describe as very . . . *human*.

Lee's essential humanity is revealed in the way his ignominy reaches him. Perpetually darting suspicious glances at those around him, the inveterate loner nurses the secret of his debilitating cowardice. Separated from the world of men by his own sensitivity to the horror of death (witness the scene of his terrifying dream) and to the shame of hiding not the fear in his gut (Vin candidly acknowledges his own sweaty-palmed fear) but the lack of 'manliness' to overcome it (witness his self-disgust in the fly-catching scene), Lee evidences reactions that are all too human, running a gamut from panic to self-pity. The latter is more acceptable here than in Chet Gwynne's case since Lee at least entertains full (horrified) awareness of what is happening to him. His humanity is manifest in his regret over his break with the world of men as symbolised by his solitude, this regret being proved by his ultimate sacrifice to reintegrate himself with his fellows.

When this regret becomes bitter despair, one only finds this understandable because, for all his moodiness, Lee is the most credible, most palpably human of the Seven: take the confessional scene of his realisation of his degradation (describing himself as "the deserter hiding out in the middle of a battlefield"). To most audiences this scene will suffice to represent Lee as a man whose actions spring not from mere selfishness but from paralysing cowardice (literally: notice how motionless he is as he grips the wall during the gun-play) and will therefore, if not condone his previous non-participation, at least make it understandable. Indeed, one could easily make out a case for Lee being the sanest and most rational member of the group while already the most sympathetically vulnerable. For often the wild cowboy antics and ludicrous foolhardiness of Chico (standing out in full hail of gun-fire for sheer bravado and getting his hat blown off), the typical tough cowboy image of Chris ("There's one thing I can do. I can kill the very first man who talks of quitting. The very first man, so help me, I'll blow his head off") and the comic-strip prowess of the others (e.g. Britt's marksmanship with hand gun or knife) seem unreal and much more the attributes of folk heroes or movie cowboys than of human beings with their frailties and imperfections. Only Lee behaves rationally: he has no personal cause to defend (like would-be homesteader Vin), no bones to pick (like Chris, outraged by injustice), no thrills to seek (like Britt, so good he can only compete with himself), nothing to prove (like the virility-asserting Chico), no gold to seek (like greedy Harry Luck), no personal involvement (like O'Reilly and the young boys), for all he wants is peace and anonymity in continuation of existence. So Lee is the only truly credible member of the Seven, for the reasons for and the solution of his predicament are clearly defined and completely logical. His are the only truly human depths of all the Seven: the others make splendid movie heroes but remain palpably no more than that, whereas Lee almost comes alive from the celluloid, so intense is Vaughn's handling of Lee's essential humanity, and does indeed become a symbol of rational cowardice. This is intensified by the fact that Lee's character decidedly leans toward the . . . *tragic*.

Lee is not an archetypal loner for its own sake in Vaughn's interpretation. This element is just a feature of the picture Vaughn composes to make Lee credible as a figure of inherent and great tragedy, a man doomed to die who had won the right to live. If up to a certain point Lee is only a sympathetic yet slightly miserable figure, from the time of the Seven's expulsion by Calvera on he becomes a tragic figure. This cannot be emphasised too strongly, for upon re-viewing the film one finds that this element underscores every one of Vaughn's appearances in the film hitherto. All the cowardice, fear, philosophical detachment and bitter grimacing are in retrospect seen in a new light as intimations of fatality. Lee, whom a contemporary piece of film publicity material ironically enough described as "the man the newspapers said had been killed", intuitively senses his encroaching death, or rather Vaughn the actor seeks to convey Lee's tragic potential in his sympathetic characterisation. In this light, Lee's reluctance to aid his fellows is much less unpardonable, for one feels in watching that almost inscrutable face that the knowledge that exposure to gunfire will surely lead to extinction is what prevents him from mobilising himself into action, an inhibition that costs him a nocturnal attack of bad conscience.

The tragic element is that he is quite right, for the very first time he risks himself he is indeed killed, and that he knows he is right, and that yet despite this he is willing to return and face almost certain death at the village, simply because he feels at this stage that he can hide no longer nor be a man apart any more. It is a moment of irrevocable commitment. Chris allows him to leave: "Go on, Lee. You don't owe anything to anybody." Almost chillingly (the chill of death?), Lee whispers in reply "Except to myself". Now, from this moment onward, Lee has paid the price and is truly one of the Seven, yet we feel, as does Lee, that the price will cost him everything, and still he is willing to risk it. It is an important moral choice for Lee as a man, probably his first truly noble gesture. The tragedy is that in rejecting a lifetime of cowardly selfishness Lee, mindful of the probable consequences, commits a selfless act that *immediately* does cost him his life. It is sad to die having only just become a worthwhile man, or as Robert Warshow put it: "The Westerner is . . . seeking not to extend his dominion but only to assert his personal value, and his tragedy lies in the fact that even this circumscribed demand cannot be fully realised."

Lee, as played by Robert Vaughn, is a figure of tragic dimensions, for his cowardice and fear are matched by his inwardness and agony of conscience and are completely vindicated by his ultimate heroism, all the more valuable for not coming easily to him (note his moment's hesitation before bursting into the room, forcing himself to do it). The result is that his death seems unnecessarily cruel and unjust, for he was robbed of the chance to be good once he had made the decision, which is the unkindest cut of all and the sort of unfairness that would happen in life, not in the movies where good of any kind is usually rewarded. Again in Vaughn's portrayal we forget that we are witnessing cinema, we feel that this is real. Yet in a small way it *is* rewarded. After rescuing the people in the room, Lee like a new man surveys the action with head held high and pride, if not in his chest, perhaps in ours. It only lasts a few seconds before the fatal shot rings out tolling his death knell, yet they are the finest of Lee's life. "Now once more, one might say, courage fits this face."

In the tragic light of the intense style in which this character is delineated by Vaughn, it becomes rather more than conjecture to see a suicidal element in Lee's character culminating in a death wish. Under this view, Lee largely went to Ixcatlan in the first place in order to satisfy that death wish, which, paradoxically, was the result of an inescapable and morbid fear of death. For as Chris says at the end of the second sequel to *The Magnificent Seven* (George Kennedy in *Guns of the Magnificent Seven*): "The coward dies many times, the brave only once." The death wish is made explicit in the significance Vaughn has Lee read into the peasants' innocuous remark "Only the dead are without fear", as conveyed by the dawning realisation Vaughn summons on his face. London's *Monthly Film Bulletin* in its contemporary review actually detected Freudian significance in Lee's black gloves and nightmares, although John Sturges is sceptical about this: "Gunfighters often wore black gloves which seemed suited to the high style Lee affected." This death wish allows Lee his only freedom of choice, the choice of when to die and, because the decision is so personal, his last possibility of self-assertion.

Although as Wittgenstein has argued "Death is not an event in life: we do not live to experience death", the decision to die *is* an event in life and Lee's screen life is constructed so that he shall experience that decision. This event is an exercise of the will and as such alters for Lee "the limits of the world . . . In short the effect must be that it becomes an altogether different world." For "The world of the happy man is a different one from that of the unhappy man". Thus Lee's decision to fulfill his death wish *is* an event that changes his life, for as long as he has left to live: it cures his maladjustment, reintegrates him with the group, affords him a world in which destinies are freely chosen rather than one in which external conditions determine a behaviour he himself despises, and promises that the end shall come *magnificently*. His tragedy is heightened by the fact that his death is not even the one he would have hoped for, since, its heroic aspects aside, his death comes from an apparently gratuitous bullet, not from the more honourable gun duel with a specific opponent, and is thus an 'absurd' accident that, culminating with his face distorted along the rough brick wall of a God-forsaken Mexican village, is ultimately sordid in its tragedy. And yet, although Lee only inhabits "an altogether different world" for what is, temporally speaking, a very short time, his decision is still worthwhile since in another sense, more profound, he inhabits it eternally, for a period beyond time. For this world, the world of the happy man, is the very first world in his screen life that he has really *lived* in (before, he was not truly The Vengeful One that in his heroic last action he became, but only "the deserter hiding out in the middle of a battlefield"; ironically, it is also the world he dies in) and only in this present world can he be said to live, and "If we take eternity to mean not infinite temporal duration but timelessness, then eternal life belongs to those who live in the present". In sum, the final value of a new lease of life cannot be counted in seconds.

These have been some of the more prominent traits in Lee's character and they enable us to consider its particular import, which, because of the conviction of Vaughn's style of playing, consists in mythic qualities of universal significance, by means of which the motivation behind Lee's behaviour is completely laid bare. Having seen what Vaughn's style and what Lee's character consist in, let us come to a final assessment of Vaughn's achievement by examining some of the qualities that count for the import of the character, their relation to myth and their universal significance.

Existential freedom . . . The dilemma Lee undergoes right up to the moment of his final commitment is clearly existential in character (as opposed to a purely moral dilemma such as that faced by Vaughn's Kreuger in *The Bridge at Remagen*). It is an existential dilemma because its object is to determine the most viable course of conduct for the future. According to Sartre: "If man is what he is, bad faith is for ever impossible . . . in order for me not to be cowardly, I must in some way also be cowardly . . . at once both be and not be totally and in all respects a coward." Thus the choice Lee makes ("Except to myself"), in its candour and moral courage, forms an act of "good faith" that, at the price of his life, does not "flee what it cannot flee". It would be wrong to say that Lee escapes from the impossible choice between bad faith and probable death by plunging into violent action, since this is simply what he is averse to, but it is right to put it that in accepting to go to Ixcatlan in the first place he put himself into a context of violent action that would finally force him to exercise his freedom, make a choice of conduct and thus resolve his dilemma once and for all. As hell together seems better than hell alone, Lee manifests his freedom by legitimately joining the Seven in volunteering to return, though he knows he is doomed to fail in finding what he really wants (*la vraie vie est absente*) and will have to accept death. Lee's freedom is only made more poignant by its circumscription and is responsible for showing how courage can be 'lodged' in features expressive of fear. This courage is portrayed on screen in the fleeting and illusory but still deeply felt moment of peace as Lee surveys the violent action with head held high, integrated at last with this absurd world by meeting it on its own terms. Lee may still be afraid and his features may still be capable of an expression of fear, but the serenity Vaughn employs in these moments is the kind of peace only obtained at the price of great courage, a courage it is impossible to detach from even this fearful man, the truest kind of courage that his actions in good faith have implacably lodged in his features, the courage of existential freedom.

Moral heroism . . . There is not time to make much of this in the film, yet Vaughn unmistakably conveys it in Lee's ultimate honesty and integrity, qualities suggested by Vaughn's candid persona rather than any scripting. It is further apparent in his articulation of the fact that he feels he *owes* something to himself. He not only needs or desires a better life, free from self-disgust, but knows it to be morally right. He feels a moral obligation, if only to himself, for himself and by himself, and has the heroism to fulfil it. Lee is a moral hero none the less for being concerned solely with self, with sacrificing himself from self-centred motives and not primarily, although this is an incidental end result, for the benefit of others, as with Kreuger. Ultimately, indeed, considerations of future horror and degradation are sufficiently to the fore to make Lee's dilemma itself mainly existential, not moral, in character, but the moral heroism he manifests in solving that dilemma is by no means negligible. This is the heroism that is much more profound than the others' schoolboy bravery.

Unprecedented complexity . . . Lee strikes us less as a mercenary than as a complex intellectual gunslinger, largely because of the cerebrality, surprising in this action genre, that Vaughn stresses, e.g. he invests Lee with the morality noted above plus the ability to articulate it to himself. Then there is the great lucidity of that articulation, remarked upon by Astre and Hoarau and expressed in introspective moments of self-examination. This thoughtful demeanour defines him, within the limits of his self, as intellectually orientated, even if his complexity is owed mainly to the deep inner resources of his own (i.e. Vaughn's) soul. Drawing on this, Lee naturally becomes one of the cinema's first really successful complex intellectual gunslingers. But cerebrality is only one facet of his complexity; there are apparent contradictions. Outwardly noble and detached, he is yet inwardly gnawed and consumed by self-disgust; and while indisputably a villain credited with a violent past, he is sufficiently complex in Vaughn's execution to be also a man of great allure and personal honour who allows his enemies the chance to draw. These contradictions help explain Lee's motivation, suggesting as they do a man more misguided than evil to whom, perhaps, society could only offer the gun as a tool of trade.

There is even a difficulty classifying Lee: is he a hero, an anti-hero, a villain, a moral hero, or all of these at the same time? Such ambivalence extends even to our judgement of his rationality, which depends on our own viewpoint. Because, opposed to the view of Lee prior to his self-sacrifice as a symbol of rational cowardice, if one locates Lee's symbolic qualifications rather in laying down his life to escape from his cowardice, then one will concur with the words of Paul Newman in *The Rack* who, faced with an impossible choice like Lee's, sorrowfully chose cowardice: "In every man's life there comes a moment of choice and if he chooses rightly it is a moment of magnificence and if he chooses wrongly it is a moment he will regret all his life." Immediately this formulation strikes one as applicable to Lee and it is odd that the words used should prove so relevant: Lee's choosing rightly is doubly a moment of 'magnificence' since it is also what makes him at last an authentic member of *The Magnificent Seven*. But if, on the other hand, one holds that Lee's choice was more foolish than correct since it cost him his life, cowardice being more rational, one might prefer to see his position as rather more analogous to the death of Porthos in Dumas' *Twenty Years After*. Porthos placed his bomb, lit it, ran away, and suddenly began to think, to wonder how it was possible for him to place one foot in front of the other . . . and, doubting, stopped running and so died. How, one may ask, is this analogous to Lee? Well, Lee's nagging scruples lead him to acknowledge a moral obligation just as Porthos' Zeno-derived perplexity leads him to a philosophical scepticism: if both have reached higher awareness that can in each case be assimilated within the sphere of philosophical thought, then whoever considers Lee's final actions as tantamount to suicidal madness will recognise the aptness of the remark on Porthos: "The first time he thought, he died as a result." Namely, in the words of Thomas Gray, ". . . where ignorance is bliss, 'Tis folly to be wise."

Now, how do these qualities relate to myth? They do so by illustrating a new archetype in delineating Lee's dilemma. For existential freedom, moral heroism and unprecedented complexity raise Lee from the level of Western fiction to the level of Western cinematic myth, insofar as these qualities revealed in his response to his dilemma establish him as an archetypal anti-hero of a more ambivalent kind than seen before, and only rivalled since by William Berger in spaghetti Westerns. They do so because they have a more profound correspondence with the realm of myth than the mere fact that Sturges' film has its origins in samurai mythology: they at once both invent and reinvent it. For Lee invents myth insofar as he is a non-traditional villain; he merely reinvents myth insofar as he is a traditional anti-hero (e.g. his Billy The Kid in *Tales of Wells Fargo* or his Edward 'The Kid' Campbell in *Good Day for a Hanging*). Shrouded in ambivalence, Lee is a non-traditional *villain* insofar as his virtues outweigh his faults, his major fault being also what his moral redemption ultimately arises from as a result of the heroism he manifests in facing up to his existential freedom. And yet it cannot be denied that he is a traditional anti-hero, a 'bad man'. If Lee is raised to mythic proportions, it is by actions revealing qualities relating to myth that illustrate an ambivalent new archetype in this genre. There are no antecedents in Western cinematic history for him to conform to. Not only is the full realisation of the overwhelming nature of fear unparalleled but Lee himself is the first successful complex intellectual gunslinger, an anti-hero on the level of myth who becomes by redemption a moral hero. So, Lee represents a departure from the archetypal anti-hero insofar as he is an ambivalent villain. Vaughn's cerebral style suggests the highly conscious aspect of Lee's awareness of existential dilemma, an aspect that lends credence to the element of moral heroism that makes Lee too ambivalent and complex a character to fit neatly into traditional villain or traditional anti-hero moulds. A new archetype of ambivalent morality and intellectual complexity has been created, prefiguring by half a decade the 'new' hero of the Italian Western whose ambivalence and complexity would be consciously emphasised, with mystery being substituted for motivation. But Lee is a more engaging figure than his cold-blooded successors.

For the particular import of Lee's mythic qualities arose precisely from the fact that Vaughn's style of premeditation and intuitive poeticising raised Lee to a level of universal significance as regards his *motivation*. Mystery may shroud a particular individual but it cannot be universally applied and so holds no mythic significance, whereas the motivation carefully if economically laid bare in Lee's existential dilemma *is* universally applicable. It mirrors the universal dialectic between mere being versus living. For what is it that makes this anti-hero with mythic qualities a tragic moral hero other than his solution to his dilemma, namely the decision to *live* come what may, to face death in the course of living, to buy some life at the price of death (its inevitable concomitant) rather than go on merely being, in bad faith, without pride or the comradeship of his fellows, tormented by dreams, breaking his contract and failing to meet the qualifying test of his manhood that the conflict at Ixcatlan poses? Vaughn's achievement is to have intuitively grasped the true existential subject of his material and to have poeticised its tragedy in a cerebral style. For his style adduces mythic qualities which, in turn, sketch in a complexity of motivation so fascinating that Lee's character assumes an import of universal significance. His dilemma of the 1880s is seen to be as widespread today, he himself is real and tragic enough to identify and sympathise with, and we can only hope that ultimately we would have the moral courage to emulate his striking and noble example in similar conditions. And if one must die, so be it: one of the film's final compositions is of four graves together, for only Chris, Vin and Chico survived. We do not know which one is Lee's, for the graves are unmarked, but it does not matter, for at last, even if in death, Lee belongs!

JOHN STURGES' COMMENT ON THE ABOVE ESSAY:
The above essay was submitted to John Sturges in May 1980 for his comment. Apart from the particular comments cited in the text, he commented generally as follows: "*It was interesting to read your essay which I thought was well written and very perceptive. You'll understand that, like most of us who make films, I work from a very free, emotional and gut reaction to what I'm seeing and putting together rather than an intellectual one, so the nature and complexity of your observations and comments are often far beyond what I thought then or now.*"

ROBERT VAUGHN'S COMMENT ON THE ABOVE ESSAY:
The essay was then submitted — along with all of John Sturges' comments — to Robert Vaughn in December 1980, and the following January he commented: "*Your comments in Chapter 5 of a critical nature about my performance in THE MAGNIFICENT SEVEN are of course analysis and not subject to revision on my part, because they are not in the area of biographical data. But I enjoyed reading it immensely. I think it's extremely well-done.*"

References

Ethics by Spinoza (Hafner Library of Classics)
Philosophical Investigations by Ludwig Wittgenstein (Basil Blackwell, Oxford 1972)
Voyage au bout de la nuit by Louis-Ferdinand Céline (translated by Erika Ostrovsky in *Cèline and His Vision* by Erika Ostrovsky, New York University Press 1967)
Only Victims: A Study of Showbusiness Blacklisting by Robert Vaughn (G.P. Putnam's Sons, New York 1972)
Fear Eats the Soul by Rainer Werner Fassbinder (West German film, 1974)
The Robert Vaughn Story, Part Two: Death in Dallas and the birth of 'U.N.C.L.E.' by Robert Vaughn (*TV Times*, London 29 September 1973); Vaughn has told me that this three-part story was actually ghostwritten from a taped interview by a *TV Times* freelance writer
Westerns: A Preview Special edited by Eric Warman and Tom Vallance (Golden Pleasure Books, London)
Hollywood in the Sixties by John Baxter (Tantivy Press, London 1972)
Univers du Western by Georges-Albert Astre and Albert-Patrick Hoarau (Cinema Club, Editions Seghers, Paris 1973)
Mutual Admiration by Peter Conrad (The Observer Review, London 31 August 1975: review of the book *Max and Will* edited by Mary M. Lago and Karl Beckson, John Murray (Publishers) Ltd 1975)
The Magnificent Seven Original Pressbook (United Artists 1960)
Movie Chronicle: The Westerner by Robert Warshow, reprinted in *Focus on the Western* edited by Jack Nachbar (Prentice Hall Inc., New Jersey 1974)
Tractatus Logico-Philosophicus by Ludwig Wittgenstein (Routledge & Kegan Paul Ltd., London 1969)
Being and Nothingness: An Essay on Phenomenological Ontology by Jean-Paul Sartre (Methuen & Co. Ltd., London 1972)
Une Saison en Enfer by Arthur Rimbaud, in *Rimbaud: Complete Works, Selected Letters*, Translation, Introduction and Notes by Wallace Fowlie (Phoenix Books, The University of Chicago Press, 1967)
Remarks concerning the death of Porthos from *Godard on Godard*, Translation and commentary by Tom Milne (Secker and Warburg, London 1972)

6: Robert Vaughn's Stylistic Techniques

Any analysis of Vaughn's style must comprehend its differences and development. On the one hand, his purely intuitive approach to performance, and on the other hand, his cerebral approach: not to mention his fluctuation between the two. Vaughn's intuitive approach concerns reliance on instinct and the rightness of certain gestures and expressions dictated by the moment, reactions demonstrating the character's personality highly emotively. It occurs mainly in the passionate performances of the earlier phase of Vaughn's career, although he has never abandoned it (the intuitive approach is highly evident in his death scene in *Blast*), and is conveyed mainly by such emotive techniques as revealing the soul in the eyes (Chet Gwynne, Lee).

The most rewarding example of this early, mainly intuitive approach arose from his unexpected casting in an episode of *Zorro* as a Spanish American peasant orange-grower in old California.

Spark of Revenge, a 1958 episode of the children's adventure series *Zorro*, is fairly typical of Vaughn's exuberant television work of the period and a sign of how television proved a richer source of roles than the cinema. Vaughn, with a pencil-thin moustache, plays Miguel Roverto who, having threatened Don Hilario for withholding water despite a drought, is falsely accused of Hilario's murder until Zorro catches the real culprits. The plot was thus fairly elementary and largely action-oriented, as one would expect from director William Witney, veteran of serials and Westerns, but thankfully devoid of the usual buffoonery featured in this series, generally centred around the comic Sergeant Garcia. Against this setting, a youthful purity shines through in Vaughn's performance, which notably gives the part more passion than it deserves.

The role only permits one or two quiet moments of intensity between comic strip action (which, in the final fight, Vaughn revels in quite appropriately: note his devilishly funny grin of satisfaction as he swiftly turns after punching his opponent through the doorway) but, despite the need to maintain a Spanish accent (which he manages convincingly, particularly with the words "loaded", "do", "water", "fair" and "happy"), Vaughn actually does begin to suspend disbelief. In part this is simply because his physical appearance is highly acceptable, casting doubts upon his unsuitability for the Latin lead in *Cry Tough*! Such images carry weight as that of Miguel standing moodily watching the smouldering ashes of his house, with his face dirtied by smoke and perspiration on his face reflecting the flickering of the embers; offsetting the solemnity of his expression, the thin moustache effectively evokes the latin stereotype of the movies. But suspension of disbelief is principally achieved by the conviction of his playing, which, whatever the level of the material, is the hallmark of vintage early Vaughn.

The chief example is the dialogue when Don Diego (Zorro) offers Miguel money to rebuild his home. Miguel turns and rests his hands against the mantel of the fireplace, looking down at the burning logs. From a right profile to full facial close-up of an astonishingly young Vaughn, Miguel pours out his sorrow: "My orange trees . . . (Vaughn pauses slightly) . . . one by one they are dying for lack of water. It is a sad thing, Don Diego . . . (pause) . . . to see a poor little tree dying, nothing you can do to help it". . . "People do not understand . . . (a long pause) . . . a tree it is a living thing (Vaughn stresses 'living thing' with passion and then continues more rapidly). . . its roots they reach out for water, when they cannot find it. . . (Vaughn pauses for dramatic effect) . . . slowly it dies." His next reply to Don Diego is spoken much faster, because Miguel is losing patience: "I will not let my trees die, it is not fair. . . (Vaughn stresses 'not fair'). . . Somehow I will get water."

One is almost touched by the peasant's plight. The exact exploitation of speech rhythm, of emphasis of key words and of dramatic pauses, coupled with the determined set of Vaughn's features, suffices, temporarily, to make one stop *accepting* a Hollywood actor pretending to be a peasant and *feel* the hopelessness of Miguel's position. Almost immediately, the script reverts to blood-and-thunder dramatics, and again one is watching Vaughn be a dashing movie actor, with a certain swashbuckling appeal that clearly shows the 'heroic' promise that was fulfilled in avuncular years to come. Nevertheless, Vaughn's versatility and capabilities with the right material have, however briefly, again been proved.

This early *Zorro* show demonstrates Vaughn to be already quite a wily actor, in that the various screen techniques he would later perfect are already in evidence here, particularly the furtive glance. When he slips into the meeting between Don Hilario and Don Diego, he confronts Mauridio and Tonio and his eyes shift from one to the other to check their violence and then he stares (expressing contained rage) unflinchingly at Don Hilario with no other facial expression (the stiff upper eyebrow) but, instead of protruding his chin as the older, bolder Vaughn would have done (particularly the 'wages of sin' characters such as Charles Clay), the young Vaughn lowers his chin, his forehead comes forward and the stare of his eyes on Don Hilario is thereby deepened. Having got his message across, he then looks away; thereafter, his glances dart furtively. The eyes flash with anger, however, as Wahl would note of the character he played in *The Venetian Affair*.

The other main reaction Vaughn would use again is the suppressed ironical laugh of disbelief, consisting of an intake of breath as if to say something in reply and then thinking better of it, smiling and lowering the head instead as if to concede a point but suggesting that the point is not worth discussing or that it has left him speechless. In this reaction, here to Don Diego's advice to accept his misfortune as his home smoulders, one plainly sees the makings of the actor of *The Venetian Affair* (see the rejection by Giulia) and *Bullitt* (see Lt. Bullitt's criticisms). Typical too is the narrowing of the eyes to indicate a process of deliberation, when Zorro rides off expecting him to follow in the hope they may clear his name.

Despite Vaughn's physical dynamism and emotional power, *Spark of Revenge* is not art. Nevertheless, there is an unconscious poetic symmetry to the episode, thanks to Witney's two most memorable framings of Vaughn, which occur at the beginning and end of the episode respectively. The first has Vaughn on all fours on the ground, Mauridio and Tonio having poured his barrels of water all over him and ridden off leaving him in the mud. Vaughn, with a lost expression, spreads his hands around on the surface of the mud, almost caressing it, as if thereby to retrieve some of the lost water.

The second has Vaughn gloriously kneeling in a downpour of rain, his arms outstretched, his face smiling wide. The image is a poetic echo — indeed, poetic reversal — of the earlier scene, and the final cut to the figure of Zorro implies that his intervention has been a cleansing and life-restoring one. Miguel is still wet and in the mud but from a posture of humiliation in the dirt he is given a dignified posture very like that of an act of worship beneath the cleansing downpour. This transformation from one posture to a very similar one of greater dignity as a result of heroic action would be more tragically represented in the climax of Vaughn's performance in *The Magnificent Seven*.

Vaughn was particularly pleased when I told him of my high regard for this performance and said: "I recall that very fondly and I remember seeing it at Natalie Wood and Robert Wagner's house when they were married the first time. Because they wanted me to be in a film, *All the Fine Young Cannibals*, a role that George Hamilton ultimately did. And I went there that night to discuss that, and mainly I tried to get away from them to watch this show that was being aired that night, but I've never seen it since. But I remember enjoying it. I remember it was such an odd thing for me to be cast in. I remember at the time that I was so delighted at not being cast in the *No Time to Be Young* 'hostile' thing. I don't remember what I did in terms of coaching, but I know I was very happy to have a crack at doing something this off-beat, for me anyway, as that role. I'd love to see that again because I remember it very vividly. I remember it fondly and I'd be curious to see it."

Then there is the calculated, more cerebral approach, realised in subtle, premeditated screen actions, which in the middle phase of Vaughn's career went hand in hand with the intuitive approach. For example, the restraint in Vaughn's performances of Lee and Kreuger erupts into an outflow of emotion. The only emotion Chalmers let himself show was anger, but *Bullitt* is still an excellent example of the middle phase of Vaughn's career.

It was Vaughn's persuasiveness as the sneaky Walter Chalmers, assistant District Attorney grooming himself for public office, that created what some associates of his feel is a latter-day George Sanders image: the sneaky, smarmy, power figure, the affluent businessman, head of a corporation or, especially, the politician. For, in a relatively small part, Vaughn's screen authority eclipsed even the dynamic star, Steve McQueen, and precipitated an immediate and quite shocking leap forward in public appreciation of Robert Vaughn's stature as an actor. He works so well within the scheme of the film because his style here is unobtrusive yet too dynamic (Chalmers is an exceptionally charming man) and compulsive (there is none of the light relief Vaughn would bring to later ruthless men such as Neilson) not to make one fascinated by the character. Audience feeling towards Chalmers remains at all times rather ambivalent, recognising how despicable he is yet unable to conquer a grudging but substantial admiration. Vaughn plays up this effect with the authority of his interpretation: e.g. the delivery of dialogue with the head tilted forward to accentuate a long-held unblinking stare. The best example of this is the scene where Chalmers faces Bullitt behind a sliding glass partition. Angry about having his witness hospitalised, Vaughn's Chalmers purses his lips, holds the long stare of a pair of inscrutable brown eyes and pauses for breath not once as he says he will personally officiate at Bullitt's public crucifixion if the witness does not recover.

Vaughn's faultless vocal and facial representation of Chalmers' intimidating personality even has the normally imperturbable McQueen taken aback. McQueen is uncharacteristically cowed (gulping at the start of this encounter), nervous and unaggressive in this scene, and is even still on the defensive in their last meeting (feeling the need to account for his obstruction by saying "Let's get one thing clear, Chalmers. I don't like you"), unable to refuse to acknowledge the superior force of Vaughn's Chalmers. For though Chalmers may be characteristically sedate, as befits a man of his public and professional stature, and is therefore rightly absent from all action or violence (Renick's shooting, the car chase) or if present (the airport shooting of Ross) is only a passive onlooker, yet he *is* characterised by great inner reserves of ferocity and acuity. Vaughn summons these reserves from the channels of his own thought, honed by introspection (note Chalmers' attitude as he awaits the duty nurse, an attitude of complete self-absorption).

Overall, though, Vaughn's Chalmers lacks doubt or fear. This is the assurance of a man with a realisation of his own security, both financial and social. Both *The Magnificent Seven* and *The Bridge at Remagen* concern man's faithfulness to his own conscience and what it costs, but *Bullitt* is concerned precisely with the negation of any such concept, for even in defeat Chalmers is a winner. Post-Watergate, Vaughn's quietly chilling portrayal becomes all too real.

The characterisation provided by many of the action-packed episodes of *The Protectors* was negligible, and much of the depiction of Harry Rule's personality is simply the result of certain mannerisms and reactions Vaughn brings to fairly lifeless situations in the scripts. For instance, it is Vaughn's facial reactions that bring interest to the routine kidnap plot of *Bagman* which was shot in Copenhagen. An example of how Vaughn's acting deepens the significance of the script occurs in the last few minutes of the episode, from the man accosting Harry for money in return for information, to Harry's observance of Christian's death and Evi's safety. The older Vaughn's increasing capacity for impatience bordered on rage at the mercenary informant's disregard for Evi's life, Vaughn employing the sternest facial expressions he could muster. This contrasted strongly with the dispassionate execution of Christian, Vaughn's entirely unregretful observance of his death and his walk across the roof to observe Evi being put aboard the boat: a symbolic representation of Rule's interest in life rather than death. The self-preservation instinct revealed in the cautious, quick, darting glances of Rule's eyes, immediately upon shooting Christian and before he knows him to be no longer a threat, becomes dislodged by a gaze of serenity, revealing order restored and innocence *protected* (represented by Evi's safe return to her family).

Finally, in Vaughn's mature phase, he completes the transition to dispassionate, utterly controlled and cerebral passivity, that is less of a 'performance' and more a matter of 'incarnating' a role, e.g. many of his 'wages of sin' characters. A typically elliptical technique to convey this cerebrality is the undemonstrative stiff upper eyebrow in the most eyebrow-raising situations. This was most apparent in performances following *The Towering Inferno*, such as in the *Columbo* show *Last Salute to the Commodore*.

In *Last Salute to the Commodore*, the rather imperial majesty of the older Vaughn's stolid presence was well conveyed solely by economical direction (best exemplified in the framing of the shot where Vaughn's Charles Clay stands on board with his head held haughtily back, his chin high in the air, symbolically dominating Columbo and the Sgt. who remain physically on a lower level on the left of the frame: the silence of Clay throughout only confirms his solitary aloofness from the enquiry being conducted). Director Patrick McGoohan also had the intelligence not just to make use of this kind of presence Vaughn is capable of projecting (given a chance) but even to send it up, which gave McGoohan the best moments in the show.

The first concerned the transportation of Clay for questioning in Columbo's small sports car. With the Sgt. in the back, Columbo squashes in beside Clay who is seated beside rookie cop Mac who is not used to driving a car requiring manual gear changes with a lever. The situation rumples both Clay's person and his dignity, which Vaughn conveyed very well by giving frowning looks and raising his arms to tug himself away from Columbo who was sprawling to get a watch out of his pocket, without falling foul of Mac's gear lever. The other scene was when Clay got a man on the phone for Columbo who plonked down on the sofa beside him, comically sprawling over Clay and pulling the telephone wire taut across his chest, in which captive situation he dared put his left arm familiarly around Clay's shoulder. Vaughn reacted with his usual distaste and contained exasperation, shifting his ground, looking with condescension at Columbo's hand on his shoulder and moving the telephone wire up to free himself a little.

McGoohan did not overlook some of the usual features of Vaughn's television appearances. He employed effectively enough Vaughn's natural authority and capacity for stern dominance in the scene where Clay shouts impatiently at his alcoholic wife not to drink; his loser connotations (his wife a drunk, his own murder); his excellent duplicity (the lies Clay tells in the morgue scene); his introspective sense of defeat (at those lies being exposed by Columbo who leaves Vaughn looking downcast in non-committal silence); and hint of Chalmersesque eminence grise (when calling Swanny an idiot). There was also the interest of seeing Vaughn in a frog suit. And like so many of the rather dishonest 'wages of sin' characters Vaughn has played on television, this time he was again a sophisticate surrounded by luxury and beauty.

Of course, this is only a very rough outline of stylistic development, and there are countless incidents of, say, passivity in an early role, or intuitiveness in a 'wages of sin' character, as one might imagine. But it offers a workable model of the development wrought by Vaughn's stylistic techniques, which are worth considering.

(a) The furtive glance

We have seen that, in the case of Robert Vaughn, the actor's dualistic screen persona causes there to be set up throughout his work a series of antinomies between the charm of virtue and the charisma of evil. These opposing currents find their resolution in the ambivalence of most Vaughn characters, notably Walter Chalmers. Now, Vaughn achieved the extraordinary ambivalence of the character by pitting a masterly element of his technique against the compelling stop-at-nothing tactics that made Chalmers fascinating: namely, furtiveness.

For Vaughn is an acknowledged master of the furtive glance, as Barry Norman once noted (London's *Daily Mail* 22nd March 1966): "Mr. Vaughn's mouth has a tremendous sense of humour, bending itself into an appreciative grin at the slightest provocation. Somehow, though, his eyes rarely seem to get the joke. Cautious, reserved things, Mr. Vaughn's eyes". A compensation for sensitivity in Vaughn heroes and a sign of duplicity in Vaughn villains, this particular technique well conveyed the double-dealing of Chalmers. Thus the natural furtiveness this actor employs gives rise to the ambivalence of his characters, a quality that is a particularly Vaughnian ambiance. One has only to look at his emotionally vulnerable heroes such as Fenner whose furtiveness was a guard against pain, specifically the pain of sexual humiliation as the scene of rejection by Giulia and as the tentativeness of his approach made clear. Claire and Fenner sit noticeably apart on her couch and he smiles sadly at his own little joke (about San Francisco being right next to Detroit) which emphasises his self-protective isolation. His furtive longing for love Fenner expresses verbally in the disconsolate words of the poetry he continues reciting but Vaughn renders visually in his furtive downcast gaze while reciting. It is as if communication when less direct is less personal and hence affords less risk of painful failure if one's partner is not receptive. Luckily, Claire is.

Throughout *The Protectors* the furtive glance was repeatedly in evidence. For archetypal Vaughn hero Rule, it was certainly used as a compensation for sensitivity (e.g. the furtive glance at the plane bearing his wife and son away in Jeremy Summers' close-up of Vaughn's face at the end of *With a Little Help from My Friends*). But it was also often used in far less noteworthy and relevant dramatic contexts simply as a non-demonstrative, elliptical way of conveying suspicion. There are scores of examples, for instance *Wam — Part Two*, again directed by Summers, a director very sensitive to the possibilities of Vaughn's face. When the Commissar is questioning Mackay in Rule's presence to determine whether he was the blackmailer they conceded to on the two-way radio, Mackay says "It wasn't me". Summers then cuts to Rule who suspects Mackay, which Vaughn conveys in a furtiveness of glance that consists of a hard stare broken by a lateral eye movement down. The latter suggests either that Rule is cloaking his fascinated observance of Mackay's reactions or, more likely, has taken in all he needs and now wishes to assimilate it.

In fact, the origin of this technique may simply have been merely young Vaughn's intuitive expression of caution (note his pose on the *No Time to Be Young* poster) but with the evolution of the eminence grise syndrome's more sinister motivations (concurrent with the home Vaughnianus' increasing capacity for calculated deception) this caution took on the veneer of furtiveness (note the close shot of scheming Charles Clay in his car outside Otis' house after Wayne Taylor's departure).

In *Last Salute to the Commodore*, Patrick McGoohan did a long exterior camera pan left over the harbour at night to come to rest on the window of the Commodore's house where Vaughn pulled back the curtain and filled the screen with a highly circumspect glance (having discovered the body, as we later learn) that, in McGoohan's persistent attention, proved one of his most furtive ever. This technique was also often employed to convey the shiftiness of Frank Flaherty in *Washington: Behind Closed Doors*, usually while listening to the ravings of the President.

The furtiveness of glance effects a distanciation between the Vaughnian protagonist and his immediate environment which protects from exposure that which in the hero we take to be (i) sensitivity, (ii) duplicity, or (iii) suspicion (the detection of any of which would be anathema to the homo Vaughnianus). The furtiveness of glance is therefore one of Vaughn's major modes of conveying the (i) moral dilemma, rejection in love, yearning for affection, (ii) loser (charisma of evil), and (iii) existential terror motifs.

Vaughn took this technique to such lengths in *The Venetian Affair* that Robert Robinson (London's *Sunday Telegraph* 27th November 1966) wrote: "Robert Vaughn makes acting a continuous variation on a single emotion, complacency, and when talking to other actors, appears to be addressing their ties." The latter certainly *is* noticeable in Fenner's first meetings with Rosenfeld and Sandra, and when I asked Jerry Thorpe, the director of the film, if he had been aware that Vaughn was doing this, he replied: "This characteristic was a deliberate choice. Some poker players never take their eyes off the cards, while others intimidate their opponents through eye contact." But 'complacency' is the wrong word to attribute to the cause of this distanciation. For 'complacency' suggests lack of involvement whereas the homo Vaughnianus — perfectly exemplified by Fenner — suffers, as we have seen, from an excess of feeling that his sensitivity cannot endure and thus he must, if he is to survive, choke off at source all emotional intercourse with the distanciation of furtive behaviour. Paradoxically, it is the raw honesty of his emotions that forces the homo Vaughnianus into covering this vulnerability with a veneer of furtiveness: those tiny eye movements are thus an integral part of Vaughn's cultural mythus.

(b) The stiff upper eyebrow

Vaughn expresses the stoicism of his nature through the use of what may be called 'the stiff upper eyebrow' when his protagonists are in adversity. This is a deliberate imposition of calm on primal agony or of self-discipline on inner turbulence, and is thus a technique more usually associated with the more dispassionate aspects of Vaughn's style, with his cerebrality and calculated passivity of 'impersonation' rather than 'performance' (though *TV Guide* did note of Vaughn as early as February 1964: "Self-discipline is apparent in his acting, which a co-worker says is rigidly controlled down to the smallest flick of an eyebrow").

Vaughn employs an impassivity (with Lee almost an inscrutability) in the face of danger, whether Rule being slammed against a wall (*The Big Hit*) or Parker threatened with fire (*The Towering Inferno*): in the latter case, this impassivity led Valerie Jenkins (London's *Evening Standard*) to deem Vaughn "expressionless". But he is not expressionless. Quite apart from the message of the lips and eyes, Vaughn literally employs stiff upper eyebrows to countenance horror with equanimity. This technique, which at its most effective is accompanied by a lifting of the chin in defiance and a not-wholly fearless gaze into the camera, is perhaps best exemplified in the blowtorch scene in *See No Evil* in which the aforementioned blowtorch is brought closer and closer to Rule's face. Rule is startled and stares at the flame but his gaze is ultimately a steely one because of the stiffness of his eyebrow that shows him to be in control of the fear he feels.

Other examples, similarly from Vaughn's later work, when the mature Vaughn was increasingly trading in nonchalance for gravity, are the *Columbo* shows *Troubled Waters* and *Last Salute to the Commodore*. There is the moment of Hayden Danziger's imperturbability in which he realises he cannot lie his way out, Vaughn's expression deliberative but unruffled. McGoohan's direction of Charles Clay seemed at times a deliberate attempt to emphasise and exploit Vaughn's stiff upper eyebrow technique, largely in terms of camera composition and framing. When Charles and Columbo arrive at the yawl for the first time, McGoohan has Columbo on a higher plane, causing Charles to look up to him: Vaughn thus tilts back his head, his chin comes forward and he prepares us for the magisterial presence that the stiff upper eyebrow stance of the following sequence establishes so forcefully as to be consciously intended, if not actually articulated.

The sequence consists of an amazingly protracted medium shot of Vaughn standing imperiously on board on the right of the frame, the imperviousness of his attitude only emphasised by Columbo's being seated on the left and Sgt. Kramer's crouching down on the extreme left. Since at this point the audience is certain that Charles is the murderer, the continued camera emphasis on this solitary, immobile figure's stolid refusal to involve himself in the physical search of the yawl which Columbo conducts draws attention to the put-upon expression of his face that, in its contained exasperation, is highlighted by the stiff upper eyebrow. Note also Vaughn's cautiously immobile regard of the grenade in *The Protectors — The First Circle*.

(c) The pursing of the lips
More of a trait than a technique, the pursing of the lips in Vaughn's work expresses either judiciousness or anguish; or, perhaps, judiciousness in the face of anguish. In *Bullitt* Chalmers pursed his lips in reaction to the setback to his plans that Ross' death caused; in *Police Woman — Generation of Evil* Lou Malik pursed his lips in frustration in the phone booth scene. In extreme anguish the homo Vaughnianus will go beyond pursing his lips to biting them, e.g. Rule looking at the article on his victim at Kahan's in *With a Little Help from My Friends*. All in all, it is a trait indicative of the kind of extreme seriousness evinced by Vaughn in *The Protectors — A Kind of Wild Justice* when he visits Kate and shakes his head at her misguided defence of her father. When I asked Walter Doniger, who directed Vaughn on television and in *Unwed Mother*, to identify any particularly Vaughnian mannerisms, he identified the pursing of the lips and the use of the voice.

(d) The soul in the eyes
The soul revealed in the eyes is a technique that is both the complement and the contrary to his furtive glance, and is, incidentally, one of Vaughn's truly incomparable and unrivalled achievements in screen acting. The most effective examples of it come in the greatest Vaughn performances, and the connection may be causal: Chet Gwynne, Lee, Klaus Everard, Jim Melford, Lee, Fenner, Kreuger, etc. Since this technique is a celluloid capturing of deep emotional sensitivity and therefore all the more reliant on dramatic context, particular examination of it is best left to the individual studies of Vaughnian characters such as Lee. But in a general fashion, without reference to particular examples, which could not do justice to the literally hundreds of times Vaughn has wrought this filmic miracle, this opthalmic transubstantiation, let us remark upon this peculiarly Vaughnian phenomenon.

"Drink to me only with thine eyes" could be the epithet for Vaughn's spiritual love affair with the camera as conducted with his eyes. The raw, naked centre of feeling his eyes constitute is matched only by the fascinated horror of the spectator of his work who witnesses a human soul dissolving its emotional defences. His eyes are so alive, so vulnerable, so hungry for experience that one immediately is struck by a profundity both of intelligence and of feeling that is exceptionally rare. Whereas the furtive glance is a desire to hide feelings, a dishonest attempt to mask sensitivity, duplicity or suspicion and effect a distanciation, the soul in the eyes is an honest attempt to reveal sensitivity, to negate duplicity and suspicion, to come to terms with the world and find acceptance there. Every pent-up longing for affection, every unspoken wish, every unformulated desire is reflected in the deep pools of Vaughn's tragically beautiful eyes, the surfaces of which are rippled by moments of doubt and pain.

It is one of Vaughn's particular strengths that his thoughts 'photograph' so clearly. It is a rare quality among screen actors, at this degree of effectiveness at least, and requires great willingness to expose vulnerability to the probing camera without a hint of dishonesty. Before Vaughn, the master of this quality was probably Van Johnson (e.g. *The End of the Affair* passim, or seeing the girl who stood him up dining with someone else in *Weekend at the Waldorf*). However, with a handful of performances Vaughn took it to incomparable heights and appropriated Johnson's mantle. Indeed, in certain performances it is not even so much that his thoughts photograph as that he *is* photographed thought or, in other words, pure cerebrality on celluloid (Fenner, Bergen, etc.). Despite this, the soul in the eyes is too heartfelt to be premeditated and remains supremely an example of Vaughn's intuitive style.

The sorrow of Robert Vaughn's gaze into the camera when rejected by his father in *The Big Show*, when realising that in death alone is there no fear in *The Magnificent Seven*, or when holding his dead wife's head in his hands in *The Venetian Affair* is the most supremely affecting aesthetic experience of which the cinema is capable. The soul in the eyes thus stands revealed as the pinnacle of the intuitive aspects of Vaughn's style (his emotionalism as opposed to intellectualism). It is this that has led co-workers such as Shane Rimmer to remark to me that, although Vaughn does not talk much socially on the set, "you get the impression there's a lot going on there". Where the director has had the intelligence to grasp the unique power of Vaughn's eyes, the finest Vaughn performances have resulted. Thus Jerry Thorpe of *The Venetian Affair* has remarked: "Robert Vaughn is an intellect. His eyes are the explicit reflection of a largely internalised personality. Milt Krasner, the Cinematographer, and I agreed to use an 'eye light' on Mr. Vaughn whenever possible." It was the cunning use of techniques to accentuate Vaughn's essential qualities that made *The Venetian Affair* so remarkable an elucidation of Vaughnian screen techniques such as the soul in the eyes.

(e) The use of the voice

In certain inflections, Vaughn's voice sounds rather Gaelic. Listen to his inflection of 'girls' in the line "It's a club for girls" in *To Trap a Spy*.

In one of the most exquisite moments of *The Venetian Affair*, Vaughn recites poetry. Claire, depressed over the death of her boss, sits by Fenner and, subdued, begins: "The world which seems to lie before us like a land of dreams so various so beautiful so new. . ." Fenner breaks in: "Hath really neither love nor joy nor light nor certitude nor peace nor help for pain". Vaughn intones this with the weariness of a decimated man, providing us with an excellent example of his ability to phrase meaningfully. He begins rapidly "Hath really neither" to forestall Claire's continuing, pronouncing "neither" rather strikingly (the 'e' is long in the first syllable), pausing very slightly for dramatic effect before "love nor joy" which he brackets together (as if they were the same thing). Again he pauses, brackets together "nor light nor certitude" as if they were less important than "nor peace", before which he pauses and again, notably, after it, isolating it very poignantly in the light of his own condition, hinting in his soothing and characteristic hissing 's' sound (described by Vaughn's publicist Jerry Pam as a slight sibilance) with which he ends the word at his own longing for peace. Then, in muted tones of sorrow, he finishes "nor help for pain" which Claire accompanies him in reciting, significantly since she *is* his help for pain — and they then find solace with each other. In the framework of *The Venetian Affair* a

obert Vaughn in James Dean-style pose in his first top-billed role in the cinema, Buddy Root in **o Time to Be Young** *(1957).*
ourtesy of Columbia Pictures Industries Inc.

Bob Ford shoots Jesse James (Henry Brandon) in Robert Vaughn's first billed role in the cinema, in **Hell's Crossroads** *(1957).*
Courtesy of Republic Pictures Corporation, owner and distributor.

The Boy is attacked by a wild dog in Roger Corman's fascinating **Teenage Caveman** *(1958).*
Courtesy of Arkoff International Pictures.

Edward 'The Kid' Campbell, typical of Vaughn's early roles as charismatic gunmen in Westerns, in **Good Day for a Hanging** *(1959).*
Courtesy of Columbia Pictures Industries Inc.

The caddish young Don Bigelow in **Unwed Mother**, *a 1958 Allied Artists production.*

The sensitive husband Jim Melford in **The Caretakers** *(1962). Courtesy of United Artists Pictures.*

Lee, *The Vengeful One in* **The Magnificent Seven** *(1960).*
Courtesy of United Artists Pictures.

Robert Vaughn in his much-praised performance as the conspirator Casca in the 1970 remake of Shakespeare's ***Julius Caesar****.*
Courtesy of Republic Pictures Corporation, owner and distributor.

Above: *Casca strikes the first blow to kill Caesar (Sir John Gielgud) in* **Julius Caesar** *(1970).*
Courtesy of Republic Pictures Corporation, owner and distributor.

Right: *The villainous Col. Donald Rogers exhibits the stiff upper eyebrow stance in* **Brass Target**.

The compassionate Dr. Michael Bergen in **The Mind of Mr. Soames** *(1969). Courtesy of Columbia Pictures Industries Inc.*

A rarity in the cinema: Robert Vaughn as comedian, in ***The Statue*** *(1970).*
Courtesy of Panoceanic Films on behalf of Cinerama Inc.

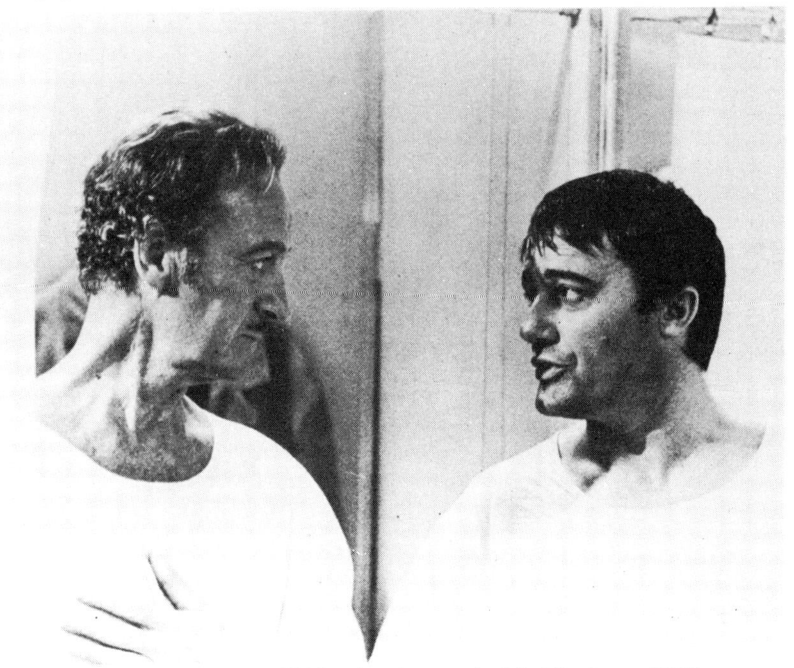

Ray Whiteley with Alex Bolt (David Niven) at the steam bath in ***The Statue*** *(1970).*
Courtesy of Panoceanic Films on behalf of Cinerama Inc.

The tragic Bill Fenner in the hostile world of **The Venetian Affair**.

character spouting poetry could have seemed ridiculous but the rapture of Vaughn's tones and his sensitive phrasing confer an unsurpassable emotive grace. The film's director, Jerry Thorpe, was aware of this and told me he found it Vaughn's most characteristic feature as a screen actor: "He speaks with very little lip movement, I believe this is due to dental problems as a child. Minimal mouth movement tends to limit inflection, create monotones, which I believe best defines Mr. Vaughn's unique style."

Not only is there a slight sibilance when pronouncing the letter 's' (noticeable in the word 'letters' in the cable car scene in *The Protectors — The Quick Brown Fox*) but Vaughn's vowel sounds tend to be emphasised: note especially the emphasis he gives to the 'u' sound in the word 'evolution' in *Demon Seed*. When Vaughn combines dramatic emphasis of key words with dramatic pauses between words, the effect is powerful, e.g. when Frank Flaherty promotes Hank in the second part of *Washington: Behind Closed Doors* and Vaughn's delivery creates menance in the words "I want to know . . . EVERYTHING . . . that's going on . . . LOYALTY. . . Hank!"

In his portrayal of Harry S. Truman in *Portrait — The Man from Independence*, Vaughn studied film of Truman speaking. Although aware that the voice would be a very important element in the impersonation, Vaughn decided against an exact imitation, as he argued Truman's voice was most distinctive in speech making and his portrayal involved no speeches, and in ordinary talk was "nondescript". So Vaughn developed what he called "the Minneapolis flat sound, where eens are frequently used to replace ings. They say walkeen instead of walking, for instance." This 'Minneapolis flat sound' can sometimes be detected in other performances.

The voice of Harry Rule (i.e. Vaughn) was analysed by a mimic (played by Shane Rimmer) in *Vocal* and described as "good modulation, well-registered, good speech pattern". *One of Our Spies is Missing* shows Vaughn so confident in the role of Napoleon Solo that he even dares to affect an English uppercrust accent in one scene ("How'd you like to go for a little drive in the country?", he asks with comical inflections) and a broad Scots accent to Scottish co-star David McCallum ("Aye, well, thanks for lettin' me know, lad").

Vaughn drew great praise for supplying the voice of the computer that rapes Julie Christie in *Demon Seed*, which was shot in the summer of 1976. Vaughn refused billing on the credits, simply to see if, despite its electronic distortion, people would recognise his voice. Everyone did, and the 'secret' did not last past the preview. Yet Vaughn remembers that the producers did not know what they wanted, so he ended up saying all of his lines in several different ways, with different inflections and phrasing, and let them choose what they thought best. In the finished film, his work cannot be praised too highly as his voice alone creates all the terror in the film. Geoff Brown (London's *Radio Times* 2-8 October 1982) wrote: "Proteus' thoughts are unctuously voiced by Robert Vaughn, who strikes suave terror with simple remarks like 'Why?'"

Surprisingly, Stuart Burge, who directed Vaughn in the film remake of Shakespeare's *Julius Caesar*, has told me that he thought Vaughn's very Americanism helped his delivery of Shakespearean speech: "On the whole that was an advantage. I feel the natural American stress on the syllables of a word in the iambic line conforms probably more nearly to the original Jacobean than does present day English, and anyway we were fortunate to have actors of Robert Vaughn's calibre in many of the parts. He was extremely accomplished in the role." Christopher Lee was also in the cast and later singled Vaughn out as being outstanding, and cited the opportunity to work with Vaughn again as one of his reasons for appearing in *Starship Invasions*.

Among occasions when Vaughn has been obliged to adopt an accent far removed to his own, one should select particularly: an acceptably languorous Spanish accent in *Zorro — Spark of Revenge*; a creditable Southern accent in *Police Woman — Blast*, e.g. "Wher ya going?"; an eccentric English accent in *The Protectors — Sugar and Spice* ("Awfully sorry that I was shawt with you earlier" . . . "Dawgs can't get hoof and mouth"). And colleague John Shaner attributed the effectiveness of the young Vaughn's transformation into Scrooge in his *Christmas Carol* stage show mainly to his use of his voice: it superbly conveyed grouchiness, prefiguring later vocal elaborations of the eminence grise syndrome.

Not everyone is in agreement here. For director Walter Doniger, Vaughn's "over-careful modulation of his voice" is one of his most distinctive mannerisms. Yet Max Arnow told me his voice has played no part in his success, and Jerry Pam even thinks that it may have proved a hindrance! Nevertheless, his voice's success in conveying ruthlessness and hostility has powerfully reinforced the eminence grise syndrome. It has been less prominent in aiding the icon syndrome, where the burden falls on Vaughn's features and conduct, although its lilting rhythm has been asborbed into his 'smooth' public image. The lazy, despairing lilt is in itself indicative of Fenner's detachment and can thus contribute to the examination of the politics of misery.

By means of these techniques, Vaughn subverts the entertainment value of the action genre, by opening further, interior, dimensions to the subject. On screen, Vaughn carries this out when a character distances himself from his environment by introspection, sometimes for the purpose of making a difficult moral choice, momentarily suspending the charm of virtue and charisma of evil in a pool of reflection. He makes the action genre revert to stasis for a moment, by means of judicious eye movements, set against an immobility of facial expression: notably the furtive glance.

One of the classic moments of Vaughnian stasis occurred under the sensitive direction of Charles Crichton. After the murder of scientist Irina at the end of *The Protectors — The Last Frontier*, Vaughn's acting equalled Crichton's skill in the 'piece of time' rendering the stasis of regretful reflection, when British Intelligence man Jones tells Rule of the necessity of her death, as she was a valuable political prize, and states that no one will ever know which side was responsible. Jones is standing behind Rule, who stares straight ahead a little above the camera in moral outrage. Jones departs, and there is a close-up of Vaughn's face, with the camera slightly angled upwards. In the ensuing moment of stasis, Vaughn once again proves himself a master of suggestive understatement.

The grim inexpressiveness of his regard is epitomised by the fixed position of his eyes and he modifies it only (but tellingly) by breaking the hardness of his stare with a movement of his eyes in a sweeping glance to the side. This glance is not furtive but thoughtful and is indicative of a process of deliberation completed and the regretful adoption of an attitude (no stranger to divorcee Rule) of bitter resignation.

This interpretation is confirmed in the subsequent fixed camera set-up, in which Rule walks away alone through the now almost deserted airport, to go and continue his often distasteful duties, the emptiness of the airport reflecting the emptiness of his heart at what he has seen: not only a classic 'loner' scene and splendid example of conscience in the typical homo Vaughnianus, but also the summation of one of the most telling renderings of dramatic stasis in Vaughn's career since the aftermath of Lee's fly-catching.

It is to be noted that Vaughn's insinuation of this moment of stasis into the narrative arises naturally out of the dramatic context yet is less significant as characterisation (e.g. Rule's moral stance) than as a film acting style. Here the stasis anticipates but is itself the object of anticipation: a cycle so smoothly executed as to seem to have left some frames out (e.g. of an emotional outburst by Rule) and hence his style constitutes a cinematic ellipsis. Vaughn leaves one with the impression that more has happened than actually meets the eye. Maybe one blinked at the wrong moment, or the celluloid leapt a few frames, but one is left in no doubt that Rule suffered a trauma over Irina's murder. A trauma that the soul in Vaughn's eyes made one feel and experience, yet Vaughn was a model of elliptical performance. This phenomenon, at this degree peculiar to Vaughn, is something of a breakthrough in film acting communication. Indeed, in more complicated works like *The Bridge at Remagen*, Vaughn's style can be analysed down into a whole continuous series of ellipses. All Vaughn's screen techniques share this elliptical quality, creating an enigmatic style, suggestive of great sensitivity, pain and warmth (Kreuger, Fenner, Bergen), hidden behind an air of cold and remote intellectualism and longing to break out. Vaughn's politics of misery derives in part from the strength of his wall of reserve; his nobility derives from the undiminished strength of those emotions.

Vaughn's "cold mask of intellectual resolve" (as novelist Michael Avallone described Napoleon Solo's face) may do no more to convey emotional turbulence in a character's internal life than allow a narrowing of the eyelids, a drawing of breath, a slight grimace, a flaring of nostrils or a pursing of the lips. In *The Venetian Affair*, he employed often a bitter grin of despair (as when Rosenfeld warns his men to step on Fenner's face if he gets in their way, or when Giulia rejects him); while the deep feeling Rule was capable of was effectively (but, undeniably, elliptically) conveyed by no more than eye movements in a particular dramatic situation (the finales of *With a Little Help from My Friends* and *The Last Frontier*).

I asked Charles Crichton, the director of such classic films as *The Lavender Hill Mob*, if he could tell me how he managed to pick up on such nuances as Vaughn's use of eye movements and he told me: "*The Protectors* is a longish time ago and my memory is dim. I do remember vividly that Robert Vaughn seemed unhappy when I first came to the series. I think there was a tendency at that time for television directors in this country to tell artistes to move to 'A' or to 'B' simply to suit their preconceived camera angles. We all preconceive our camera angles, but it is essential that artistes should feel happy and comfortable with the moves we *suggest*. Therefore they need discussion time and rehearsal time and we must adjust to them and they may find it possible to adjust to us. (Nearly all good artistes understand how much the camera can help them.) The camera should be the servant of the artiste – and of the mood of the story – but the artiste should never be the servant of the camera. I suspect that it is because I work this way that Robert and I got on well together – and I did enjoy working with him."

The outwardly dignified and passive homo Vaughnianus continually threatens to break down in the manner Vaughn describes and in some cases has actually done so (quite spectacularly): Chet Gwynne at his imprisonment, Fenner at the knowledge he must help find Sandra (his face becoming in the Venetian night a silhouette of agony) and later under the influence of the drug (breaking down hysterically in his padded cell), Rule at the death of Zeke, etc. The very fact that the homo Vaughnianus does sometimes suffer a great break in the wall of his intellectualism is significant. It confirms the correctness of our reading the techniques Vaughn employs throughout performances where the character is not explicitly allowed to give his latent emotionalism full sway (e.g. Solo) as elliptical signs of the dialectic between intellectualism and emotionalism. Vaughn moves elliptically from the stylistic representation of one syndrome to the other, making the unceasing fluctuation too smooth even to notice. Our admiration for Vaughn heroes is carried over to charismatic men of evil imperceptibly, while his heroes can suddenly brutalise our sensibilities (Solo and Rule). It is as if the 'persistence of vision' illusion on which motion pictures were founded applies to our emotions and seems to extend to our hearts. Nevertheless, be it real or apparent, the effect upon audiences is the same. This achievement, metaphor for the possibility of a stylistic reconciliation between emotionalism and intellectualism (the failure to achieve which destroyed Lee and Kreuger), reveals the stylistic uniqueness with which in Vaughn's work these polarities can be both fully explored and yet unified within one personality, i.e. elliptically.

7: Robert Vaughn As Action Hero and Director — Aspects of *The Man from U.N.C.L.E.*, *The Protectors* and *Police Woman*

On the basis of the first episode of *The Man from U.N.C.L.E.*, *Time* magazine wrote: "Solo is authentic Bond with a private label, but he is not 007. He is 006⅞." But only months later it conceded: "Given the mass audience of television, the actor who plays Solo may soon be even more celebrated than Sean Connery, who plays Bond in the movies." And this was indeed what happened. Why? Because the charmingly ironic personality with which Vaughn imbued Solo in the early years of the series was preferable to Bond's ruthless one-dimensionality.

Robert Vaughn's dynamic creation of Napoleon Solo utilised a combination of the cat-like agility Vaughn possessed as an action hero, as evidenced in the alacrity with which he darts to the side at the first sound of life in the pre-credits sequence of *The Helicopter Spies,* and the moral authority conveyed by Vaughn's inherent intellectualism. This rare combination arguably made Napoleon Solo, in his better scripts, as fitting an archetype of the Sixties' ideal male as the Humphrey Bogart hero was of the dour Forties', not only free of but also antithetical to James Bond's sadism and snobbery. London's *Daily Mail* attributed this to class when it wrote of Napoleon Solo and Illya Kuryakin in 1966: "They are not of the upper classes; merely well-dressed men of indeterminate social backgrounds." Walter Doniger has told me that he actually considered Vaughn to be an intellectual variation on Bogart but legendary director John Brahm told me: "Oh, that is such a *personal* attitude! I didn't *study* Vaughn, so to speak, as he came to me day after day after day. The parts he played were limited to the kind of thing we did. I have the feeling that he is a more-sided actor and did not have the full chance to show anything. He did not in this part (Napoleon Solo) have the chance to really develop his potential. I felt always that he had possibilities and unusual vitality and unusual drive and I felt he was never given a wide enough range as an actor. I thought that he was a natural. He really responded to my direction in a natural way. I don't think that his direction did things to him in an outstanding way or developed him. He had a natural gift and natural vitality but I could not say that I was the person who developed it. He had a natural personality that just came through."

The cultish director Charles Haas worked with Vaughn on one episode of *The*

Man from U.N.C.L.E. and recalled for me: "We shot four or five days on M-G-M sound stages, and one or two days on location in the San Fernando Valley. As I recall, the final script was not ready until a day or so before shooting, Vaughn learned the lines day by day, we rehearsed until we were ready with each scene (no pre-production rehearsals), we took as many takes as were needed to get the scene right." He found in Vaughn as a performer a "hard edge on film which overlays his charm. A hard, brittle and angry tinge which limits his attractiveness without being sufficiently released and free to give him the energy of a great 'heavy'. This is not a characterisation of Bob — only a *nuance* of his nature. I question whether he could impose himself on an audience with the power of a Scott or Brando — but even that tentative judgement may reflect his never having played General Patton or Stanley Kowalski. His nature is such that had he felt that any idea of mine violated the character, he would have said so and explained why. I had a comedy idea which he questioned. (I no longer remember what it was.) And did it anyway. *He was right.* From an audience point of view I would say that David McCallum passed through celluloid with charm more intact than Robert Vaughn. Relations were smooth, but they were as different from each other as night and day."

James Sheldon, who also directed one *U.N.C.L.E.* episode, slightly contradicts Haas but had known Vaughn socially for some time previously: "I think David was warmer and friendlier but Bob was the Rock of Gibraltar! I think Bob personally is too private a gentleman and finds it difficult to 'let it all hang out' like George C. Scott. I think Bob could be better than Scott. With the right part, like Patton for Scott, he could still make it!" Sheldon directed Vaughn again in 1979 in the television film *The Gossip Columnist* and found that Vaughn needed to be "prodded to be warmer": "I wanted him to be warm and innocent appearing. 'You got the wrong actor', Vaughn told me when I told him. But he did try and he was very good."

Writer Sam Rolfe originally strongly envisioned Napoleon Solo as a Cary Grant type, a happy state of affairs for Vaughn who admired few Hollywood performers himself but did greatly admire Cary Grant (as well as Rex Harrison and Anne Bancroft). I asked Rolfe if he had indeed found Vaughn's interpretation to be like Cary Grant, and he laughed: "No, it was . . . Cary Grant Vaughn-ised!" Charles Haas is of the same opinion: "Robert Vaughn is so different in nature and impact from Cary Grant that the question has no great meaning. Perhaps one might say that he played Robert Vaughn playing a Cary Grant figure. That is about as close as any actor could come without resorting to imitation and pastiche." Jerry Pam agrees but puts it down more to the quality of the scripts than Vaughn's essential nature: "The role he played was such a spoof. He didn't come across like that. The writing wasn't that good. It was okay, but it wasn't like Cary Grant's writing. If it had been like Cary Grant's writing, maybe he would have come across like that." But even if Vaughn did not come across as exactly a Cary Grant type, he certainly invested Napoleon Solo with a fascinatingly ambivalent mixture of strength and charm that is wholly and characteristically Vaughnian, as is apparent from viewing his previous work.

For, notwithstanding Ian Fleming's seminal contribution in the naming of 'Napoleon Solo' and writer Sam Rolfe's detailed elaboration of the character, the conception of Solo was finally personalised with the casting of Robert Vaughn. The result was a supposed carbon copy that bore little resemblance to the original, so it seems that we should attribute the Bond-like elements in Solo's make-up to Fleming, the difference in particular role, details and behaviour from Bond to Sam Rolfe more than to any of the subsequent writers of the show, and the general difference in personality and appeal to Robert Vaughn.

Apart from the often complex screen relationship between Vaughn and David McCallum, men with personalities as different as those of the men they portrayed, an important element in the success of *The Man from U.N.C.L.E.* was Vaughn's handling of Solo's relationship with his daily colleagues. Although the show embodied an extravagant fantasy, Vaughn enhanced its credibility in that he provided the focus for a set of everyday relationships that, in one way or another, mirrored the working lives of all those who watched the series. The viewer could easily identify with the humanity Vaughn brought to Solo's dealings with others, notably his occasional hesitancy, slight uneasiness and efforts to be charming, all qualities not readily apparent in Sean Connery's portrayal of James Bond.

For one thing, anyone working directly for someone of an older generation could appreciate Vaughn's occasional discomfiture, and tactful but hangdog silence, at Solo's boss Waverly's frequent reclamation of his off-duty time. Vaughn brought the same qualities to Solo's response to having his memory of old files tested as if in a school examination in *One of Our Spies is Missing,* his embarrassment at being scolded for an error in judgement in *To Trap a Spy* or to hearing that he had exceeded his clothing allowance by getting too many suits ruined on missions. The headmasterly bearing of Leo G. Carroll as Waverly brought out the whole question of how a young 'swinger' responds to the discipline of an older set of standards, and Vaughn seems to have intuitively sensed the ironic and comic possibilities for Waverly's mock outrage at his modernism and Solo's subsequent guilty embarrassment. Such subtleties naturally required sensitive interpretations of character by both actors, which they delivered: Alfred Hitchcock once selected Leo G. Carroll as his favourite actor. Let us now look at specific examples of the incisiveness of Robert Vaughn's interpretation.

To Trap a Spy was an artificial construction, taking the American pilot 50 minute episode *The Vulcan Affair* and adding extra footage by way of afterthought to create a viable cinema feature. Writer Sam Rolfe has told me that he would have written a very different film had he known from the beginning he was to write a cinema feature, and explained how difficult it was to invent forty minutes of extra plot that could be coherently inserted into the television footage. He also faced the difficulty of finding locations around the M-G-M Culver City studios that would blend in with the existing material. Nevertheless, the new scenes, featuring Luciana Paluzzi as Angela, were extremely successful, and seem to have been borrowed by the Bond series for

Thunderball, in which Luciana Paluzzi is again seduced, rejected and lured into the path of a bullet. Perhaps this is only fair, since *The Vulcan Affair* borrowed from the film *Dr. No*: the infiltration of the enemy's stronghold to thwart his plans, with the hero's eventual capture, incarceration and escape to destroy his enemy.

Historically, the most important feature of the film is that it contains one of Robert Vaughn's most beguilingly charming performances, admittedly aided by Rolfe's witty, occasionally sexy, flirtation/seduction dialogue. It gave Vaughn a greater dramatic range as Solo than he would later enjoy. He is not just impeccably slick but also angry ("I don't like to be kept waiting"), shocked (at Angela's death), anxious (fear on Solo's face when he sees the shadow of a plant guard) and poignant (the mirror scene with Elaine). Vaughn is, even more than usual, highly expressive in this film. He frowns deeply at his superior Allison's criticism of his having killed the intruder, looks rather wary at the summons into the office and adopts an ironic facial attitude at Allison's impatience with him: he smiles to himself, allowing his lower lip to protrude when Allison finishes, which appears to be symptomatic of a deliberative disengagement from criticism.

Vaughn reacts facially to first meeting Elaine. When she refers to Vulcan in a critical tone as "serious", Vaughn looks down. It is as if, Solo being an occasionally serious man himself, he cannot concur with that being an undesirable quality. And so, when she goes on to call Vulcan "strange" — an adjective that colleagues such as Elke Sommer would use about Vaughn for his being "so serious" as Sommer put it — Vaughn moves his eyebrows as if to 'agree' in mocking fashion. All very rich embellishment by Vaughn of an otherwise ordinary scene.

Vaughn's Solo winks throughout. There are good examples in the first scene with Maggie, and when he tells Elaine to pretend she is now a wealthy woman. At the words "Oil wells", his left eye winks very slightly. And again in the scene in Elaine's hotel room when she awakes. The charming wink was a mannerism Vaughn would retain throughout many of the television episodes in years to come, as it was typical of Solo's flashy personality. However, when Elaine regards Solo in horror at Ashumen's collapse, erroneously thinking that Solo has tricked her into killing him, Vaughn's eyes are quizzical and his mouth is agape, which is strongly expressive of his concern for her loyalty.

Let us conclude our look at Vaughn's work in *To Trap a Spy* with three examples of notable screen reactions. In deliberation at finding Lancer's paper in the fire, Vaughn's eyes look up and his mouth moves, an expressive reaction as effective as it is economical. When Angela's trap is sprung, his look is savage, his eyes are wild and his mouth is snarling. Looking for a means of escape from the steam and seeing the joint in the pipe, Vaughn represents Solo's process of thought very graphically with a grimace and eye movements around the room that come to rest of a sudden, which is no less than Vaughn's purely cinematic representation of suddenly finding an answer.

The following seven *U.N.C.L.E.* cinema features, not counting Vaughn's jokey appearance as Solo in the Doris Day spy spoof *The Glass Bottom Boat,* in which Vaughn again delivers a furtive glance, all have their moments but do not repay critical attention to anything like the same degree as *To Trap a Spy*. The best of these was undoubtedly *The Spy With My Face*, to which our attention will be confined. Exciting and sexy, *The Spy With My Face* lacked the excellence of *To Trap a Spy* in terms of script. Vaughn appears particularly jubilant throughout the film, grinning and smiling even at quite inappropriate times, which was part of Vaughn's conscious decision to play Solo as a "Mr. Slick" who "faces work with a smile, THRUSH with a smile, love with a smile, death with a smile", as Vaughn put it at the time. However, these scenes, including his entering Sandy's apartment and his regarding himself nude in Serena's bathroom mirror, do point up the extraordinary charisma he exuded as Napoleon Solo, and Vaughn's playing here is supported by a witty script that allows this portrayal to be a fairly definitive example of Vaughn's interpretation of Solo at its best. More than any other cinema film in his career, *The Spy With My Face* attempts quite deliberately to construct a sex symbol image for Robert Vaughn and succeeds memorably, particularly in the scenes of his seduction of Sandy on her bed, in which he suggests very sensual foods to her between kisses, and Serena's joining him nude in the shower with the ambiguous reference to his pistol: "How can I attack you when you're pointing that thing at me?"

Generally speaking, the television episodes of *The Man from U.N.C.L.E.* were superior to the big screen efforts and it would be as well to consider one of them, albeit not one of the classic episodes such as *The Terbuf Affair* or *The Never Never Affair*. The day before Vaughn performed Hamlet's soliloquy on *Jimmy Durante Meets the Lively Arts*, broadcast on 30 October 1965, he was seen in *Time* magazine's favourite *U.N.C.L.E.* episode from the second season, *The Arabian Affair*. *Time* was amused by its exploitation of David McCallum's partial resemblance to Peter O'Toole in a plot that saw Illya passing himself off as the son of Lawrence of Arabia! In fact, *The Arabian Affair* offers a good example of the gradual erosion of what initially gave the series its manic inspiration. Vaughn, luckily, is especially vigorous in fighting the creeping senility of the whole conception, turning in an ever-sharp delineation of Solo. He forces a picture of the agent's strong personality, a blend of lively charm and strength of purpose, to emerge from wafer-thin material. Solo's impact in this episode is a triumph of Vaughn's facial mobility over tawdry situations. For the few laughs *The Arabian Affair* does provide arise not from writer Peter Allan Fields' would-be satirical dialogue but simply from Vaughn's wry facial expressions of superiority when he cons THRUSH guards, his dainty arranging of his THRUSH headgear and his twee expression when ribbing Illya about his "dress".

As entertainment, *The Arabian Affair* is, then, one of the less impressive entries in the *U.N.C.L.E.* series. As an example of Vaughn's craft as an actor, it is altogether more rewarding. Certain moments communicate Vaughn's presence very strongly, and their sequence conveys the perennial Vaughnian fluctuations of mood. This disjunction between the iconic and eminence grise aspects of Napoleon Solo's heroic make-up is principally effected by Vaughn's dynamic handling of two well-directed scenes. Both scenes involve Solo's use of coercion to gain co-operation, but Vaughn interprets them very differently. The first offers the very summit of Vaughn's easy, ironical charm, despite the portent of the dialogue (murder and treachery). If we look at the actual words he uses in this scene and note the facial expressions the actor has chosen to accompany certain key phrases, we will see how the emphasis of his particular interpretation creates values lacking in the scripted dialogue. Solo warns David Lewin: "Now Mr. Lewin, my crystal ball has it that THRUSH is going to favour you with a retirement dinner and a gold pocket watch for 31 years of self-sacrificing loyalty. Is that correct? . . . Now as your brand new friendly U.N.C.L.E. insurance agent, I'd like to tell you . . . Mr. Lewin, would you please not interrupt my sales pitch? . . . Now the moment one retires from THRUSH, he not only ceases to be an asset, you become a distinct liability. Because you know all those dark, dirty little secrets, don't you? Now we know you're going to retire but if you'll peruse this carefully drawn file, I think you'll notice that they're also going to kill you. Go ahead, examine it. I'm certain you'll find U.N.C.L.E.'s fringe benefits far superior. Take a look, please. Go ahead, examine it."

Within the few moments of this dialogue, Vaughn produces the best acting in the show. He breathes life into these words in several highly effective, if simple, ways. At "is going to favour", Vaughn narrows his eyes to embellish the delivery with a hint of shrewdness. At "secrets, don't you?", Vaughn delivers a smile of great cunning, which contrasts interestingly with the shrewdness in the eyes. At "kill you", Vaughn heightens the impact of the words by reacting unexpectedly: he grins and his eye twinkles. At "far superior", he lays great stress on pronunciation of the word "far", making it understood that there is no comparison to make between life and death. In these modest ways, Vaughn not only supercedes the aridity of the writing. He also establishes the witty charisma of Napoleon Solo as super salesman. It was such momentary renditions of Solo's plausible aspects that brought the character to life and made him inseparable from Vaughn's interpretation in the same way that James Bond, for most people, was inseparable from Sean Connery's interpretation.

All the greater, then, is the impact of one brutal scene exemplifying the toughness that gave the classic U.N.C.L.E./THRUSH confrontations their bite. Vaughn's chilling representation of Solo as a self-confessed "very well-dressed and very nervous homicidal maniac" is a brave attempt to offset the blandness and unrelieved farce that was beginning to dominate the show. Solo as eminence grise arises in one shocking composition in which the agent holds the barrel of a THRUSH gun against a guard's forehead. Vaughn's expression is ferocious and he grimly delivers the tough message: "All right, musclehead, do we get that steel bathtub open or do I perform a very messy frontal lobotomy?" No sign of the 'sales pitch' Solo, no smiles or twinkles: a visage of pure steel. He later pins the man's neck to the floor with his foot. Thereafter, the actor fluctuates back to easygoing charm again with no difficulty.

Throughout the whole of *The Arabian Affair* Vaughn shows himself to be an aware actor. He never enters a room without glancing around it circumspectly. He fills up idle moments with little actions, e.g. playing with the food before being discovered in the kitchen. He uses lively eye movements to convey the meaning of the phrase "unexpected death benefits", and winks at the words "get hold of a little old THRUSH man" to convey that this is a euphemism: all examples of Vaughn's polished craftsmanship.

It is important to remember, when judging Vaughn's work in the later episodes of *The Man from U.N.C.L.E.*, that he was also heavily involved in campaigning against the Vietnam war. A typical speech is printed in the Appendix to this book. I asked Vaughn how he was able to do this as well as carry the leading role in a hit television series, which presumably involved a great deal of learning scripts, only to learn: "I never read them. Or took them home. *U.N.C.L.E.* stories were always the same. They never changed. They would change the locale and I'd wear a turban but they were always the same story. It was the same character. David did what he did, he wore noses and things, and I was the straight guy. Occasionally, I put on a hat to make a big deal. So I never had to read the scripts. For most actors with very few exceptions, you shoot in such limited amounts . . . a page or two or three, maybe five at the most. If there are five people in a five page scene, you only speak every forty seconds or something, and you say a couple of lines. Once you've rehearsed the scene and got the blocking — and I connect blocking very much with lines — once I've actually done the staging of it for the lighting, I know it. I don't know why I know it, but most actors do. David Janssen, even in his last drunken days, could do it."

I felt Vaughn was under-rating his performance, but he maintained that *The Man from U.N.C.L.E.* was not a demanding show for an actor: "There was nothing demanding in that except having to change clothes ten times a day. That was the most demanding thing . . . I'm not under-rating my performance. I'm just saying that the demand was not that great. The greatest problem was having to change clothes so much. You know, we don't shoot in sequence and I was forever getting into a tux and getting out of a tux and into some jumpsuit, catsuit or whatever you call it and so on." Yet this indicates that, if he did not look down on his own performance, he looked down on the show. John Hackett, who was dialogue director on the show for a year, both confirms what Vaughn has said and offers a major reason why Vaughn perhaps looked down on the show: "I'd be hard pressed to remember a time of him studying a script. He seemed to be able to almost literally look at it once and know it. And he was always totally precise on his lines. He'd walk on and *GO*! It might even have allowed something that might not have been there . . . a spontaneity. It seems to have been something that worked for him. While he was doing *U.N.C.L.E.*, he was working on his Doctorate and on his Vietnam protest, which were two things intellectually that were beyond the content of *U.N.C.L.E.* So if he looks down on *U.N.C.L.E.*, it's because of these other things that were so driving in his life at that time. To come from the indignation of babies and women being blown to bits . . . You're getting some information about that, and someone knocks on your dressing room door and says 'Ready to shoot, Mr Vaughn'. And he walks away from that kind of intense horror into something as adventurous and frivolous as *U.N.C.L.E.* You can understand why he might look down on it." It is gratifying, then, with the renewed interest in the original *U.N.C.L.E.* series sparked by *The Return of The Man from U.N.C.L.E.: The Fifteen Years Later Affair*, that Vaughn was happy to host an affectionate retrospective on the original show aired on television in Connecticut where Vaughn presently lives.

In the essentially parodic 1983 television film *The Return of The Man from U.N.C.L.E.*, Vaughn's portrayal of an ageing Napoleon Solo bore little stylistic comparison to the 'Mr. Slick' approach he had adopted in the Sixties and was, if anything, closer to the Harry Rule of *The Protectors*, especially in his lack of flirtatiousness with women. The film contains one genuinely affecting scene in which Vaughn and David McCallum walk through the teeming streets of Manhattan seemingly unnoticed by genuine passersby, the same city in which the two actors were mobbed when the series was on the air in the Sixties. The impact of this scene derives partly from seeing the old partnership, so often filmed in the M-G-M Culver City studio version of New York City, actually in the reality of the location, but also from the convincing note of feeling Vaughn injects into his conversation with McCallum when he says "We shared a lot of things in the past". Until this moment in the film, Vaughn had represented Solo as very cold in his dealings with everyone but there is a feeling of nostalgia in the best sense that is evoked by the softness Vaughn injects at this moment, seeing his old partner for the first time in fifteen years, particularly as McCallum is representing Illya Kuryakin as resistant to the renewal of their friendship. As Robert Vaughn and David McCallum had themselves never met during the previous fifteen years, the scene carries a double sense of reality unfortunately not duplicated in the rest of the film.

In the early Seventies series *The Protectors,* which was shot on European locations, Vaughn presented a non-romantic resilient image that made detective Harry Rule strikingly different to his interpretation of Napoleon Solo. Although a less accomplished series than *The Man from U.N.C.L.E.*, it repays greater attention on account of Vaughn's development of a more mature representation of the action hero and the tension-laden dynamics of his increasingly sophisticated acting relationship with the camera. For, by stark contrast with the optimistic Sixties fantasy of *The Man from U.N.C.L.E., The Protectors* favoured a clinical psychological realism. Excessive psychological examination of incidental protagonists took place in *For the Rest of Your Natural* and *The First Circle* but the *entire* series probed Harry Rule in his frequent moments of stress and unhappiness. This enabled Vaughn to give one of the most introspective performances of a television action series hero ever aired.

All throughout the series Vaughn lends a rather stolid and occasionally impassive presence to Rule. The style of his playing suits the content in being a lot less light-hearted than his Solo. Vaughn continually stresses Rule's deliberative thought processes, e.g. in his pursing of his lips slowly to form the words "Okay, we'll do what we can" when agreeing to help Krassinkov in *Balance of Terror*. In certain instances, he invents his own "thinker pose", e.g. in the vigil scene in *Balance of Terror* he is seated, silent, eyes cast down and his fingers interlaced under his chin. The latter mannerism occurs again in *For the Rest of Your Natural* as he ponders on Caroline's safety. In similar vein, at

Kahan's in *With a Little Help from My Friends* his fingers are interlaced and resting on his temple. A particularly memorable mannerism for deliberation was his putting his thumb up on his forehead upon discovery of the car-and-projector trickery in *Thinkback*, in which episode Vaughn also conveyed that Rule visibly thinks before he speaks (note the very measured replies he gives to the police from his hospital bed, pausing every few moments as if to consider how to put it).

And then Vaughn has a small repertoire of stylistic tricks for economically suggesting moods and aspects of character. To convey Rule's decisiveness, Vaughn only needs to speak more quickly than usual (e.g. in the cable car scene with Helga in *The Quick Brown Fox*). Vaughn's unflinching stare, with which Rule transfixes his subject, completes the effect powerfully. This steely gaze complemented the stiff upper eyebrow to convey Rule's stubbornness when threatened with the blowtorch in *See No Evil*. In *Border Line*, Vaughn rubs his eyes and scratches his forehead to convey Rule's weariness as he sits by Ilona in the chapel. A judicious softening of his voice ("And a good person") well conveys Rule's understanding of Ilona's dilemma.

But perhaps Vaughn's most effective stylistic contribution is his constant understatement. In *Bagman*, when he tells Caroline that he means to get his glasses changed, she advises him to get one of those big magnifying glasses to make him look more like Sherlock Holmes. With delightful understatement, he just looks at her. Vaughn's continual understatement gives the character a credibility that the silliest scripts do not destroy. Charles W. Eckert in *Film Comment* (May-June 1973) has written: "The hero who is central to the detective action film is an embodied dilemma: if this dilemma were resolved by filmmakers and viewers the hero would cease to attract them." The dilemma Harry Rule embodies is the dialectic between two opposing character traits with which Vaughn imbued the performance: these were identified in the original ATV Press Release announcing the show as "cold tough unapproachability" and "an understanding sensitivity". This dilemma is conveyed by the precision of Vaughn's screen acting throughout the series, some examples of which will now be considered.

Shadbolt is of interest for examples of Vaughn's technique in conveying existential terror. The latter element accompanies the shift from Rule as intellectual (the bespectacled thinker engrossed in *Newsweek*, seated immobile) to man of action (the chase through the quarry) albeit a quick-witted one (the escape from the shack), a shift caused by the mechanics of the plot and visually symbolised in the slow and deliberative way Vaughn removes his glasses and folds them flat. This action readies him for danger and is accompanied by existential terror: thus as he removes his glasses at the sight of Shadbolt's gun, his expression is nervous, he swallows in consternation and then *smiles* ironically — as if to disguise (or release) his terror. There are various other examples. When he has picked himself up after leaping from the train, Rule dives behind some bushes and then, terror-sticken, looks back up at the disappearing train to see if he is pursued, Vaughn's *sharpest* expression rendering his features more angular, accentuating desperation. When Rule hides behind the shack and permits himself a breather, having unbalanced Shadbolt momentarily, Vaughn conveys existential terror in having his mouth wide open and breathing heavily, almost heaving: instinctive, *body* acting (contrasting with Vaughn's more usual cerebral style).

Three other moments were of particular interest to Vaughn students. (1) Director John Hough's close-up of Harry's realisation that he is being watched. From the train corridor Shadbolt is staring at Harry. Cut to close-up of Harry reading his magazine. Seconds elapse and slowly his eyes lift: a capturing of the process of incipient suspicion and follow-through investigation. (2) A series of reaction shots. In thoughtfulness (as to why Shadbolt is revealing his plans) Vaughn narrows his eyes ("There has to be a reason"). When Shadbolt mentions the girl who will give him an alibi, Vaughn expresses curiosity by moving both of his eyes very slightly from side to side a couple of times as if trying to read Shadbolt's face for information. At Shadbolt's explanation of his plans, Vaughn smiles in professional admiration ("All planned out"). Curious again as to why Shadbolt has lengthened the odds ("Why?") Vaughn narrows his eyes once more. At his realisation of Shadbolt's vanity, he smiles, and of his amateurism he sneers. (3) The finale, surprisingly moving in the light of the contrived nature of much of the former and relying for its effectiveness upon the seriousness only Vaughn's gravity could provide, which concerned the depressing realisation on Harry's part that this may well happen again and again ("Any idea who hired him?" asks the Inspector. "No, I haven't. Or if he's the last" replies Harry: a typically downbeat *Protectors* ending).

Baubles, Bangles and Beads was a story of jewellery hi-jacking and gang double-cross, rendered watchable by director Jeremy Summers' interesting framings of Vaughn against Danish locations. As Harry listens to the tape in his first scene, Summers slowly zooms in on Vaughn's face with his eyes narrowing and lips pursing in reaction. At the shipping control station, Summers frames Harry and Caroline against an enormous ship gliding across behind them in the harbour, then cuts to a lovely close-up of Harry looking round for a vantage point for Caroline; he spies a tower. Summers varied the angles at which he explored Vaughn's face. When Harry is approaching the wall at the beginning of the second half, the camera looks down on him as if it were mounted on the wall, whereas when Harry arrives in the woods to find an observation point, Summers' camera is on the ground looking up as Harry cautiously stops and looks round each way. As for Vaughn's performance, there was one striking moment when Harry complains that the baddies are having it all their own way and slams the aerial of the two-way radio in with his palm with a very grim expression, which provides as good an example of the potential for bitterness in Harry Rule as it does of Vaughn's authoritative screen presence.

In *Burning Bush*, there was a good example of Vaughn's ability to portray in wholly elliptical terms an idea striking Harry. When Ferris tells Harry of his concern for his daughter, Vaughn's expression is appropriately concerned, his eyes lowered as he pours Ferris a drink. As Harry hands Ferris his glass, however, director Don Leaver's close-up of Vaughn's face reveals a sudden preoccupied stillness, Vaughn's eyes yawning chasms of thought, his face moving to the right to fill the frame with expression of the plan emerging in his mind which was prompted by the alcohol: to pose as a drunk to get to Ferris' daughter. There was a certain fascination in the following shot of Harry as a tramp on a North London bench, acting as a drunk. There was the characteristic Vaughnian sniff of distress (a rapid intake of breath through the nostrils) after the word "guidance" when he is being interviewed by the sect head, and his usual 'thinking man' pose when exploring the prayer room during which he rests a finger of each hand on his lips.

In *Border Line*, Vaughn sported a dark blue raincoat that made him more than ever almost a Bogart figure, the laconic tough 'tec. Director Charles Crichton employed some highly aesthetic close-ups of Vaughn, who was interestingly subdued throughout this performance, notably the framing of Vaughn's face toward camera with the back of Zoltan's head on the left and the back of Ilona's head on the right as they plead with Harry: Vaughn's face moving back and forth from one to the other well rendered Rule's strong but fair personality. Vaughn's screen actions themselves help the characterisation, the rubbing of his eyes and scratching of his forehead during a moment of peace in the chapel well conveying strain and worry, or, at Ilona's plaintive "You called the police?", his mouth opening to reply, no sound emerging and his looking away slightly a convincing representation of embarrassment. An elegaic, funereal music score effectively underlines the emotional tone of the proceedings.

Sugar and Spice was one of the most charming and wholly satisfying episodes of the entire series and, he indicated to me, one of Vaughn's personal favourites. This was perhaps Vaughn's most paternalistic performance; as he wore his glasses and lectured to little Vicky whom he was guarding, it looked like father and daughter. Charles Crichton picked up this nuance, as in the scene when Harry asks her not to draw the curtains back, actually for safety reasons but alleging a headache, and she sits him down, takes his glasses off, puts them in his top pocket and massages the sides of his head; again, when he puts Vicky to bed and takes her glass from her; and, above all, at the end. She is on the stairs and he looks up and tells her she can go out at last. She cannot believe it and he asks, after all the obvious untruths he has had to tell her for her own good, "Have I ever lied to you?" She, impishly, nods and Harry smiles, puts his cane around her neck and pulls her down. Crichton's final shot is very moving and highly lyrical. Harry walks down a country lane hand in hand with Vicky. He walks like an old gentleman, she gleefully dances. Its appeal lies not only, if certainly, in the evocation of father and daughter, but also in the sense of Vaughn's own encroaching paternalism and middle-age. No longer the lithe young girl-chasing, hell-raising bachelor image of Napoleon Solo days, now the sedate, paternal, affectionate, quiet and gentle father figure of *Sugar and Spice*. In this long-shot, Crichton contributed perhaps the single most moving image of the entire series. Crichton comments: "Of course, a carefully conceived long-shot can be as emotive as a close-up. (Charlie Chaplin, the tramp, walking into the sunset). The director has the fun of deciding when to use which or what."

It must be borne in mind, when viewing *The Protectors*, that whereas Vaughn was generally happy with the production conditions he enjoyed on *The Man from U.N.C.L.E.*, this was not the case with *The Protectors,* which he told the Press was "tasteless junk" even while it was being aired for the first time! Shane Rimmer, who wrote *Blockbuster,* acted in *Vocal* and acted in and wrote the excellent *Zeke's Blues* (a script he originally wrote for Tony Curtis and adapted for Vaughn), has told me that if Vaughn was unhappy, it did not show in his relations with the crew. Vaughn has told me: "The crew may have thought I was all right to work with, but Gerry Anderson (the producer) didn't like me at all. Nor did I like him. The conflict started before I ever started the show because what they sent me as a pilot script could have been a cartoon. Guy jumping out of an airplane, changing positions or something, that was the pilot! And I said, 'Well . . .' Once again, I was escaping the Vietnamese war which I was exhausted with at that time, and this was a chance to live in Europe for a year with a fine situation. I assumed if I brought Sherwood Price (Vaughn's business partner and long-time acting colleague) along that they would be able to comprehend that what they were doing was not *The Avengers,* and what I wanted them to do WAS *The Avengers* or something like that, and if we all got together and reasoned together, then we could do something. Well, it never happened. What I wanted them to do, which I could never get through — I don't know how many ways I could have said it and how many memos I sent — was the oddest and most unique thing, which was subsequently done by Richard Widmark in a show that he did in England: what was odd about England to an American living there. And there are many things that are odd and that could have incorporated a great deal of humour into the script. Plus making Harry Rule not just trenchcoat and gun, have them give him a little home life . . . something other than those chaotic plots. I couldn't understand them when I read them, I couldn't understand them when I did them, I never understood them when I saw them on the air. They had five or six running characters in a twenty-two minute show! Then the frustration grew and grew and grew, and then Lew Grade sold the show for a second year without anyone ever seeing the first year, because if they had, they wouldn't have sold it for a second year, and so I was stuck. I was literally exiled and incarcerated for two years with that show and it was very, very frustrating because I couldn't get anybody to get on the wavelength that what they were doing was as bad as the critics said it was." Actually, *Variety* (20th September 1972) wrote of the first episode *20,000 ft. to Die*: "Vaughn still impresses with a sophisticated low-key performance."

Vaughn agreed that his expectations were perhaps too high and also that the series improves on repeated viewings: "Oddly enough, I've seen it a few times since then somewhere else in the world in English and I thought 'It wasn't that bad. What was I . . . ?' My wife said the same thing. She said 'I don't know what you're complaining about. That's as good as anything we have on American television.'" When I suggested that the series even contained some of his best work, he responded: "There are a couple of shows where I recall that the scripts touched me, a couple with children (*Sugar and Spice*) and Hannah Gordon (*With a Little Help from My Friends*)."

Even if Vaughn had not intended Harry Rule to be regarded as melancholic, he did intend this flashy detective to be portrayed with unusual gravity: "We intended to do that, Sherwood and I. By the way he dressed. And, although he was in the general genre of the agent-spy-detective thing, to make him as opposite from Napoleon Solo as we possibly could. That's what our intention was, from the day we got the wardrobe on. May have been dull, but . . . !"

Despite the feelings Vaughn has expressed about *The Protectors*, his co-star Nyree Dawn Porter finished her two years' work on the show with a deep affection for Vaughn and has tried to explain for me why he ran into conflict with the producers: "I enjoyed working with Robert Vaughn and my husband and I are delighted to call him, and his lovely wife, our friends. He is a strong personality and a great individual — I think these qualities reflect in his work and, of course, in his relationships. If you have a strong personality people are bound to react 'strongly' towards (or against) you. I react strongly towards Bob — apart from which I am very very fond of the guy!" Vaughn, in turn, sent her a charming greeting on film when she featured on *This is Your Life* on television in London, in the company of his young son Cassidy whom he advised "Never cover your face when you're on camera, son" to the amusement of the studio audience.

When Vaughn himself was given the chance to direct an episode, after criticising the show to the producers, it was significant that, surprisingly, he turned this rather grim show into a light comedy. Lord Grade, who commissioned the series and was angered by Vaughn's forthright public criticism of it, said of this episode: "This was a disaster, the worst episode I've ever seen of *anything*." Although it was not a great episode, this was hardly a fair summation, as we shall see by examining it now.

The Pantheon of great American comedy directors: Charles Chaplin, Harry d'Abbadie d'Arrast, Preston Sturges, Billy Wilder, Frank Tashlin . . . Robert Vaughn? No, not on the basis of *It Could Be Practically Anywhere on the Island*, an uneasily atypical episode of *The Protectors*. Yet the set-piece of the finale not only continues the lineage of American slapstick comedy generally, as do the earlier scenes the lineage of American satirical comedy, but also bears direct comparison with a scene in Preston Sturges' *Sullivan's Travels*. Comparisons may be odious but do show that not even an acknowledged master of film comedy could invigorate a tired gag any better than Vaughn did.

In *Sullivan's Travels* (1941), Veronica Lake struggles as Joel McCrea holds her under the arms and a butler holds her feet. The butler gets edged into the swimming pool, taking Lake and McCrea in behind him. A second butler comes over to the pool to offer a helping hand to the first and is himself pulled in. In *It Could . . .* (1973), Felix is pursued by Jonathan, who overbalances at the edge of the swimming pool and falls in. Hotel pool users then rush forward and, in poetic justice, lift Felix bodily and toss him in. This precipitates a general pushing and leaping into the pool. Mary joins in and then extends her hand from the poolside to help Felix out and ends up being pulled in by him. Harry and Linda arrive belatedly and the manager pushes Harry in for fun but is himself pushed in by Linda in return. In doing this, Linda loses her footing and topples into the pool, too.

Now certainly neither sequence is desperately funny, but the point is that Vaughn's direction is not in any evident way less competent than Sturges', and is decidedly more exuberant. In the former, four people end up in the pool; in the latter, the number is forty! Sturges' camera remains close to the actors but Vaughn takes a vantage over the pool, his camera looking down on the chaos to fill its perspective with motion, and then moves to ground level for a medium long-shot in one take of Linda pushing and herself falling. Vaughn's actors communicate such light-heartedness that, though not hilarious, the sequence is sufficiently jovial to avoid a charge of silliness. To have elicited conviction in comedy despite the unoriginal nature of the material is creditable for an actor whose directing experience was limited to plays, home movies and documentary.

Relying on traditional comic ingredients (kookie people, overacting, slapstick, absurd plot), Vaughn nevertheless possesses real economy in presenting them, which is best rendered in little directorial touches such as the knee-level view of seemingly endless suitcases being carried through the hotel entrance at Linda's arrival: as effective an indication of feminine self-indulgence as Vaughn's suggestion of a politician's pomposity in *The Towering Inferno*. When Felix buys Linda a "rusty nail", the costliness of the drink, her "personal plumes", her monied self-possession and her indignation that Felix's tuxedo is rented are as evocative of class distinctions as any of the scenes (e.g. between Fredric March and the butler) in d'Arrast's *Laughter* (1930).

The few Maltese exteriors Vaughn uses are interestingly atmospheric, largely as a result of his framing. The camera pans with the car containing Felix and Mary which halts on the road down below. She gets out and opens the door for Felix who walks off to the left. The camera moves with him until he leaves the edge of the frame; Mary and the car have left the right of the frame. Vaughn lingers for a few seconds on the frame, empty but for landscape, before cutting away. There is an Antonioni-like desolation to the composition as well as a feeling for space, reinforced both by the lack of narrative significance and by the suggestion of windy, inclement weather. Later, Vaughn frames Flynn looking for Muffin against a craggy Maltese coastline and a rough sea. Framing again plays a part in the attractiveness of the very first image of the second half. The camera moves very slightly — it is almost a tremble — to frame more centrally the hotel exterior, on the road before which a horse-drawn carriage is being driven. Like all Vaughn's exterior shots, it hints at an aliveness to architecture, be it natural or man-made, that could and should have been exploited further.

It Could . . . can also be construed as a paean of praise to the woman the director was soon to marry, Linda Staab. Largely this is conveyed by camera set-ups which emphasise her undeniable appeal. When she enters the lounge at the beginning of the second half wearing a tight blue trouser suit, Vaughn's camera is positioned behind her as she approaches Harry and the shot captures the sensual movement of her derriere. Later, to underline the value of the reward Linda offers ("a great big hug"), Vaughn emphasises her cleavage by having the camera low and angled up in her direction and the frame is therefore filled by that particular facet of her appeal. The episode's greatest asset, Linda Staab is also, on the evidence of certain scenes, such as her taken-aback reaction to Harry's question about Muffin ("Sex?") as she replies "No . . . she's just a puppy!", quite a convincing and delightful actress.

The fact that Vaughn cast himself, Linda and his partner Sherwood Price as Felix shows that he did not mean this directorial effort to be taken too seriously. It compares interestingly, therefore, with his more serious direction of the tough *Police Woman* television series, for an episode entitled *The Melting Point of Ice* in which he did not appear. This opportunity arose for Vaughn during the filming of the outstanding *Police Woman* episode *Blast* when he told the producer, Douglas Benton, that he would like to direct an episode. Benton had known Vaughn from his earliest work in television when he worked for Benton's friend John Brahm in *Screen Director's Playhouse — The Bitter Waters* and other shows. Benton had also produced *The Girl from U.N.C.L.E.*, in which Vaughn guested opposite Boris Karloff (*The Mother Muffin Affair*).

Blast ranks among the best of Vaughn's post-*Remagen* performances. He played Andrew Simms, a charming ex-convict running a girlie bar who is involved in blackmail and murder, in the investigation of which Sgt. Pepper Anderson, the Police Woman of the title, gets emotionally involved with him. The part was well-written, utilising Vaughn's talent to the full, calling for vulnerability yet eruption into toughness, great charm yet sadness, as well as requiring a Southern accent which Vaughn sustained very well. The flirtation scenes between Simms and Pepper were touching, making her upset at his death highly credible (although her usual preference, to judge by other episodes, seemed rather the James Darren type or the Alex Cord type). Clever characterisation of Simms, who always wanted to be somebody, to own property, to have people look up to him, to "live with pride" and "do good things", striving to achieve this by "making good contacts" to get on a football team, made his protracted death scene especially moving, enacted with great emotion by Vaughn (hopelessly wounded, he still cons himself pathetically "Gonna make it . . . making good contacts"). The drama of the episode was heightened by a very good score. Director Alvin Ganzer, astonishingly, has no recollection of the show whatsoever, so great is his disdain for directing television shows rather than films. There are perhaps some ramifications for the auteur theory that it is the producer of the show who is the one who recognises the importance of this performance.

Benton deems *Blast* "one of the most successful segments we made in the first year" and the death scene played by Vaughn "one of the best moments in the whole series". He recalls that it was the Police Woman herself, series star Angie Dickinson, who asked him to get Robert Vaughn for the role of Andrew Simms: "She was always looking for opportunities to work with him. He was a favourite of Angie's. She thought he was the best actor we ever had as a guest on *Police Woman*." I put it to Benton that Simms seemed to me one of Vaughn's best performances of the late Seventies and asked how much of his own personality he thought Vaughn brought to it: "I agree with your assessment. I think the writer gave Bob more opportunities. The character was not just a dog heavy — he was an idealist whose idealism had gone sour. Simms had within him the materials to be an outstanding human being, but somewhere the mix had gone wrong and he (Simms) understood this. What makes Vaughn such a superior actor is that he can understand that type of personality and project it. Vaughn is such a powerful actor that he virtually creates the character for the audience as he interprets it in any film he appears in." Benton recalls that they printed the third take of the superbly moving death scene.

Of Vaughn's technique and potential, Benton had this to say: "Whatever mannerisms Bob uses in bringing a character to life are things that he does as a part of his own personality. If he is using tricks or mannerisms, he is so good at it that you never see where the actor ends and the character begins. I think Vaughn has fulfilled his potential as an actor in the sense that he's done every role he's been offered as well as it could have been played. But who knows? Maybe someone in a little garret in the Bronx is writing the definitive Robert Vaughn part at this very minute. If Vaughn will do it as well as he has the opportunity to do, he will find values in the role that no one else can. What Robert has that most acting rockets lack is the fact that he will be working as a popular and in-demand character actor until he drops. Whereas most of the so-called 'television stars' of the *Man from U.N.C.L.E.* period will appear as footnotes in *The Filmgoer's Companion*." Vaughn's recent signing to the highly popular television series, *The A-Team,* bears out Benton's forecast.

Angie Dickinson was very enthusiastic about the idea of Vaughn directing an episode and when they found a script they thought he might like, they offered it to him and he accepted as soon as he was available. He also acted in another episode, *Generation of Evil*, in the more routine role of a crooked casino owner Lou Malik, along with such veteran colleagues as Sherwood Price and Tony Carbone and director Corey Allen. Benton recalls Vaughn's approach to direction: "The major problem was that he had set up a scene where, when a character looked one way he saw one vista that was in actual fact twenty miles from the vista he saw when he looked the other way! Therefore, Bob had to be very careful about his entrances and exits, and he was meticulous about being sure that everything 'matched'. It seemed to me that he was much more concerned with this than he was the way the actors performed, and that like all experienced television directors, he had more or less cast the performance by putting his friends in the parts, knowing exactly what they would do when he said 'Action!' Angie and Earl (Holliman, the co-star), both admirers of Vaughn, worked very hard to help as much as they could."

Of the finished episode *The Melting Point of Ice,* Benton comments: "It's hard to judge a director on one picture, but he got through it on schedule, the acting and movement were good, and he showed a good camera eye. There's no doubt that with experience he would make a first-rate director. But I don't know whether he would be any better or any different from a hundred first-rate television directors. I do know that as Robert Vaughn the actor he is unique. And therefore in my mind, Vaughn is an actor who directs rather than a director who acts." I asked Benton to compare Vaughn's directorial style with that of two *Police Woman* regular directors, John Newland and the late Barry Shear, who had directed Vaughn in *The Spy With My Face* and *The Karate Killer* respectively: "That would be comparing a rookie with an old pro. He is not ye as smooth as John Newland, nor does he generate the dramatic drive of a Barry Shear. I think he was more interested in proving that he could make the picture for the money and in the time he was allotted (far more important in the television business) than to stand anyone on his ear visually, and he succeeded."

I asked Vaughn why his Andrew Simms contained such passion while other performances of this era were very cold, devoid of passion. Vaughn's reply is highly significant in explaining these apparent fluctuations in his approach, which led even a great admirer of Vaughn's, the distinguished Director of Photography Gerald Perry Finnerman, to tell me that he thought Vaughn had "laid back" somewhat in the late Seventies. This had been my own feeling during the *Brass Target/Last Salute to the Commodore* era, though it is certainly not the case in the Eighties with Vaughn's excellently dynamic performances in *Superman III*, *The Return of The Man from U.N.C.L.E.* and *Black Moon Rising*, to name but three. Vaughn countered my suggestion that some of his late Seventies performances lacked passion: "I think there would be (more passion) if I got the parts. I mean, if I got a *Young Philadelphians* or something like that again. I don't get emotional parts. I get coldness, rage and Presidents." So it was not deliberate? "No, I'm not doing it deliberately, but if that's what you say you see, then that's what you see. I mean, I'm not consciously trying to be passionless. You see, I react to language. That's what really sets me off. That's why I've gone back to Shakespeare. If I find language that to me seems to sound like people talking to people, or a person talking to another person, I am enchanted enough to embellish on it. If the language is what I call computer talk, as most television shows are, I do it to the best I can, because I'm going to give as much as the writer gave, which is *zip*!"

So why was *Blast* so good? "Well, I think it was because it had a whole background of the guy being a dirt farmer who worked his way to the top and I think it was the language there I responded to. I won't question what Doug (Benton) said, but I think the understanding of it really isn't in my head at all. I mean I don't look at it and say 'o yeah!' It just happens or it doesn't, based upon the language. I'm sure I never thought about that for one second. I mean I *know* I didn't. It just organically happens or it doesn't, according to the language."

Thus it was that John Hackett could tell me of a scene he saw in 1980 on television, which he could not identify but which I suspect was in the television film *Mirror, Mirror*: "He had a scene in bed with an actress. I saw a quality in him. It was a centre of truth in that one scene that was a deeper dimension to his relating to women than I've ever seen. The technique of Bob as an actor had gone. He was open, vulnerable, he was quiet, sensitive. I've known him all these years and seen an awful lot of his work and here was just this *other* quality that he hadn't been able to use, and when he was able to use it in this scene, he used it beautifully. It was so nicely done that I thought I'd like to have been able to see more of that in his acting, more of this side. It even surprised *me*!"

8: The Actor As Moral Philosopher — Robert Vaughn as Major Paul Kreuger in *The Bridge at Remagen* (1968)

MAJOR PAUL KREUGER

The last enemy that shall be destroyed
is death. Corinthians XV, 26

But who's the enemy? Major Kreuger (d. 1945)

Paul Kreuger undergoes a crisis that reminds one of Lee. The analogy is unsurprising, as William Roberts wrote both parts, serviced in each by the creative realisations of Robert Vaughn. Generally, either certain qualities in a scripted character appeal to Vaughn (one might note his reason for accepting the part of Harry Rule: "he seemed to be a guy very much like myself") or he invests a given script with these qualities. Kreuger is the outcome of both processes, with Vaughn reading moral dilemma into situations where lesser actors might have settled for confusion.

For the particular emphasis bestowed by Vaughn on the behaviour of Kreuger is a moral one: how faithful should a man be to his own conscience if there is grave personal (or even national) risk? His duty means the avoidance of such risks and it is the effect that a direct conflict of duty and conscience has upon the motivation and destiny of this character that forms the film's core. In Vaughn's interpretation, the character becomes more significant than the drama in which he is engaged — as is common with Vaughn protagonists. Chapter 5 describes the scene in *The Magnificent Seven* where Lee has to commit himself one way or the other and adopt a course of action that so far he has secretly avoided: the finality of his decision is portrayed by that last moment of hesitation in which Vaughn suggests a man summoning up the power to force himself to do something. Similarly in *The Bridge at Remagen* Vaughn portrays a man who has to make a commitment one way or the other and, as with Lee, each alternative is highly unattractive. But whereas up to the moment of his commitment Lee has been dodging his duty, has been fighting shy of responsibility, insofar as he has been fighting at all, and avoiding the course of action that he finally adopts, Kreuger avoids the course of action he has adopted *after* he has made his commitment. He puts off as long as he can obeying the orders he has been sent to execute, to blow up the Ludendorff Bridge as soon as possible, after promising to allow his countrymen time to pass over the bridge to safety. Thus *his* moment of commitment comes at the beginning of the film, after Gen. von Brock has explained the situation on the map to Paul, given him his official instructions while pointing out what their literal execution would entail, and asked him what he intends to do; whereas Lee's moment comes at the end of his film.

So while the forms of their dilemmas are not the same, since for Lee it is a choice between running away and living as a coward or else facing up to life and probably death, but at least as a brave man accepted to die amongst good company; and for Paul Kreuger it is a choice between doing his duty as a faithful but mindless Nazi officer under orders or else doing what his conscience tells him is right; yet their predicaments *are* similar, since each is faced with a profound moral problem. In each case there are two incompatible courses of action one of which each man feels morally bound to follow (making a positive stand against tyranny; allowing one's countrymen to get to safety) while in each case the respective other course of action would be the more typical, safer thing to do (behaving according to character, i.e. in cowardly fashion; obeying official orders, i.e. the immediate destruction of the Bridge). Of course, Kreuger's tragedy consists in thinking his courses of action to be compatible: "One can only do one's duty . . . DELAY!" And this leads to his ruin.

Nor again in these parallel cases are the two men's practical solutions to their quandry the same: nor would one expect this of two men who are really opposites, for does not Lee start off a disillusioned coward and die an illusioned almost-hero or a coward on the brink of heroism, whereas Kreuger is a loyal distinguished hero who dies a somewhat disillusioned (for as he prepares to face the firing squad, passing planes cause him to ask whose they are: upon being told they are enemy planes, he muses with his last words "But who's the enemy?") but no less heroic figure? Also, Lee commits himself whole-heartedly to what he would like (to be able) to do, namely to flee; whereas Kreuger takes what he knows he ought to do (i.e. his duty as a loyal German Major) and what he would like to do (i.e. act according to his conscience as a man who loves the people of his country) and fatally attempts to combine the two, playing off the latter at the expense of the former. Yet what these two men have in common as regards the solutions they offer to the choices they have to make is the personal disaster their highly-motivated decisions bring upon them. Both are typical Vaughn losers. Kreuger is for many reasons the more tragic of the two, although in ways less pitiable: let us look at the destiny and behaviour of this "doomed 'good German'" (London's *Observer*) in order to see why this state of affairs pertains.

More tragic and yet less pitiable? How can this be so? It is a question of character: Lee is much less in control of his own destiny, he is a hunted, hounded figure haunted by his own lack of worth, a miserable man in a situation not of his choosing, a "deserter hiding out in the middle of a battlefield" because anywhere else he would be found. A definite, even definitive, loser, though not necessarily by choice: a couple of times he seeks acceptance, as when he tries to join in the conversation of the others after drinking alone, idly boasting to try to impress them, and in his final decision not to desert the group. Kreuger, on the other hand, is very much in control of his own destiny: a very strong man who expects to be obeyed, a strict disciplinarian, a staunch and loyal Nazi aristocrat, a respected hero, slightly world-weary, a loner seemingly by choice, in a situation, whatismore, very much of his own choice and well able to handle it.

If Lee is a man whom external forces put into a situation where his own internal forces urge him towards his destruction, then Kreuger is a man whose own internal forces put him into a situation where external forces destroy him. An unavoidable dilemma is created for Lee whereas Kreuger creates his own dilemma by attempting to alter the ordered course of events to suit his own requirements. The difference is simply that Lee is not free as regards his actions whereas Kreuger has complete liberty: he is in charge. Besides, Lee comes across in *The Magnificent Seven* as a likeable man: although credited with a villainous past, he is a reserved man, full of self-reproach whom we only ever see fire his gun in fair combat. Kreuger, however, smashes a valuable ornamental piece in front of its proud owner's eyes (when that man's cowardice angers him) and later, admittedly under stress, shoots two deserters in cold blood in an effort to maintain discipline. Both because he can be himself quite ruthless and because he could have avoided his own destruction had he either acted differently or been more careful (not to mention the fact that all his actions are in the service of an evil regime), we find Kreuger less deserving of our pity than Lee: indeed, once Lee has made his choice, he (as well as the audience) does know his death to be almost certain, whereas the news of Kreuger's eventual court martial leaves him speechless with surprise. There are certain intimations to the audience of the end of this "doomed" German throughout the film, but Kreuger hardly ever seems aware that he is heading for disaster, confident as he is. Yet not being quite as sympathetic a figure as Lee does not prevent him being more tragic (or even more admirable). He is more tragic by virtue of the very fact that his destruction was of his own making and not unavoidable as in Lee's case.

The risk Kreuger runs is not shouldered for any motives of personal benefit: he does not need to edify his image of himself in his own eyes. It is a purely altruistic act, placing his life on the line that others, who would even be ignorant of his action, may be safe. It is a selfless and humanitarian code of conduct, motivated purely by the dictates of personal conscience. We noted before that just prior to Lee's death it seems that his ultimate courage *is* rewarded in some way, since once before he dies he can hold his head high. Kreuger's is much more tragic a destiny, since a patriotism so sincere it cares about individual lives leads only to execution as a traitor. And it is a lonely death: condemned by those to whom he belongs, he is stranded between two armies. Another 'deserter hiding out in the middle of a battlefield'.

In a haunting scene early on, the director indicates that Kreuger is a marked man: shortly after agreeing to disobey the Fuhrer's orders, he is forced to observe a roadside execution by firing squad. The look of fear and horror on the face of this humanitarian man subtly suggests to the audience, in the light of the dangerous situation he has placed himself in, that the same thing may happen to him. Furthermore, when he is told by an officer that the man is a German being shot for desertion and the officer adds "It is better to die facing the enemy than the firing squad", Vaughn's numbed look of shock brings home to us the sense that Kreuger may only for the first time be realising the personal implications of his heroic brand of treason.

It is above all this scene that makes the execution of Kreuger seem to have been determined: by his own actions, he will find himself facing such a squad. The fear he shows does not mean that he will not die consistently with his behaviour in life, i.e. nobly, and there is both considerable dramatic tension and spectator sympathy as Kreuger is marched to the execution post by (apologetic!) soldiers of his own army. He is allowed a last cigarette, starts to ponder upon who "the enemy" really is, takes a last long drag on the cigarette, looks up to the sky for the last time, not even a tranquil sky but a sky full of planes, yet maybe for Kreuger a reassuring sky, since those planes are hostile to the Nazis, whom he now perhaps recognises as the true enemy, and waits for the bullets to smash into his body. He awaits "the last enemy", as Richard Hillary, himself a fatality to the Nazis, put it. Lee's death in *The Magnificent Seven* was poignant enough but Kreuger's is more horrific because he has to wait those long seconds for the rifles to ready, aim and fire, whereas for Lee the bullet came out of the blue. It is even more so because of the look on Kreuger's face when the bullets smash into him: it is a look of horrific disbelief, above all a look of surprise. It is as if he had not thought it could be that painful. And the aristocratic young figure that stood there so elegantly with his cigarette holder a moment before, who faced the firing squad with nonchalance, is flung violently back by the bullets' impact, dying clumsily and painfully. It is that someone so brave can die with such a look of painful shock that makes the demise of Major Kreuger a deeply moving experience. Nor does the intensity of Vaughn's portrayal, witnessed by Guillermin's unflinching camera, spare us the upsetting pathos of the final, spasmodic flutter of life streaming out of Paul Kreuger's body (comparable to the disturbing lingering close-up of the eyes of Col. Donald Rogers fixed in death in *Brass Target*). When one also considers that it was his selfless and humanitarian ideals that led this brave and noble soldier to such an ignominious end, the tragic status of the character created by this actor is confirmed to supercede that of even his previous character Lee.

Vaughn's portrayal of the world-weary Kreuger reveals new dimensions to the character throughout. He begins as an earnest, wry soldier with a haughtiness natural to one of his aristocratic birth and lent by Vaughn's naturally reserved presence. With the subsequent accumulation of worry, he "struts moodily" (London's *News of the World*). He also evinces both authoritativeness and patriotism (in the smashing of the ornament and remark about the owner's son), to a desperate degree (the shooting of the two deserters). On the more sympathetic side, there is personal bravery (under fire on the Bridge) and concern for others (before detonation).

Then comes the mind-boggling sequence, superbly acted by Vaughn, where Kreuger, having unnecessarily shot two of his own kind in the back in a vain effort to retain discipline and realising his efforts to hold the Bridge are doomed to failure, erupts in a memorable scene of what Wells termed "mind at the end of its tether". James Stewart has spoken of the job of a film actor being to create 'moments', short celluloid incidents or situations with an indefinable magic or appeal that remain forever in the memory almost with a life of their own. Of all the 'moments' Vaughn has created, the moment when it all becomes too much for the misguided but noble Major Kreuger remains perhaps the most affecting. In this amazing scene, he supercedes the intensity of previous moments like Jim Melford's bewildered account of his wife's attitude towards him in *The Caretakers* or Lee's night of fear in *The Magnificent Seven* and acts at a pitch that is almost distressing to watch.

The horror at having had to take life, the absurdity of trying to maintain discipline, the knowledge that he is directly responsible for the invasion of his country, the fear of the mob's violent reaction: these are the elements that cause Kreuger, up until now a very cool and restrained man, to erupt violently to the point where Vaughn's masterly exposition reveals the brink of insanity, followed by his rapid descent from this plateau into a state of almost mindless passivity, admirably conveyed by Vaughn's body becoming limp and swaying as he is jostled by the mob. It is a state of physical surrender that complements his surrender of authority, no longer giving orders but only begging favours. Kreuger's disintegration is pitiful, an eruption of inner turmoil that Vaughn's triumph in the role makes frighteningly realistic.

In *Bullitt*, individuals between whom there is no external condition for conflict (Frank Bullitt and Walter Chalmers are meant to be on the same side) adopt the opposed stances of good and evil, so there is a personality clash. But Kreuger and his American antagonist Hartman, played by George Segal, who is himself disenchanted with the war, are much more complex in motivation and behaviour because the conflict is external: they do not adopt their stances, but wrestle with them. It is this that makes Kreuger's fate dramatically more important than the loss of the bridge, permitting Vaughn a performance that virtually plumbs the depths of human moral consciousness.

And from the complexity Vaughn brings to this human arises considerable philosophical interest: Kreuger was torn between what his duty told him was right and what his conscience told him was right. Was his decision to delay the right one? It might seem that it was if it can be shown that his means were morally justified by his particular end. Recent philosophers have taken exception to this oversimple utilitarianism. John Dewey, for one, has repudiated the "refusal to note the plural effects that flow from any act, a refusal adopted in order that we may justify an act by picking out that one consequence which will enable us to do what we wish to do and for which we feel the need of justification." Dewey emphasises the "varied consequences" because in his view "there is no such thing as the single all-important end."

Along these lines, one could argue that it is arbitrary to deem the salvation of the 50,000 as *the* consequence of Kreuger's decision which morally justifies putting his entire country in jeopardy, for there were many other consequences which in sum vitiate that justification (e.g. the high death toll unavoidable in keeping the Bridge intact, the time allowed to the Allies to reconsider their tactics and decide not to destroy the Bridge but capture it, the lowering of general morale as the Allies could be seen to be literally at their threshold, etc.). Of course, we have not even considered yet the actual consequences of his decision owing to unforeseen contingencies such as the poor quality of the explosives and the inadequacy of his troops: we have only considered what the consequences would have been had all gone according to plan, i.e. the antecedently probable consequences. Consideration of the actual consequences obviously adversely affects the justification of Kreuger's decision.

For G.E. Moore wrote: "whether an action is right or wrong *always* depends upon its *actual* consequences. There seems no sufficient reason for holding either that it depends on the intrinsic nature of the action, or that it depends upon the motive, or even that it depends on the *probable* consequences." However, as Moore makes a special point of distinguishing the notions of 'right' and 'morally praiseworthy', and 'wrong' and 'morally blameworthy', even to say Kreuger was wrong would be no moral condemnation and would not seem to affect his justification; it would only be a non-moral comment on the actual consequences of his action. But we still want to ask if Kreuger has a moral duty to act as he did and to ask if his end, the greatest possible saving of life, justified his means, putting millions in possible, and as it happens actual, jeopardy for the sake of a few: as Moore makes clear below though, even a non-moral comment on the actual consequences of Kreuger's action *would* affect his justification and so the two things we are asking are not, as one might have thought, the same, for Kreuger could have had a moral duty to act as he did without his action being morally justified!

Moore explains: "if any being absolutely *knew* that one action would have better total consequences than another, then it *would* always be his duty to choose the former rather than the latter. But what such people would point out is that this hypothetical case is hardly ever, if ever, realised among us men. We hardly ever, if ever, *know for certain* which among the courses open to us *will* produce the best consequences. Some accident, which we could not possibly have foreseen, may always falsify the most careful calculations, and make an action, which we had every reason to think would have the best results, *actually* have worse ones than some alternative would have had. Suppose, then, that a that Vaughn's German accent occasionally fails to convince, especially in the extraordinary emphasis on the first syllable of "useful" in his reply "That would be very useful", and he did not bother with a German accent in *Inside the Third Reich* (none of the British and American cast did), but even if his performance lacks the technical perfection of his work in *Bullitt*, Vaughn's playing is yet more impressive for having an all-out passionate intensity entirely lacking in Chalmers and must rank with *The Magnificent Seven*, *The Caretakers* and *The Venetian Affair* as his finest screen work.

References

Human Nature and Conduct: An Introduction to Social Psychology by John Dewey (Henry Holt and Company, New York 1935)
Ethics by G.E. Moore (Oxford University Press 1978)

9: The Wages of Sin

When Vaughn was beginning to make the transition from leading man to character actor, he began to be typecast as 'wages of sin' characters, that is to say affluent, ruthless power figures who benefit well from their corruption. Sometimes they wield political power, sometimes they run corporations or even film studios as in *S.O.B.* and *The Studio Murders*. Walter Chalmers in *Bullitt* began the trend, but it was after the relative failure of *The Protectors* and his role as Senator Parker in *The Towering Inferno* that, for a while, Vaughn seemed to deal exclusively in such characters. He played these parts in television shows like *Police Woman, Columbo, The Feather and Father Gang,* television films like *The Woman Hunter, The Islander* and the superb *A Question of Honor*, and cinema films like *Superman III* and *Black Moon Rising*. Let us consider some of these many performances of villainy for the sake of material gain.

Vaughn's Ed Fuller in *Kiss Me, Kill Me* was an advertising executive, implicated in the cover-up of a sex killing of a young girl by his male lover! It boasted the extraordinary sight of the immaculately dressed Vaughn pleading with his boyfriend to come to a party with him in the environs of a seedy gay disco. Fuller was Vaughn's first portrayal of homosexuality and remained morally neutral; his next portrayal, in *Brass Target*, was less sympathetic. Even so, the humourless portrait of Fuller culminates in his presentation as somewhat repellent a personality, with none of the surface attractiveness of men like Chalmers.

What redeems Vaughn's performance with this circumscribed material is simply a greater solemnity and passion behind the usual eminence grise histrionics than displayed in playing other 'wages of sin' roles, e.g. in *Nightmare at Pendragon's Castle*, etc. This muted energy conveys Fuller's hypertension and hints at Fuller's essential neurosis (Vaughn came to represent a number of eminence grise figures as essentially neurotic, the sharpest portrayal being the hawk-eyed treachery-seeking Frank Flaherty in *Washington: Behind Closed Doors*). Vaughn presents this in the character's obsessive fidgeting and use of his hands: playing with the tray at the police station as he answers questions, repeated and very noticeable brushing his lips with his fingers when Stella comes to question him, scratching his left hand when Stella enters his apartment at the end, etc. The two sudden and very brief smiles as Fuller pleads with Douglas to come to a party reveal, in the threatening surroundings, Fuller's failure of confidence. The character's general over-aggressiveness (also a feature

This is still perhaps more than can be said for the production as a whole, which, despite various similarities, never quite managed to be the *Gone With the Wind* of the television era it would have liked to be. In large measure this was due to the often vulgar style of director/writer Douglas Heyes whose films have been as routine as the many television series he has directed. But it was a resounding popular success. A resounding *critical* success was *Washington: Behind Closed Doors*, for which Vaughn won a television 'Oscar', The Emmy Award.

Shane Rimmer, a former colleague of Vaughn, once told me: "I thought he was terrific in *Washington* because in something like that you have so little time, and he really registered, him and Robards. There's a coldness there . . . He *was* Washington." Rather, it is more relevant to the limitations of this role that the conception of the character at no point allows for the introduction of any of the recurrent motifs that generally elicit Vaughn's most affecting (as opposed to merely 'effective') performances.

Episode One allowed Vaughn to flesh out Flaherty fully, although the forcefulness of his personality was continually undercut by the subservience of his role; but his dynamism was conveyed in Flaherty's fast movements and reflexes (re. Press photographers) and ultra-efficiency (he smoothly draws back coverlet, closes curtains, pours a drink, proffers sleeping pills and shuts the bedroom door for the exhausted Monckton with all the automatic rapidity of one who has done the same thing so many times before). Vaughn presents Flaherty as extremely image conscious in little touches: adjusting his tie in the mirror as Monckton washes upon waking, always immaculately dressed, smiling throughout Monckton's public speech while on platform, with a little hint of flamboyance (the swing of the body as he hits his fist into his palm to start up the band). Yet the image is successively revealed to be as false as the sincerity with which (with a sickly smile) he tells an interviewee "Call me Frank, it's easier" (very reminiscent of Chalmers' "Please call me Walter"). While Vaughn presents Flaherty as predictably implacable (chewing out Hank for his oversight with his expression extremely stern and his unblinking stare slightly reading Hank's reaction), authoritative and smug, he also conveys thoughtfulness (nodding his head slowly and biting his lip) and vulnerability to Monckton's reproaches (registering dismay with a hangdog look). Vaughn continually overcomes the fact that his is not an especially verbal part by means of subtly elliptical reactions: e.g. having left Monckton with the Director of the F.B.I., he returns to a colleague and merely flops his wrist loosely in reaction to the high-level intrigue taking place, which perfectly conveys the impressive nature of the meeting.

Episode Two also contained much effective characterisation of Flaherty, confirming our suspicions that he was a mean bastard in various forceful scenes. There is the uncompassionate demotion of Dorothy with a veiled threat that leaves her distraught; rudeness ("Get to the point, don't give me any chit-chat"); brutal dismissal of long-serving Bailey ("This . . . is GARBAGE . . . You're just a waste of time Bailey. All you want to do is kiss up to a bunch of lousy reporters"); his lying to Mrs. Monckton and ominous stare at Dorothy for disloyalty. These actions are despicable enough in themselves, but Vaughn's subtle facial and vocal inflections render them especially invidious. For example, when Flaherty asks Hank to keep an eye on Bob ("I want to know what he's cooking up"), Vaughn's eyes narrow slightly — indicative of his slyness and probing Hank's compliance. When first criticising Bob over a leak to the Press ("Except you gave Wisnofsky a little something extra, didn't you?"), Vaughn's left eye narrows slightly in contempt and his raised upper lip causes two fierce creases round his mouth, making Flaherty's face particularly formidable. When Bailey presents his report and Flaherty asks "What did you have in mind with this?", Vaughn injects especial distaste into the word 'this' which he also isolates very slightly from the rest of the sentence, well conveying Flaherty's brand of malicious sarcasm. Vaughn's final satisfied smile suggests that Flaherty derived a sadistic pleasure in the dismissal.

Episode Three proved the initial failure of momentum regarding the presentation of Flaherty. His role becomes more passive, although his lines still convey corruption. In only one very brief scene does the full extent of his nastiness come across, when he criticises the guest list of the television show run by Adam's wife. Vaughn conveys Flaherty's viciousness with sharp, emphatic enunciation, his eyes stony still and leaving all expression to his lip muscles: "Nothing but a bunch of lefties. You'd better start sitting on your wife." Adam's protestations are cut short with "I think that covers it . . Thank you": a medium close-up of the cold containment of anger in a hidden sneer on Vaughn's face as he dismisses Adam with this mock politeness remains a leading illustration of the eminence grise syndrome.

Episode Four was little more satisfying. Although Flaherty remained in the background in the first scene, Vaughn still attended to his reactions economically (opening his hands, looking at them and putting them in his pocket, etc.). Later came an amusing facial expression of incredulousness over the use of a dog to enhance Monckton's image; note also the adjustment of his tie upon arrival at the demonstrator-ridden airport, which again conveys Flaherty's image-consciousness, as well as the consistency of Vaughn's portrayal. Vaughn's most memorable attitude in the episode was that in which Flaherty adopted a seeming attitude of adjudication: his feet were up on his desk, he reclined with two fingers against his lips and listened until ready to comment, occasionally scratching his right hand or holding his finger.

Sadly, the remaining episodes left unfulfilled the original intimations of Flaherty being the real power behind Monckton, who grew in dominance ("well, you haven't delivered, Frank!"). Nevertheless, Flaherty remains one of the fullest possible depictions of the eminence grise syndrome in Vaughn's career.

When Vaughn played the superficially similar role of Gordon Cain, the President's Chief of Staff, in *Hangar 18,* he portrayed a much more independent character who showed initiative and quick-witted self-reliance, albeit with a smile as sneaky as Flaherty's. Not overtly as bad a man as Flaherty but still manipulative: "We've got to keep this thing bottled up", he says about the UFO that has landed. A good example of Vaughn's capacity for fury on screen comes when two Government agents are killed and Cain explodes in anger. Vaughn smilingly complained to me that he was generally being offered "coldness, rage and Presidents" at this time and Flaherty, Cain et al are typical examples of the first two types of role.

Vaughn continued to earn his bread-and-butter by appearing in routine television pilots, such as for the unappetising and eventually short-lived series *The Eddie Capra Mysteries*. The pilot of this series, *Nightmare at Pendragon's Castle*, wasted Vaughn as publishing tycoon and eminence grise Charles Pendragon. A brief role poorly conceived and written, Charles Pendragon is of little interest to Vaughn students. The few unusual features of the performance include a slightly demoniacal quality to the character in the early scenes, achieved by Vaughn's allowing his eye a slight twinge of contained rage. This demoniacal quality is eventually depicted graphically in the flashback after his death, when we see him rampaging in lust, which makes Pendragon one of Vaughn's few sexually rampant characters (Solo never used force). There are little hints that Vaughn could not take this character, who describes himself as "obsessively single-minded", entirely seriously: certainly, the character's pretentious Arthurian sword-in-the-stone antics were highly implausible (even then, the unusual manifestations of Pendragon's mania were never developed or explored, merely accepted). Such hints are the amusing look of surprise and the general flailing when he is shot: definitely a tendency to camp it up! It is of some incidental interest that the contrived exaggeration of this death scene ends with Vaughn in a crouched attitude not dissimilar to that of Lee at the end of *The Magnificent Seven*. Which is not to say that this performance, directed by James Frawley, had any of the eminence of The Vengeful One. Richard Afton (London's *Evening News*) called this pilot "a convoluted concoction of pretentious rubbish"!

Actor Jackie Cooper, the former child star who played Perry White in Vaughn's *Superman III*, directed Vaughn in a 'wages of sin' role as a fashion photographer in *Murder at F-Stop 11*, an episode of the light comedy series *The Feather and Father Gang*. It was Cooper who suggested Vaughn, whom he had met first in 1965 or so at a party when he knew only his work in *The Man from U.N.C.L.E.* and discovered they were both staunch Democrats, for the part of Winslow to producers Bill Driskill and Robert Mintz. The part of Winslow had a surface glamour that hid corruption, and Cooper was conscious of Vaughn's excellence at expressing what Walter Doniger defines as his "feeding off his own dichotomy of evil and good". Cooper told me: "That is the reason we wanted him for the part." *Murder at F-Stop 11* was shot in five days in 1976. Cooper was happy with the final result: "It was one of the better episodes, I thought. Bob's performance gave the role more importance. He fit the role, in my opinion, and took direction extremely well. He was very friendly — and respectful of me as the director. Very responsive. Had many good ideas. He's inventive, energetic, co-operative." I asked Cooper to characterise Vaughn and he said "Bob is not demonstrative, and I wouldn't imagine him as very affectionate. I believe he 'holds in' a great deal. I would say his intellectuality dominates his emotional capacities." Cooper isolated Vaughn's particular gifts as: "His eyes . . . and his command of the language."

For the show's Director of Photography, Gerald Perry Finnerman, this was the first time he had worked with Vaughn since he had been Assistant Cameraman (i.e. focus puller) on *The Young Philadelphians* nearly two decades before, a film in which he told me he found Vaughn "very powerful". In *Murder at F-Stop 11*, Finnerman kept the light high and did not use a fill light, in order to achieve a sparkle in the actor's eyes which gave Vaughn what Finnerman describes, appropriately for the character of Winslow, as a "snake-like look in the eyes" and made them "flare" on screen. Finnerman remembers adopting the lighting style appropriate to the actor, avoiding half-tones as unsuitable for this particular subject material, *The Feather and Father Gang* being a very light, high-key comedy show. Finnerman found Vaughn "extremely professional", "technically knowledgeable (much more so than most other actors)", and very satisfactory in "finding key lights, angles, and not shadowing other people". He felt the actor "played rather well" in this show but thought the role had not allowed him to be capable of his best. Finnerman greatly admired Vaughn's performance in *The Magnificent Seven* and told me he wished he could have worked with him on that so that he could have worked *closely* with him: "What impressed me most was his attitude. Very dedicated. A quiet, unique man. Very brilliant. He doesn't have to show off. He exudes charisma. You are very conscious of his presence." For him, Vaughn's intellectualism contributes to his impressive charisma, and he found him to be in the same mould as Efrem Zimbalist Jr. and Jeffrey Hunter, in that he was a "gentleman" and "didn't blow his horn". As both a television director in his own right and a Director of Photography who won an Emmy and two nominations and whose work includes the television series *Star Trek* and *Moonlighting*, Finnerman told me he picked and chose carefully among actors, but Vaughn particularly impressed him.

Brass Target is of interest as an extreme example of the mature Vaughn's tendency to spiritual stillness, but Col. Donald Rogers, albeit an unusual villain for Vaughn, lacks the subtle layering of personality of a Kreuger, and hence this stillness becomes an intriguing source of mystery. The distinction of the film lies principally in this element of strangeness, jointly achieved by Vaughn's highly technical performance and director John Hough's lingering emphasis on it. Typical examples are the very deliberate use of the furtive glance, to convey Rogers' circumspection at the railway tunnel, here to the left of the screen in medium close-up not once but thrice, and the stiff upper eyebrow technique when descending the stairs with John Cassavetes. Note the almost visible mental workings with which Vaughn raises his chin, a further example of the thinking man as actor. The severity of many of Vaughn's reactions in the film recalls Flaherty in *Washington: Behind Closed Doors* but Rogers' manic determination is offset by black humour. Rogers is a promiscuous homosexual and Vaughn well conveys the cruel streak of wit in his remark "Under the covers, girls, it's the house detective". Hints of eccentricity worthy of *Clay Pigeon* abound, especially in the first scene which features him in bed, but Vaughn keeps plumbing the depths, to a fascinating degree, of his capacity for screen passivity. Hough, already well-versed in Vaughn's profound skill from *The Protectors*, seemingly shared this fascination, for his camera is at certain moments content to defuse plot content by simply lingering on close-ups of Vaughn's wholly deliberative self-containment, thereby reducing the charades of this kind of thriller to a kind of other-worldliness. Such examples of Vaughn making the cinematic clock stand still in contemplation of Rogers' internal machinations include the medium close-up as he sits silently facing the camera opposite Patrick McGoohan in the train carriage after some successful plotting, a hint of a smile the only assistance to the stillness of Vaughn's gaze in conveying a mind with thoughts on the future. The long static seconds of this shot prove thought-provoking in the overall action context of *Brass Target*. Another excellent example is the final close-up of Rogers shot dead.

This death scene, with its echoes of Vaughn's death scene in *The Bridge at Remagen*, consists in the final frames of a chilling focus on the dead body of Rogers with his lifeless eyes staring at camera. The lingering of Hough's camera again calls into question the 'meaning' of the shot and emphasises the mystery at the heart of Vaughn's performance of Rogers. *Brass Target* is recommended for viewing as the ultimate example of a trend in Vaughn's late Seventies work towards internalised inscrutability, from which he has in more recent years retreated.

There have been other occasions when Vaughn has remained curiously self-contained in the performance of material that presumably did not inspire him. Of *How to Steal the World,* Elkan Allan (*Movies on Television*) wrote: "David McCallum and Robert Vaughn walk through their parts as if zombied by the nerve gas which is this particular villain's secret weapon . . . and director Sutton Roley doesn't seem to mind." But, more so than in *Brass Target*, the distance in Vaughn's performance in *How to Steal the World* is not only curious but appropriate, as it reflects a disengaged quality in Sutton Roley's generally superb direction of the entire film, notably in the dream-like scene where Vaughn awakes on a deserted boat in the middle of the sea.

It is hard to see how the lamentably tedious mini-series *The Rebels* could have inspired anyone but Vaughn's successfully villainous portrayal of traitorous assassin Seth Maclean offers another case of a man who puts the wages of sin above personal morality, as he explains before being shot in the attempt to kill Judson (played by Don Johnson): "We're plantation owners, Judson. Our wealth, our position, our system of living depends on the King's rule. Washington is an arrogant fool and he must be stopped." Vaughn's aggressive enunciation of the words "arrogant fool" well conveys Maclean's malice and, with Vaughn's deep vowel on "fool", has a memorable felicity.

Vaughn himself was enthusiastic about playing the villainous Ross Webster in *Superman III* as there could hardly be a more notorious role than the man who tried to kill Superman. Webster, the ruthless head of Webscoe Industries, is an ultimate 'wages of sin' character and the role brought Vaughn a great deal of popular appreciation, helped by the fact that his physical appearance in the film is even better than usual and his wardrobe is superb. Vaughn's first scene as Ross Webster in *Superman III* reveals his excellent timing in the delivery of lines, e.g. when he says to Simpson "My old friend, *you* are yesterday . . . whoever pulled this caper . . . is tomorrow", says of Gorman "Unless of course he is a *complete* . . . and *utter* . . . moron", and says to his subordinates "I can't have anyone with me (Vaughn frowns and his finger flicks upwards for emphasis) . . . who isn't with me." Vaughn speaks emphatically and fluently, underlining the comedic irony inherent in his words, and his confrontation with Gorman in which he attempts to communicate in jive talk such as "I can dig where you're coming from, brother" is genuinely funny. The scene that best combines Vaughn's impeccable delivery and ironic humour is the one where he is telephoned by the hapless Gorman, played by Richard Pryor, and says "I asked you to kill Superman and you're telling me you couldn't do that one simple thing" in a wonderfully deadpan tone for maximum ironic effect, dropping the telephone in disgust at Gorman's failure to accomplish such a 'simple' task. In all, *Superman III* features one of the most extrovert performances of Vaughn's mature years, even if Ross Webster is certainly not among his more multi-faceted performances.

Superman III is a comedy and Webster cannot compete in terms of chilling villainy with Vaughn's Ryland in *Black Moon Rising*. Ryland is a similar corrupt power figure but a very serious one who can watch an unco-operative business associate being strangled with a smile of satisfaction. The fact that Ryland has the humanity not to let a disobedient female protegee kill herself, even if it means allowing her to defy him, only renders even more believable the perversity with which Vaughn imbues the character. Ryland, who specialises in stealing cars, is an excellent example of a Vaughnian character who blithely profits from the wages of sin.

In *The Studio Murders*, President of the Network Doug Girard is a man of sober rationality, albeit utterly devoid of sentimentality— he refuses to cancel a lucrative television show simply because the actors are being murdered. After the third murder, Vaughn acts out the character's delivery of a very sincerely presented address to the cast of the show, his voice quavering with emotion, his sentences full of effective dramatic pauses ("It is . . . with a *deep* and abiding sorrow that I come here today"), only for his smug comment to the detective Errol (played by Barry Newman) "Does that satisfy you?" to reveal his Chalmersesque cynical duplicity. Vaughn well depicts the oily charm in Girard's handling of his employees and is on the whole a more credible mogul in this undistinguished television film than in the rather superior, if flawed, cinema film *S.O.B*. This is because *S.O.B*. (which stands for 'Standard Operational Bullshit') is a black comedy which, as one of its ways of satirising Hollywood, asks Vaughn to portray his Robert Evans-type studio chief David Blackman as a straight transvestite who makes love in ladies' underwear! What is interesting is how serious Vaughn remains when playing such farcical material. Vaughn is at his most persuasive in this performance in his discussions of financial wheeling and dealing, percentages, grosses and so forth. He is on the whole angry and impatient in his dealings with colleagues — indeed his favourite saying seems to be "you'll never work again in this town as long as you live" — unlike the equally cunning but far more approachable Doug Girard. The briefest comparison of these two performances shows how differently Vaughn can interpret similarly-conceived ruthless moguls.

10: Trends To Resolution

Just when it seemed that Vaughn might forever be limited to cold 'wages of sin' characters, there began to appear some important performances in which this casting permitted Vaughn to show warmth and tenderness as well as power and ambition. This trend to resolve the disparate strengths of Vaughn's past screen personae is highly welcome, as Vaughn could retain the intimidation of Chalmers or Flaherty but make the character more human. Thus, Harrison Crawford III in *City in Fear* is one of the most rounded, multi-dimensional performances Vaughn has given, the ruthless efficiency in the newspaper office becoming all the more realistic for seeing how vulnerable he is in the scenes with his wife when she criticises his sensationalism. Crawford's love for his daughter (he comforts her tenderly when she is scared) and his wife leads him to try to justify his misguided sensationalism in a highly rational manner, and renders his motivation for hard behaviour at work highly plausible — he is not, like Flaherty, simply a mean bastard.

This tendency to allow cold, logical precision to co-exist with personal warmth was first notable — not in *The Mind of Mr. Soames,* where Bergen was not a cold man — but in *Starship Invasions.* Although *Starship Invasions* contains a scene with a hint of the "rejection in love" motif (Vaughn looks pained when his wife criticises his obsession with UFOs), Allan Duncan is a much warmer type of man than the mature Robert Vaughn generally portrays. As the ship departs at the finale, there is a memorable composition of Vaughn tenderly clutching 'vulnerable' wife and daughter, in a classic 'father and protector of the household' stance. The striking scene, immediately prior, of his reunion with his daughter has a paternalism as touching as that at the end of *Sugar and Spice.*

The combination of Vaughnian gravity of facial expressions and vocal inflections on the one hand and plausible expert's dialogue on the other hand contributes to the definition of Duncan as a typically convincing Vaughn intellectual. His first scene, the television interview, so defines him, just as the ecological televised debate in *Centennial — The Scream of Eagles* would so define Morgan Wendell. Unfortunately, Duncan's immobility once aboard the starship severely limits his dramatic opportunities, which is principally why *Starship Invasions* is only one of Vaughn's minor films, albeit a diverting one. Nevertheless, there are a sufficient number of scenes that contribute to the Vaughnian screen persona for the film to be worth considering.

The most notable feature is the character's happy family base, and subsequent freedom from the usual neuroses of Vaughnian protagonists. Even at his wife's criticism that from being a top astronomer he has become a UFO cook, Duncan does not exhibit (other than momentarily) the typical homo Vaughnianus' sensitivity to defeat — he immediately counters this situation with a sudden grin, a sexual innuendo (harking back to Solo's happy-go-lucky approach) and an embrace.

Starship Invasions offers several examples of strong points of Vaughn's screen acting technique. His caution at the moment he looks around the starship for the first time is well conveyed by his stiff upper eyebrow stance until at his ease. Another good example of the mature Vaughn's capacity for stoicism occurs when he complies in the abduction of his friend the computer expert: director Hunt frames the solitary figure of Duncan who watches as he is led off and wears a look of weary acceptance. There is on Duncan's return a striking shot of the right side of Vaughn's face (as Duncan looks over at his wife approaching) that indicates Hunt's appreciation of Vaughn's amazing profile. Finally, once Duncan is aboard the starship, helplessly abducted, there are one or two good examples of Jerry Thorpe's remark "His eyes are the explicit reflection of a largely internalised personality", e.g. when he sits down as the alien girl passes and his eyes look up at her quizzically. The apprehension there is all internalised.

It is, indeed, true to say that Vaughn's principal posture in the film (something very unusual for the persona of an actor still carrying title roles, let alone in the context of an action-oriented sci-fi movie) is one of passive, interiorised deliberation (note Duncan's lack of resistance at being abducted, agreeing to co-operate if the aliens will return him to his family). Slight lip pursings also occur throughout the film — a technique the actor has always used to convey deliberation.

The most interesting feature of Allan Duncan is the neutrality of his status as a Vaughnian protagonist. He has no heroic status: he is an onlooker. He is not as admirable as Dr. Bergen (and the long-shot scenes of him walking and talking with the computer expert *are* rather reminiscent of *The Mind of Mr. Soames*). Nor does he have any of the sneaky or reprehensible traits of the 'wages of sin' characters. Allan Duncan is simply an intellectual whose passion is only directed to his family (and even then not excessively). It is a performance remote from ethical issues, one that again demonstrates the aptness of Jerry Thorpe's remark "Robert Vaughn is an intellect". While it might be suggested that the lack of the usual hero/villain stereotype allows Vaughn's inner personality to dominate the film to a greater extent, *Starship Invasions* is in fact too childish and lightweight a confection to permit that. One need only compare the power of Vaughn's personality as non-hero/non-villain Bill Fenner in *The Venetian Affair* to be convinced of this.

This complexity of presentation infected even a less obviously warm man, Wendell in *Centennial — The Scream of Eagles*, whose extreme rationalism militated against his sneakiness. In *The Scream of Eagles*, the twelfth part of *Centennial*, Vaughn's curious appearance as Morgan Wendell, businessman out for public office, brought nothing new, except that, while he was obviously cast in his now usual role of sneaky would-be politician, the part soon outgrew this shallow conception (and nearly all the characterisations throughout the series were shallow) and turned into more a dramatic mouthpiece for philosophical opposition to Paul Garrett, played by David Janssen: herein lay the only real curiosity and challenge in the role, the rest of which was a piece of cake for an actor so used to conveying duplicity.

Thus, early in the performance are manifestations of Chalmersesque oily charm, as in the readiness of his smile when he first greets Lew ("do the writing") or when he meets Paul to offer him a job ("let me know"). There is also a fundamental seriousness of purpose and ruthless determination (the emphatic frown as he tells Lew "I don't mean to crowd you"). Wendell certainly represents the eminence grise syndrome in the early parts of the performance. First is established his distaste with subordinates who are slow to understand his feelings: he creases his eyes as if in disgust when it is suggested that he is afraid of Paul and then, having explained himself ("Understand?"), looks from one man to another with a put-out expression as if at their not being ahead of him. Just before we see his rage at being thwarted (he sneers at Paul being a "phony Southern . . ." with a vehemence reminiscent of Frank Flaherty), Paul's rejection of the offer to work as his deputy brings a decidedly menacing parting comment ("and I'm sorry . . . for you").

The Chalmersesque duplicity speaks for itself. His first action in the film is to conceal a family secret. He tells his subordinates: "We've got a perfect set-up going here. A campaign for a real public service showcase. A chance to push an image the public wants to buy." In offering Paul a job, he already has to ask him to "duck" an issue of conscience (a suggestion typically delivered with a smooth smile). Having compromised Paul politically (he gives a very smug sudden smile of satisfaction as he then pronounces "He's not cut out for politics"), he later denies all knowledge of it; etc.

Yet the character is not really a baddie. His actions are unfair rather than evil, and his less-than-noble behaviour to safeguard his political chances is not without precedent (one thinks of Robert Kennedy's rapid departure from California at Marilyn Monroe's death). Furthermore, in running for the post of Commissioner of Resources and Priorities, he does in a misguided way express genuine ecological concern ("the great problem for Colorado in the next decade is going to be to save the state . . . to save the forests, trout, elk . . . and especially things like the rivers and the air we breathe").

And so, in the most interesting scene in the film (the long televised debate between Wendell and Paul), Wendell's Chalmersesque manifestations come to be belied by a reasoned representation of sincere feelings about the land. Wendell's conviction is conveyed by Vaughn looking directly at Paul when he wants to emphasise a point ("I believe the time is coming . . ."); and the genuine eminence grise cares only for his own aggrandisement. As an actor, Vaughn is best used in the long exchanges of dialogue (something of a feat of memory), in that "one of Hollywood's most intellectual actors" (as *Photoplay* once described him) has been chosen to present argumentatively and persuasively a certain philosophical outlook on ecology. Not only does style (Vaughn's intellectualism, suit content (philosophical argument) here. His virtuoso delivery, measured, mellow and shifting rhythmically both to emphasise key words and to project his sincerity to the viewers ("the *whole* pattern of life is *vanishing*"), also shows that Vaughn is adequate not only to generally cerebral roles (Bergen, Duncan) but also to those requiring the most taxing verbal deliveries, such as in presenting an ideological stance, as, briefly, here. In his acceptance of defeat, Wendell's misguided sincerity is confirmed: "How can people vote against progress . . . What's the matter with them?" This acceptance is engagingly portrayed by the character sucking a cigar and with a woman on his shoulder as he sits, lest we start to pity the loser: like Chalmers, he may have lost the battle, but it is no personal calamity.

It is interesting to note that the land problems here hark back to one of Vaughn's earliest television performances in the *Zorro* show *Spark of Revenge*, wherein Spanish California was plagued by drought. Between two similar themes lies the whole development of Vaughn's screen acting style, from exuberant emotionalism (such passion as the soul in the eyes when discussing his misfortunes with Don Diego/Zorro) to virtuoso intellectualism (such passivity as his response to Lew's taunt about stealing graves and as expressed by the stiff upper eyebrow technique developed with his maturity). Constant remain the most basic techniques such as the use of the voice (note the near-Irishness of his pronunciation of such words as "couple of years" when talking to his subordinates and "strength" when offering Paul the job). Vaughn filmed it in three weeks in December 1978 and enjoyed working with David Janssen, whom he knew "only very casually" beforehand but with whom he went on to make the far superior *City in Fear*.

On a completely different level, the bizarre released version of the long-delayed *Next Week Rio* under the videocassette title *Three Way Split* alternates between strange scenes of Vaughn in Venezuela and moments of absurdity, in part due to the dubbing of Vaughn's dialogue in places by an actor with a low voice nothing like Vaughn's. What survives of Vaughn's performance as fading movie actor Tony is occasionally good but his usual screen mastery seems to have been affected by the hybrid nature of this U.S./Spanish/Venezuelan co-production, if not by the intervention of the Venezuelan police who halted the production over debt problems and arrested Vaughn! There is a lyrical bedroom scene with girlfriend Anne in which Vaughn sensitively conveys Tony's confession that he is losing his touch in the intricate stunts he performs, as well as contrasting scenes in which Tony enjoys the good life on a yacht and in the restaurant after the robbery, played with Vaughn's usual exuberance. Tony is a character driven to crime by his failing career but is not truly villainous. He is an amoral playboy in the same vein as Michael in *Mirror, Mirror*, albeit a more likeable one who thinks only of Anne's safety when she is held for ransom by a gang who want the gold Inca mask he has stolen. The film contains scenes of Tony making a spaghetti Western and we see Vaughn on horseback, wearing a cowboy hat, and riding in the Caracas countryside with the same elegance he displayed in *The Magnificent Seven*, making one wish he had made more Westerns in his career. On the other hand, when Vaughn played the Western movie star Stuart Chase who turns to crime, a pure baddie role, in another bizarrely interesting production, René Clement's *Wanted: Baby Sitter,* his reaction on being offered another Western in Calabria was: "I'd rather puke than ride into another sunset!"

Of films like *Three Way Split* and *The Lucifer Complex*, Vaughn told London's *Daily Star* in 1983: "I don't mind at all that films like that never got screened. I'd mind a lot more if they were released." Yet such films are more fascinating to watch than some of the mainstream television pap in which Vaughn has appeared such as *Murder She Wrote — Murder Digs Deep.*

The afore-mentioned *Mirror, Mirror* takes the archetypal Vaughnian suave cad in the faithless grasping photographer Michael Jacoby but, by means of a tender bedroom scene in which Vaughn unashamedly evokes the character's new-found yearning for Vanessa's affection ("I need you"), effects a transition to the more vulnerable persona of Vaughn's pre-*U.N.C.L.E.* loners. This is not to say that the character actually becomes sympathetic, and indeed Vanessa, played by Lee Meriwether, ultimately causes him a cruel rejection in love by dismissing his proposal of marriage with a list of his character faults. For these characters of Vaughn's maturity remain within the eminence grise syndrome and lack iconic stature; they do, however, exhibit moments of humanity in Vaughn's interpretation that make them more intriguing than the rather one-dimensional 'wages of sin' characters.

A key example of how it is from Vaughn's singular screen acting technique that this tendency in the mature Vaughn's work to find artistic resolution between the disparate elements of character of the more human exponents of the eminence grise syndrome occurs in *Intimate Agony.* Here he plays another hard-headed, quick-tempered Vaughnian capitalist, property developer Dave Fairmont, giving a far stronger performance than in *Mirror, Mirror.* The character has great tenderness for his daughter, kissing her forehead and telling her "You're perfect", and looking extremely doleful at the realisation that she is growing up. When she finally tells him that she has lost her virginity and tries to tell him that she has contracted the venereal infection herpes, Vaughn's playing of Fairmont's pent-up reactions exhibits the legacy of his years of emotional over-containment on screen. This scene well conveys that sense of Vaughn 'checking his internal fire' as Tony Carbone has put it but the power of the scene derives from the fact that Vaughn is not simply subsuming the character's emotion to rationality or using the dominance of his intellect to control his emotions. Here the overt emotional investment of Fairmont in his daughter is already established and Vaughn is portraying a man reeling with emotional shock, in the way that Kreuger was shattered by shooting the deserters. The power of Vaughn's acting in this scene derives from the fact that the pain of Fairmont's struggle to realise that his "princess" is now a woman is fully played out in Vaughn's facial expressions and, unusually with Vaughnian protagonists, the attempt to suppress it fails. Fairmont cannot bear to hear what his daughter is telling him and bolts from her bedroom before she has even finished confiding in him. The downcast eyes and the pursing of the lips, frequent Vaughnian techniques, cannot check the raging fire within as director Paul Wendkos studies Vaughn's anguished expressions in close-up.

A parallel situation occurred in the television film *Private Sessions*, in which Vaughn's Oliver Coles also had problems with his daughter's sex life. His daughter Jennifer complains "He doesn't like any man that I fall in love with" and turns to promiscuity. Coles is far less affectionate than Fairmont and Vaughn expresses embarrassment rather than emotion when Jennifer begs him to accompany her to her analyst, though he too eventually reaches the limit of what he can bear. "You were such a perfect little girl", he tells her tearfully. On the whole, Vaughn gives a more subdued performance here than in *Intimate Agony,* possibly because Coles is more off-hand in his dealings with others and therefore less expressive of emotion.

It is a pity that Vaughn's role as Dr. Neal in *Good Luck, Miss Wyckoff* was so small, as this superbly mature study of adult sexuality which, of course, ran into trouble with the Victorian mentality of the British censor, must rank among the very best films with which Vaughn has been involved, with Anne Heywood giving the performance of her career. Dr. Neal reflects the steadfast and reassuring aspects of Vaughn's screen persona as in the dispassionate and sensitive way he carries out Miss Wyckoff's internal examination, although his cold treatment of her once she is disgraced shows him to lack the warmth of Dr. Bergen in *The Mind of Mr. Soames.*

John Bradford, the anti-semitic polio victim in the mini-series *Evergreen*, is one of the grimmest-faced personalities Vaughn has portrayed, a man full of bitterness even towards his own daughter who has married a Jew. The performance features extensive use of the stiff upper eyebrow technique in service of the older Vaughn's screen impassivity. And yet even in such an unattractive character, Vaughn allows moments of compassion and sentimentality. Treating his daughter with wariness when she visits him and closing his eyes when he learns she is pregnant — a recurrent technique used by the mature Vaughn to register a character's emotional pain — he eventually melts, saying "I don't like your hat, either" and then smiling. His sentimentality surfaces in his comment that his grandchild Eric has his mother's nose and mouth and even in the otherwise chilling scene held in close-up where Bradford goes birdwatching with Eric. While Bradford verbally instils racist ideas into the boy ("I just believe that Jews should live with their own kind. Coloureds with coloureds. Americans with Americans. Works better that way"), he actually behaves like a rather dotty, harmless old grandpa, constantly erupting into the mating call of the wood peewee bird ("Oh, there he is! Pee-wip! Pee-wip!"). This short scene, in which Eric pushes Bradford's wheelchair before a retreating camera, is a persuasive example of the easy mastery of Vaughn's mature character acting.

Necessarily outside the scope of these considerations are those pure character roles such as the various U.S. Presidents whom Robert Vaughn is in the unique position of having played: the young Teddy Roosevelt in the 1959 television episode of *Law of the Plainsman — The Dude,* Harry S. Truman in *Portrait — The Man from Independence*, Franklin Delano Roosevelt on stage and in a television film record of the stage performance *That Man in The White House:*

F.D.R., Woodrow Wilson in *Backstairs at the White House*, and Franklin Delano Roosevelt again in the television film *Murrow*.

Vaughn's brief appearance as Franklin Delano Roosevelt in the television film *Murrow* is surprisingly lively, despite his representation of Roosevelt's physical discomfort in a wheelchair. Vaughn altered the usual pattern of his speech, adopting a more clipped tone than his customary lilt and this well reflected Roosevelt's perky mood, as when he warmly confides "I think they are vices that sustain life, cigarettes and martinis." Yet, for such a brief cameo, Vaughn also manages to encompass the reflective side of Roosevelt's character, as when he recites a litany of the dead at Pearl Harbour and comments "Dammit", sniffs and repeats the ejaculation more emphatically, thereby representing Roosevelt as a sensitive man. Vaughn communicates an even more overt confidence in this performance than with his Woodrow Wilson in *Backstairs at the White House*.

This was perhaps because of Vaughn's previous experience of playing Roosevelt on stage and in the television film record of his stage performance, but also because Wilson was portrayed as a man plagued with doubts. In an expressive moment in *Backstairs at the White House*, a frowning Vaughn asks himself with his usual clarity of enunciation: "What's a schoolteacher like me . . . (pause) . . . doing with a war?" He exhales after a moment of silence and turns his head away in an effective portrayal of sadness. Vaughn's most telling opportunity for character acting occurs in a scene shortly before Wilson's collapse which director Michael O'Herlihy chose to shoot in the reflection of a mirror, as Wilson talks to his own image, a little like the mirror scene in *To Trap a Spy*. It features the strongest display of emotion in what is otherwise a rather bloodless piece of writing, as Wilson wishes he had been an actor so he could "sleep the sleep of the innocent" and suddenly erupts: "What *hypocrites* we are. I have a dinner for my enemies . . ." (he says "enemies" with exactly the same intonation as Lee in *The Magnificent Seven*) . . . "and they *come* and eat my food! Republican Senators!" Vaughn turns his head and frowns deeply in great surprise as he emphasises the words "and they *come*".

John Hackett, in fact, accords particular importance to Vaughn's appearance as the young Teddy Roosevelt, the first of his Presidential impersonations. This arose in *The Dude*, an episode of Michael Ansara's Western series *Law of the Plainsman*, in which young Roosevelt, the 'dude' of the title, set out to recover a ring stolen from him by a gang of thugs. This was broadcast by NBC the night following Vaughn's appearance as a cowboy killer in the series *Wichita Town*, such was the frequency of his appearances on television as a young actor. "I was the designated hitter for heavies in television, on Westerns particularly", Vaughn commented to me. *The Dude* was rather different, as John Hackett has told me: "This kind of wonderful, jaunty, odd duck character came out. It was unusual for him to get cast in that kind of thing. And he's always done well in those things. When he gets the chance, there's a range in him." Hackett regrets that Vaughn's roles have, with such great exceptions as Napoleon Solo, been mainly cold: "It is unfortunate because there's a playfulness within him which isn't utilised in any of this. I've seen that in some of his stage work. He has a kind of far-out character that's he's played on the stage that he just doesn't get a chance to do."

These acclaimed performances, being essentially re-creations rather than original creations, even allowing for the actor's individual interpretation of the man, are of varying degrees of excellence and in some cases such as *Backstairs at the White House* can show rather unexpected angles of Vaughn's persona such as irony and humour. They are best judged, however, for their level of success in impersonation rather than as enlargements of presentation of the homo Vaughnianus. Much the same can be said for Vaughn's costume roles such as in the historical mini-series *The Blue and the Gray* and the cameo of General Woodbridge in *The Delta Force*. These are such purely character parts that they largely stand outside the considerations of Robert Vaughn's screen creativity dealt with in this book. This is not, of course, to deny the effectiveness of these character performances in the given dramatic context. For example, in the opening scenes of *Hotel — Charades,* Vaughn had the opportunity, in the wake of Dustin Hoffman's success at female impersonation in *Tootsie,* to pass himself off as a woman and, although immediately recognisable to anyone who is familiar with his work, he gave a superbly fussy and convincing enactment of a certain pampered kind of middle-class American woman, contrasting starkly with his reversion to virile cold killer later in the episode.

Of course, the meatier the character role, the closer Vaughn brings it to the concerns of this book, and *The A-Team* offers a surprisingly meaty opportunity in this respect. Whereas Vaughn had been disappointed by the character role of Captain Raymond Rambridge in his first television series *The Lieutenant*, the character role of the retired General Hunt Stockwell in *The A-Team* is, to judge by the first few episodes, a fascinatingly ambiguous creation, combining echoes of the ruthlessness of Ryland in *Black Moon Rising*, the charisma of Chalmers in *Bullitt* (he dresses like Chalmers and moves to his limousine flanked by flunkies like Chalmers) and the slight quirkiness of Webster in *Superman III*. It is interesting to observe the effect that Vaughn's customary hard edge of reality brings to a series not noted for any leanings to realism, even if leavened a little by Vaughn's ironic depicitions of Stockwell's intermittent pomposity. Director Tony Mordente's highly dramatic use of close-ups of sections of Vaughn's face and sinister whispered Vaughnian voice-overs in *Dishpan Man* is an intelligent exploitation of Vaughn's screen strengths.

Conclusion

Our examination of Vaughn's work has shown how his elliptical style of film acting has embraced a number of characteristic motifs. It only remains to consider the question of 'authorship': Vaughn chose to play the role of Dr. Bergen in *The Mind of Mr. Soames*, for example, because he admired its sympathetic nature, yet it seems to be the brooding presence he brought to often non-verbal scenes that establishes loner, loyalty and tragic fate motifs. There are clear possibilities, given the lonely circumstances of Vaughn's childhood bereft of his parents, that these concerns keep emerging from his work because they have a private meaning for him. Charles Eckert has written that the meaning of a myth is "hidden from the narrator who rather compulsively tells and retells versions of the myth. . . If its content were not hidden from the narrators, they would have no reason to obsessively reshape it, retell it, and accord it such significance in their lives."

If a private mythology emerges in Vaughn's work, its heart is dilemma or contradiction (Lee, Fenner, Kreuger), as Levi-Strauss argues is the case with all myth. Do the motifs of Vaughn's screen work indicate the existence of private, perhaps unconscious, obsessions on his part? Vaughn himself does not know, as he has told me that he thinks his understanding of the process of interpretation of a character like Andrew Simms "really isn't in my head at all". Yet all true artistic activity reveals the inner man, and these motifs may well constitute Vaughn's unconscious search for the meaning of his own life: it is interesting to compare with this Kenneth Tynan's view that all artistic activity is a gesture against death, which Vaughn cites in his book *Only Victims*.

It is worth noting that a significant shift of emphasis in the content of Vaughn's work alerts us to a corresponding re-adaptation of style. The increasing substitution for a motif of his youth such as qualifying test of manhood by one of his maturity from that area of his work we have designated 'the wages of sin' is invariably accompanied by a corresponding stylistic substitution. For example, the intuitive approach (techniques such as the soul in the eyes) makes way for a passivity of impersonation (techniques such as the stiff upper eyebrow). Also, Vaughn may well be using certain content for the sake of style, i.e. choosing a certain type of role because it is amenable to a stylistic exploration (e.g. the furtive glance) that will bring the performance within the sphere of one of his interests such as the politics of misery, which may have a particular meaning from him: he has, for instance, claimed that he can get "very dour".

Often Vaughn's viewers are unsure whether his screen presence is one of charm or charisma: hence the ambiguity of such characters as Chalmers. Only in the rare cases where Vaughn is prevented from establishing a dualism of some kind does his work lack its customary dynamism (e.g. *The Karate Killers, The Woman Hunter*). Vaughn does not do this on an intentional or even conscious level, but that makes him no less an auteur of the finished product. The conclusive proof of Vaughn's auteur status comes from his directors, who time and again have stressed to me the fact that Vaughn uses his intellect in order, as Douglas Benton once observed, virtually to create the character for the audience. So Walter Doniger muses: "The flaw — and yet the asset — in Vaughn is his super intellectuality and its insight on his own and the world's corruption. A variant on Bogart who handled the problem with passion instead of intellect."

For Vincent Sherman, you can detect Vaughn's intellectual creativity even in his screen presence alone: "He has a strong screen presence, authority and you feel there is a brain behind what he does." Similarly, John Sturges isolates as Vaughn's distinctive gifts as a performer: "His perception and intelligence in developing the character from a concept to a performance." For Jerry Thorpe, Vaughn's performing reflects his own "internalised personality". Acting colleague Jonathan Haze agrees with Jerry Thorpe's remarks but comments that, while Roger Corman gave Vaughn no acting guidance during *Teenage Caveman*, Vaughn's internalisation "manifested itself much more into thought than into feeling", thus creating this 'intellectual caveboy' as Ed Naha has described it. Roger Corman himself has told me: "I initially spotted Vaughn performing in the play *End As a Man* and would agree with your statement that characterises Vaughn as a cerebral performer, yet not entirely. I believe that there is a basic subtextual emotional drive that Bob draws upon for his performances."

The consensus appears to be that Vaughn's intellectual interpretation of empirical reality is what forms the heart of every character performance he gives, whether Solo or Hamlet: his execution of that character's emotions is directly linked to his own intellectual insights on reality and the character's likely interaction therewith. Walter Doniger has again put this most succinctly: "He is intelligent and can use that intelligence to comprehend and then connect the intellectual insight or understanding with his emotions."

The highly sociable Vaughnian man of action is well described as an extrovert. The politician of misery, however, accords with H.J. Eysenck's description of the introverted man, who "prefers to seek salvation in his own thinking". Robert Vaughn's wholly rounded characters such as Harry Rule draw equally upon introspection and action for the satisfaction of their intellectual and emotional needs. The homo Vaughnianus does not prefer action to thought or vice versa: it would never occur to him to employ those terms of reference. His life encompasses both spheres without apparent conflict, satisfying emotionalism and intellectualism without apparent difficulty.

Of course it is only an illusion, for the homo Vaughnianus suffers great stress in trying to break down the inhibitory wall of his intellectualism to allow his emotions free rein. But Vaughn's elliptical acting style has eradicted nearly all vestige of this struggle, save the soul in the eyes, and, unless an actual breakdown occurs as it did with Chet Gwynne, it would seem that emotionalism and intellectualism do not foster antithetical longings. Have we entered the Surrealist realm where pure desire is the prime intellectual motivation? No, but Vaughn has at least pointed out what a free being managing to encompass the best of both worlds would be like. In all his screen characters, only Vaughn's elliptical style conceals the underlying conflict and permits us a glimpse of harmony between the dictates of heart and head, of what a complementary relationship between emotionalism and intellectualism would be like. Since much of the cinematic and social relevance of Vaughn's work lies in this tantalising glimpse, Vaughn's cerebral style has adduced performances of significant content.

The conditions of Vaughn's early life and the workings of objective chance, his dualisms of purpose and of temperament functioning consistently in the face of antithetical longings, the acceptance of work as what he called his "primary driving force": these ensured Vaughn's adoption of means to ends, of emotionalism whether over a screen role or over a political issue to intellectualism. It may well be the contradiction of Vaughn's own life, the "puzzlement" of which was what his mother meant to him as he once stated, that is conceptualised in the endless dilemmas of his screen characters Lee, Kreuger, Rule, etc. Vaughn polarised the dualistic elements in his own personality into two screen syndromes but, stylistically, moved towards their progressive mediation; hence a screen presence that forever fluctuates.

Vaughn's screen dynamism arises out of that constant fluctuation. It would appear that the actor has virtually interpolated his awareness of contradiction in his own life into the most mythic, and therefore most radically polarised, of arts, the cinema. The mediation between extremes continually attempted by Vaughn, who has made the illuminating observation that "Hitler and Stalin loved children and animals", is of the utmost significance, for the dynamic flux of this mediation has an unprecedented emotional impact upon audiences stunned by its intensity. Quite typical is critic Philip Jenkinson finding Lee the greatest movie depiction of cowardice: "to my mind the best movie coward was Robert Vaughn in *The Magnificent Seven*" (London's *Radio Times* 19-25th June 1976).

It may be possible to encapsulate the importance of Vaughn's acting thus: even if the mediation between the polar syndromes is never fully achieved nor the contradiction of his life ever resolved, yet the mediation itself is a metaphor for the possibility of reconciliation between emotionalism and intellectualism in our daily conduct, if only in the stylistic consistency of Vaughn's intransigent attempt to reconcile antithetical longings through the application of logic.

In this sense, Robert Vaughn's screen career offers an incomparable blueprint for finesse.

Appendix

A Speech Delivered by Robert Vaughn
at Harvard University, Cambridge, Massachusetts,
on Friday 5 May 1967.

Published by kind permission of Robert Vaughn.

First let me express my gratitude to the Dunster House Forum and Messrs. Gar Alperovitz, Cort Casady and Sandy Levinson for their gracious invitation to address the Student Body of this most distinguished of American Universities.

When I was invited to speak at Harvard I was informed of the renewed anti-war activity which has grown up in this community in recent months. Let me say that the form in which the dissent is being expressed . . . the concept of a "Vietnam Summer 1967" involving groups of volunteers, professional people, housewives and students in opposition to the Vietnam War . . . is one I wholeheartedly endorse.

It is traditional protocol in speaking engagements such as this to take a few minutes to warm up your audience with a humorous anecdote or two. It serves as a lead-in and is not an unnatural procedure, but the subject matter that brings me here today is of such a stark nature that it seems to render that whimsical approach meaningless.

I'm here today to talk about the war. A war which is directly involving almost a half-million of our men. As these inadequate words are being spoken, people are dying. Dying for something that they believe in, or think that they believe in, or wished that they were able to believe in.

Anyone who has the ability objectively to study this war will find staggering volumes of evidence against it. In this war, more than any one that we have ever been engaged in, we are faced with that perplexing dilemma — what is the truth? We are concerned here, like nations have been so many times in past history, with what are the legitimate and illegitimate exercises of power. And we are confronted with the unavoidable question as to whether or not the compromise and destruction that are necessary to win this contest are proportionate to the good which may be achieved.

It is strange to be thousands of miles away from the scene of this struggle trying to understand it. It is difficult, being so far removed, to go beyond academic argument and experience empathy. We lucky civilians here in America know nothing of the reality of war. We know nothing of the sight and stench of carnage. Ask the sane men who have experienced modern war what it is like, and you'll see a disquieting look in their eyes.

Words are small substitute for experience. Perhaps Thomas Carlyle came close when he said, "Under the sky is no uglier spectacle than two men with clenched teeth, and hellfire eyes, hacking one another's flesh, converting precious living bodies, and priceless living souls, into meaningless masses of putrescence."

War is the failure of logic and the last desperate resource of passion. War has long been an unavoidable expression of the human condition. Yet, even more unfortunately, opposing groups of combatants have never been able to perform their respective hostilities without also involving and subsequently murdering a large group of innocent bystanders who, out of indifference or enlightenment, have not cared to engage themselves in that mass hysteria of barbarism. If war cannot be considered appalling for any other reason, this corruption and slaughter of the innocents has always been grounds enough.

If certain men choose to exercise their right to die violently in their youth, for whatever reason, valid or invalid, so be it. But should it be at the expense of others who choose to exercise their right to live? The problem for the non-aggressors, those who choose to live, arises when some aggressor government elects to threaten their inherent rights, including their ultimate right to live. It is then and only then that a man does well to fight. If there is ever any justification for war it stems from the intrinsic knowledge that there can be absolutely no other way to defend a righteous cause. Let us look now at the key issues in this Vietnamese war which our government claims to be righteous cause, which, therefore, makes it honourable for us to fight.

The United States government, basing its decisions on certain assumptions, has committed our political and military might to a steadily expanding struggle in Southeast Asia. William Winter, the distinguished journalist from San Francisco, has labelled those decisions "fallacious assumptions". If, indeed, these assumptions that created our involvement are seriously challengeable, or even wrong, then U.S. policy is open to grave questioning. Using William Winter's general categories we will review briefly our Vietnam "assumptions."

First, The Legal Argument: "The United States has a 'commitment' to South Vietnam."

Secretary Rusk said, "We have a very simple commitment to South Vietnam. It derives out of a Southeast Asia treaty, out of the bilateral arrangements that President Eisenhower made with the government of South Vietnam, out of regular authorisations and appropriations of the Congress of last August (1964), out of the most formal declarations of three Presidents of both political parties."

Let us consider first the Southeast Asia treaty which Secretary Rusk speaks of — and which, by the way, Vietnam was never a party to. It was devised by John Foster Dulles in 1954 after the French defeat in Indochina. It was both a military alliance based on the fear of the "domino theory" and a strategic move that would enable us to retain a military foothold in Southeast Asia.

Mr. Dulles invited to Manila the Southeast Asian governments of India, Pakistan, Ceylon, Burma, Thailand, Indonesia and the Philippines. However, India chose to pass up this opportunity to join the American military alliance, as did Ceylon, as did Burma, as did Indonesia. As a point of fact, only the three governments that already had military pacts with the United States and depended on the U.S. for support showed up: Pakistan, Thailand and the Philippines.

Of the several non-Asian SEATO countries, Britain and France have refused involvement on the grounds that there is no Vietnam war commitment possible under the articles of the SEATO Treaty. And there was certainly no provision in that treaty for interfering in someone else's Civil War. And, the Hawks' view to the contrary, it was deemed a Civil War not only by President Kennedy but by the leading American authorities on international law, who collectively prepared a statement based on their investigations which was printed in the New York Times of January 15th, 1967, under the title "U.S. Intervention in Vietnam is Illegal".

Rusk's second point has to do with the appropriations of the Congress of August, 1964, which were passed in response to the Tonkin Gulf episode and, as it has been pointed out, was not a specific authorisation for a large-scale land war. Besides which, it was an act of respect to the President — and in no way a "commitment" by the United States to anybody in Southeast Asia. We might do well to stress that our foreign aid policy has not hitherto included an automatic obligation to war on behalf of those recipient nations to whom we extend our financial aid.

The third point Mr. Rusk refers to is that our commitment to South Vietnam resulted from "The most formal declarations of three Presidents of both political parties." President Eisenhower, the first of the three in question, commenced the alleged "commitment" theory by writing a letter to President Diem on October 23rd of 1954, offering aid to the new government. But, President Eisenhower himself definitely stated that the aid he had offered was only economic! And as late as September the 2nd 1963, less than three months before his death, President Kennedy said, "In the final analysis, it is their war. They are the ones who have to win it or lose it. We can give them equipment, we can send our men out there as advisers, but they have to win it, the people of Vietnam."

It is a curious fact that nowhere in the major speeches, documents, communiques and press conferences bearing on this subject since 1950 can one find the words "commitment", "obligation", or "pledge" used to describe our relation to South Vietnam . . . until the Johnson administration. Yet this administration's now-familiar refrain has been that our whole policy has continued unchanged since 1954.

So we see that the background of the term "commitment" is indeed hazy in the light of historical fact. Eisenhower and Kennedy attempted to avoid the problems we find ourselves in today. Eisenhower, in fact, said that we ought not to become involved in a big land war in Asia. As did General MacArthur, and General Gavin and General Ridgeway.

So the final point on this alleged "commitment" theory is: When we resort to invoking this term, to whom are we relating it? To the Saigon government? We must remind ourselves that the Saigon government, starting with President Diem, has been our own creation. And as Professor Hans Morgenthau points out, "In a sense we have contracted with ourselves, and I do not regard this as a valid foundation for our presence in South Vietnam." President Johnson, to anyone's knowledge, has not brought any further definition to the problem, usually saying simply, as he did in his John Hopkins speech of April 7, 1965, "Why are we in Vietnam? We are there because we have a promise to keep".

Furthermore, when Secretary Rusk appeared before the Senate Foreign

Relations Committee's hearings on Vietnam, and was challenged to define the grounds of our "commitment", he made the following impatient reply, "Now there's no need to parse these commitments in great detail. The fact is we know we have a commitment. The South Vietnamese know we have a commitment. The Communist world knows we have a commitment. The rest of the world knows it. Now this means that the integrity of the American commitment is at the heart of this problem." He was so right about our integrity but contrary to the meaning he intended.

Next, The Political Argument: "We must stop aggression!"

The term "aggression", as usually defined in international agreements, refers to one nation's unprovoked attack upon another. Or, the imposition of one country's rule upon another by open force. In the case of the country of Vietnam there are not two nations at all, but one. As a result of the Geneva Conference of 1954, Vietnam was temporarily separated into two zones, North and South, thus allowing opposing factions to regroup, to prepare for the nationwide free elections that would take place in 1956. When we, the United States, together with the Saigon government under the dictatorship of Diem, prevented these internationally sanctioned elections, the Southern guerillas, representing the will of 80 percent of the population, formed up again in order to resist this latest suppression of their freedom. When we violated the Geneva Accords by sending in military assistance to back Diem and then escalated that assistance, the guerillas turned to their former leader Ho Chi Minh for help. When he sent that help to offset our illegal intrusion, we labelled that action "aggression".

The argument from the "Right"would probably be that Communist influence goes back farther than our noticeable appearance on the scene with Diem; back, in other words, to the Viet Minh. Quite so. But then our influence goes back also. It goes back to our two billion dollar financing of the French in their war against the Vietnamese. Back even to the now seemingly incongruous fact that we supported Ho Chi Minh in his resistance to the Japanese.

Too often, in trying to determine influences, we can follow a receding trail back to a disappearing point, and in so doing the truth becomes bogged down in such a conflicting set of intangibles that reasonable, progressive answers to the problem are made largely impossible. The issue, then, must ultimately refer itself to which country first broke international law and which broke it more often. The International Control Commission, which was set up by the Geneva Conference in order to determine those infractions, states that while both sides committed violations, the United States and South Vietnam committed the greater part of them. Viewed in this light, we are forced to again re-ask the question, "Who, then, is the aggressor?"

Next, The Religious Argument: "We must stop communism!"

I use the word religious advisedly because a certain paranoia about communism has taken form in this country which has acquired the overtones of a holy crusade. Senator Fulbright described the irony in 1964, saying, "It has become one of the 'self-evident truths' of the postwar era that just as the President resides in Washington and the Pope in Rome, the devil resides immutably in Moscow."

It is not necessary to quote the radicals to prove the point. It is not necessary to repeat the illogicality of the Joseph McCarthy inquisition or the muddled thinking of Billy James Hargis, or the irrationality of the Birch Society's Robert Welch. No, there is ample evidence in the attitudes of more conventional national leaders. Lately we have heard General Westmoreland alluding in all seriousness to the war in Vietnam as a latter-day Christian crusade. We note Billy Graham flying his banner in the ranks of the Hawks. We see elected representatives of the people, certain U.S. Senators, Presidential candidates, former Vice Presidents, manifesting the same emotional substitutes to thought. We observe that Cardinal Spellman, deaf to the words of his own Pope, has somehow misplaced the arsenal of God and fervently rattles in its stead the sword of Mars.

Like all the "anti-isms", anti-communism is not a policy but an expedient to conceal the fact that we have no policy. Communism, whatever its spiritual limitations, is not the bastard-child of Satan. It is an ideology, and an ideology cannot be killed with a gun. If we seek to stop communism, war is proving to be the wrong way to go about it. As Professor Howard Zinn put it, ". . . We are protecting Vietnam by killing its people and destroying its land. Who else would want such protection?"

This is proving to be a century of revolution. We have yet to see, in scores of places in this tumultuous world, more and more of these revolutions. A new generation of leaders is emerging who are inspiring their people with the promise of social and economic achievement. They are not to be denied this need to modernise any more than it was denied to us. In our fervour to halt the potential spread of totalitarianism, what incredible precedent are we setting in Vietnam? Is this the way we intend to counter communism? Are we to oppose inevitably emerging popular revolutions when they don't meet with our fancy, and by our opposition totally ignore the will of the people involved? Are we to prevent the spread of communism by sacrificing the principles of Democracy? Oppose them by disseminating lies to our own people; oppose them by clandestine and illegal plotting in order to set up puppet militarist governments; by breaking treaties, by giving no heed to international law, by marching our legions through the countryside of foreign continents, burning homes, laying waste to the land, and indiscriminately killing friend and foe alike in the zealous pursuit of our own ends? Can we possibly imagine that this bloody insanity will prove that the democratic way of life is more fulfilling than communism?

If we think our methods are righteous we are fooling no one but ourselves. Certainly not the rest of the world! And certainly not history!

Next, The Strategic Argument: "We must stop China!"

The assumption here is that China threatens our nation's security by her avowed desire to wage war directly against us, or by indirectly inspiring wars of national liberation around us. The facts as they stand simply do not support the assumption that China is bent upon waging wars against her neighbours.

The Rand Corporation, under contract to the United States Air Force, did an exhaustive research assignment to determine the extent of China's aggressive tendencies. To the probable irritation of the Air Force, they reported that China cannot, the records show, be so accused of aggressive tendencies.

What are the critical issues that have supposedly indicated her international aggressiveness? We usually cite the border disputes with India, Pakistan and Burma. However, these disputes were the direct results of British colonialism. The result of Britain readjusting the territorial demarcation lines of the Chinese borders. Even Chiang Kai-shek openly supported mainland China on these issues. China took back through negotiation or force what had been hers for centuries, and having done so, sought no further gains and stood fast at those points.

Then there is the oft-cited and totally misunderstood case of Tibet, a Chinese province within China that refused, among other things, to give up its practice of slavery. China, after 10 years of patience and prudence, forced Tibet to suspend that unsatisfactory practice and observe national law. Bloodshed was held at a minimum, contrary to popular propaganda.

Or we might cite the Chinese communist influence in Vietnam. However, we should do well to recall that Ho Chi Minh was waging his war of liberation long before China became a communist country. Then we fall back to citing Korea in which an invading army from the North attacked the South. But they were North Koreans, not Chinese. Sanctioned by the United Nations, our forces entered Korea to defend the South. And when we pushed beyond the 38th Parallel and up through North Korea, China warned that if we went as far as the Yalu River she would have to fight, the Yalu being China's electrical lifeline and also her national borderline. MacArthur unfortunately assumed that she was bluffing. When we pushed through the entirety of North Korea and displayed no intention of stopping at the Yalu, she fought as she said she would. When the war was over China withdrew her troops from Korean soil. Fourteen years later, the United States still has 60,000 soldiers there.

The United States and China are currently jockeying in a power play for the purpose of gaining territorial influence in Asia. And, looking at the situation objectively, the conflict has been staggeringly one-sided. For over 20 years we have been the strongest power in Asia. The United States has almost single-handedly prevented China from joining the world community of the United Nations. China has no combat troops stationed outside of her own borders. On the other hand, the United States has thousands upon thousands of soldiers in Korea, in Japan, in Formosa, in the Philippines, in Thailand, in Vietnam. And we give financial support to indigenous armies in all those areas. Our Navy churns at will through the Yellow Sea, through the North China Sea, through the South China Sea, and controls the entire Pacific Ocean. We have nuclear capabilities at dozens of striking points along China's threshold. All of which begs the question of who is threatening whom?

These very brief comments should not be misconstrued as a naive attempt to whitewash Communist China's power ambitions. Rather, simply a reminder that when China looks across her borders at this massive armament that confronts her, when she hears the voices of certain of our statesmen and military shouting, "War with China is inevitable!", we must recognise that she has excellent reasons for paranoia. The situation is narrowing down to which side is going to panic first and attack the other on the grounds of a "preventive war."

Too many of our military leaders and too many of our statesmen have too many times in the past been wrong in their judgements for us to predicate that their future decisions will suddenly be free of errors. If the impending catastrophe is to be avoided, the U.S. has the responsibility of initiating the first steps toward a sane international policy regarding this gigantic Asian country that only one generation ago was our friend and ally.

Next, The Military Argument: "Bombing the North will bring negotiations."

Bombing, as witnessed in Britain, in Germany, in Korea, has proven its ineffectiveness as an inducement to bringing the enemy to his knees. And we are now dropping as much tonnage into Vietnam as we did into Europe at the peak of the Second World War. Despite our efforts to avoid it we are causing extensive casualties among the North Vietnamese civilians. And accidentally destroying churches, hospitals and schools. In the South, it has been estimated that we have wounded a million Vietnamese children and killed a quarter of a million more. And despite this carnage, or maybe because of it, we have driven the enemy further and further away from the possibility of any discussion at the negotiating table.

It is an inescapable fact that the bombing has not only failed its alleged purpose; it is indeed prolonging the war! We must recognise that the bombing has not reduced the enemy's will to fight, has not lowered the morale in the North, has not reduced the flow of supplies South, and most certainly has not advanced the cause of peace.

And lastly, The Idealist Argument: "We are fighting for Freedom."

The question here is whose freedom are we fighting for? Certainly not our own. The Vietcong constitute no threat to our territorial freedom. Neither do the North Vietnamese. Who then? Not the 80% of the South Vietnamese people who have made it amply clear by now that they are not interested in the brand of freedom we have so far offered them. We have consistently failed to give them the one thing that they so ardently desire, restitution of the rights to their own land. Our first puppet Diem saw to that by taking away from them 85% of the land they had fought for and won against the French. The absentee landlords to this day ride out to the villages under the protection of American guns to collect exorbitant rents that keep the peasants in a perpetual state of poverty and submission. Whose freedom, then, are we fighting for? The absentee landlords?

Or maybe it's Air Marshal Ky and his Saigon staff who, with the exception of one man, are Northerners who fought with the French against their own people. Or could it be the South Vietnamese soldiers whose freedom we're fighting for? Could be. They don't seem to be very interested in fighting for it themselves. Every year they've been deserting at a staggering rate: 124,000 last year. And it is estimated that even more will make their exit this year. Or perhaps it's the very pro-American South Vietnamese black marketeers and grafters and procurers and prostitutes whose freedom we are concerned with? But that can't be, because we only recently created them ourselves by our presence there.

Then whose freedom are we fighting for? Perhaps we don't even know anymore. Let us not be naive about human nature, our attitude toward the Vietnamese contains as much opportunism as altruism. Yet there are those who would argue, with ready sophistry, that we are in Vietnam to give the people the right to vote for a freely elected government. However, the citizens who have come to the polls, and we should not forget that they are just some 20% of the population, have found only representatives of the ruling military junta on the ballots. Opposition has not been allowed any voice. Is it our intention then to seduce these people with a brand of liberty we ourselves would most emphatically reject?

Senator Young of Ohio is of the opinion that, "The primary reason for our being in Vietnam today is our proud refusal to admit a mistake in our attempt to make Vietnam a pro-American and an anti-communist state. More than anything else, we are fighting to avoid admitting failure. As Walter Lippmann bluntly put it, 'We are fighting to save face!'"

If that be so, then we must in some way reflect, and by so doing temper our preoccupation with prestige and power and the feeling that a loss of either is intolerable. We talk so fervently of saving face, without realising that face has already been lost. It has been lost irrevocably, step by step, as we have been talking peace while escalating war. Mankind has already observed our actions. Mankind has already recorded its reactions. What is done, is done, and there is no erasure possible. Face has been lost! But a nation, like a man, if inspired, can change. While there is violence in us, there is also creativity.

Change is the only worthy course of action left open to us. Only through change will we be able to initiate a compassionate and lawful conclusion to the hostilities in that small, tortured country we are ravaging. If we so treasure the opinions of mankind, its histories, having recorded our desolations, will also record our progressions.

If there is not a creative change in our attitude toward international relations it will not be due solely to the dangerously aggressive policies of President Johnson and his advisers. The mantle of guilt must also be worn by we the people who, by and large, have no empathy for what's happening in Vietnam or we wouldn't be allowing it to happen. Most of us have little interest in the matter. We're out of touch. Isolated in the most opulent country the world has ever known. We turn away with a shrug and say, "What can I do about it anyway?", or else we belong to that faction of rationalisers driven by an excess of questionable values and psychological infirmities who say, "Well, it's a dirty business but we're stuck with it! So I say let's bomb the hell out of them and get this mess over with!"

And thus we begin to see a brand of fascism parading under the guise of "Americanism." We see men compelled to swagger rather than to think.

There are many roads to barbarism. And surely America, beginning to emulate decadent societies of the past, is in the process of discovering her own slick new state of barbarity.

Truth, as usual, is one of the first casualties. It has been said that we prolong the war by opposing it — a strange logic indeed. These victims of irrationality must learn that one does not free oneself from a quagmire by foolishly plunging more deeply into it.

It has even been stated by the most militant defenders of our policies that dissension is un-American; furthermore, they are insisting, dissension is actually tantamount to treason. Are these zealots asking us to ignore the factors that have brought us to our current chaos? Are they asking us to compromise our morality and obediently contribute to a war we know to be unjust and illegal? Are they asking us to sit idly by while our young soldiers are brainwashed by their paranoid elders and packed off to kill for a mistaken cause? Are they asking us to resign ourselves passively to throwing more of America's young men into foreign graves? If respect for our Constitution, if compassion for our fellow man, if intelligent and informed opposition to the failures of our Southeast Asia policies can be deemed "treason", then the very meaning of the word has gone awry.

The majority of the American people, despite their differences of opinion, would like to see this war brought to an end. The problem is which course of action will best suit that desire. We have four approaches open to us. First: Escalation, which means an even greater increase of our troops, increased bombing North and South, our probable invasion of the North and the almost inevitable likelihood of a major confrontation with China or Russia or both.

The second approach: Reclaiming; this would avoid the dangers of escalating the war in the North, but would still involve a greater increase of our troop strength in order to reclaim all of South Vietnam for the Saigon government. This plan would involve an expansion of our "search and destroy" methods, increased defoliation of the land, extensive relocation of civilians, forced pacification of the countryside, and, after victory, the inevitable long-term occupation of what's left of that nation.

The third approach: Holding, or the "enclave theory", which would essentially be a territorial division of the South — a crazy-quilt solution in which *they* get that section, *we* get this, *they* get that city, *we* get this one. This would avoid the hazards of the two previously mentioned approaches, but would do little to solve the larger problem unless it also involved the following. . .

The fourth approach: Negotiations and Withdrawal; this would be a phased dewesternising of the war, not a Dunkirk-like retreat. It would be a planned pull out under international control including whatever is necessary to protect the anti-communist Vietnamese after the cease-fire.

When one dispassionately examines the lengthy pros and cons accompanying each of these four approaches, one discovers that for the benefit of world peace and international order we must discard the first three approaches and begin to lay the groundwork necessary for accomplishing the fourth choice: negotiations and withdrawal.

If we really want negotiations, the ways and means are still available. As Senator Robert F. Kennedy said in a speech on the Senate Floor on March 2nd of this year, "I propose that we test the sincerity of the statements of Premiere Kosygin and others asserting that if the bombardment of the North is halted, negotiations would begin".

If we sincerely seek peaceful solutions for Vietnam, I believe we will find inestimable support from not only Premiere Kosygin, but Secretary General U. Thant, Pope Paul VI, President de Gaulle and a vast host of world leaders and interested nations.

Without further delay we must take the following specific steps:

1. Unconditional termination of bombings in North Vietnam.
2. De-escalation of military operations in South Vietnam starting with the cessation of offensive operations.
3. Recognition of the National Liberation Front as possessing belligerent status, and hence negotiating status, equal to that of the Saigon regime.
4. We also must initiate the reconvening of the Geneva Conference, preferably in some Asiatic city, with our commitment to negotiate on the basis of the 1954 Geneva Accords, including the withdrawal of all foreign military forces and the elimination of all foreign bases in South and North Vietnam, within a specified period of time, and the re-unification of the entire country through free elections.

The war can be ended when we as a country will it to be ended. It is not beyond control.

If this nation still has a choice about its destiny, it hinges on the element of time and the point of no return. Have we not yet learned by experience? Have not the governments involved displayed enough prejudicial blindness, enough inane pride, enough intellectual rigidity? With the threat of the Third World War in the balance how much further can we escalate this war under the delusion that we are promoting peace? Have there not been enough lies to make us recognise the need for truth? Have not yet enough men died, enough women been slaughtered, enough babies burned?

When are we going to find the courage to rediscover our honour?

When, in the name of justice, are we going to wake up!

Screen Credits

THE MAN FROM U.N.C.L.E.

The Vulcan Affair (Don Medford)
The Iowa Scuba Affair (Richard Donner)
The Quadripartite Affair (Richard Donner)
The Shark Affair (Marc Daniels)
The Deadly Games Affair (Alvin Ganzer)
The Green Opal Affair (John Peyser)
The Giuoco Piano Affair (Richard Donner)
The Double Affair (John Newland)
The Project Strigas Affair (Joseph Sargent)
The Finny Foot Affair (Marc Daniels)
The Neptune Affair (Vincent McEveety)
The Dove Affair (John Peyser)
The King Of Knaves Affair (Michael O'Herlihy)
The Terbuf Affair (Richard Donner)
The Deadly Decoy Affair (Alvin Ganzer)
The Fiddlesticks Affair (Theodore J. Flicker)
The Yellow Scarf Affair (Ron Winston)
The Mad, Mad Tea Party Affair (Seymour Robbie)
The Secret Sceptre Affair (Marc Daniels)
The Bow-Wow Affair (Sherman Marks)
The Four Steps Affair (Alvin Ganzer)
The See Paris And Die Affair (Alf Kjellin)
The Brain Killer Affair (James Goldstone)
The Hong Kong Shilling Affair (Alvin Ganzer)
The Never Never Affair (Joseph Sargent)
The Love Affair (Marc Daniels)
The Gazebo In The Maze Affair (Joseph Sargent)
The Girls From Nazarone Affair (Alvin Ganzer)
The Odd Man Affair (Joseph Sargent)
The Alexander The Greater Affair — Part One (Joseph Sargent)
The Alexander The Greater Affair — Part Two (Joseph Sargent)
The Ultimate Computer Affair (Joseph Sargent)
The Foxes And Hounds Affair (Alf Kjellin)
The Discotheque Affair (Tom Gries)
The Re-collectors Affair (Alvin Ganzer)
The Arabian Affair (E. Darrell Hallenbeck)
The Tigers Are Coming Affair (Herschel Daugherty)
The Deadly Toys Affair (John Brahm)
The Cherry Blossom Affair (Joseph Sargent)

The Virtue Affair (Jud Taylor)
The Children's Day Affair (Sherman Marks)
The Vienna-Venice Affair/The Adriatic Express Affair (Seymour Robbie)
The Yukon Affair (Alf Kjellin)
The Very Important Zombie Affair (David Alexander)
The Dippy Blonde Affair (E. Darrell Hallenbeck)
The Deadly Goddess Affair (Seymour Robbie)
The Birds And Bees Affair (Alvin Ganzer)
The Waverly Ring Affair (John Brahm)
The Bridge Of Lions Affair — Part One (E. Darrell Hallenbeck)
The Bridge Of Lions Affair — Part Two (E. Darrell Hallenbeck)
The Foreign Legion Affair (John Brahm)
The Moonglow Affair (Joseph Sargent)
The Nowhere Affair (Michael Ritchie)
The King Of Diamonds Affair (Joseph Sargent)
The Project Deephole Affair (Alex March)
The Round Table Affair (E. Darrell Hallenbeck)
The Bat Cave Affair (Alf Kjellin)
The Minus X Affair (Barry Shear)
The Indian Affairs Affair (Alf Kjellin)
The Her Master's Voice Affair (Barry Shear)
The Sort Of Do-It-Yourself Dreadful Affair (E. Darrell Hallenbeck)
The Galatea Affair (E. Darrell Hallenbeck)
The Super-Colossal Affair (Barry Shear)
The Monks Of St. Thomas Affair (Alex March)
The Pop Art Affair (George Waggner)
The Thor Affair (Sherman Marks)
The Candidate's Wife Affair (George Waggner)
The Come With Me To The Casbah Affair (E. Darrell Hallenbeck)
The Off-Broadway Affair (Sherman Marks)
The Concrete Overcoat Affair — Part One (Joseph Sargent)
The Concrete Overcoat Affair — Part Two (Joseph Sargent)
The Abominable Snowman Affair (Otto Lang)
The My Friend, The Gorilla Affair (Alexander Singer)
The Jingle Bells Affair (John Brahm)
The Flying Saucer Affair (George Waggner)
The Suburbia Affair (Charles Haas)
The Deadly Smorgasbord Affair (Barry Shear)
The Yo-Ho-Ho And A Bottle Of Rum Affair (E. Darrell Hallenbeck)
The Napoleon's Tomb Affair (John Brahm)
The It's All Greek To Me Affair (George Waggner)
The Hula Doll Affair (Eddie Saeta)
The Pieces Of Fate Affair (John Brahm)
The Matterhorn Affair (Bill Finnegan)
The Hot Number Affair (George Waggner)
The When In Roma Affair (George Waggner)

The Apple-A-Day Affair (E. Darrell Hallenbeck)
The Five Daughters Affair — Part One (Barry Shear)
The Five Daughters Affair — Part Two (Barry Shear)
The Cap And Gown Affair (George Waggner)
The Summit-5 Affair (Sutton Roley)
The Test Tube Killer Affair (E. Darrell Hallenbeck)
The 'J' For Judas Affair (Alf Kjellin)
The Prince Of Darkness Affair — Part One (Boris Sagal)
The Prince Of Darkness Affair — Part Two (Boris Sagal)
The Master's Touch Affair (John Brahm)
The Thrush Roulette Affair (Sherman Marks)
The Deadly Quest Affair (Alf Kjellin)
The Fiery Angel Affair (Richard Benedict)
The Survival School Affair (Charles Rondeau)
The Gurnius Affair (Barry Shear)
The Man From Thrush Affair (James Sheldon)
The Maze Affair (John Brahm)
The Deep Six Affair (E. Darrell Hallenbeck)
The Seven Wonders Of The World Affair — Part One (Sutton Roley)
The Seven Wonders Of The World Affair — Part Two (Sutton Roley)

THE PROTECTORS

2000 Ft. To Die (John Hough)
Brother Hood (Don Chaffey)
Disappearing Trick (Jeremy Summers)
Your Witness (Jeremy Summers)
The Quick Brown Fox (Don Chaffey)
The Numbers Game (Don Chaffey)
Triple Cross (John Hough)
A Kind Of Wild Justice (Jeremy Summers)
One And One Makes One (Don Chaffey)
See No Evil (Jeremy Summers)
Balance Of Terror (Don Chaffey)
King Con (Jeremy Summers)
The Big Hit (Roy Ward Baker)
Thinkback (Cyril Frankel)
The First Circle (Don Chaffey)
Chase (Harry Booth)
. . . With A Little Help From My Friends (Jeremy Summers)
For The Rest Of Your Natural . . . (John Hough)
The Bodyguards (Don Chaffey)
Talkdown (Jeremy Summers)
A Case For The Right (Michael Lindsay-Hogg)
A Matter Of Life And Death (Don Chaffey)
It Could Be Practically Anywhere On The Island (Robert Vaughn)
Vocal (Cyril Frankel)
It Was All Over In Leipzig (Don Chaffey)
Ceremony For The Dead (Jeremy Summers)
Sugar And Spice (Charles Crichton)
The Bridge (Jeremy Summers)
Lena (Don Leaver)
Dragon Chase (Charles Crichton)
Route 27 (Don Leaver)
Zeke's Blues (Jeremy Summers)
Goodbye George (Michael Lindsay-Hogg) — *Vaughn appears only in the credit sequences*
Decoy (Michael Lindsay-Hogg)
Implicado (Jeremy Summers)
WAM — Part One (Jeremy Summers)
WAM — Part Two (Jeremy Summers)
Trial (Charles Crichton)

The Tiger And The Goat (Jeremy Summers) — *Vaughn appears only in the credit sequences*
Shadbolt (John Hough)
Burning Bush (Don Leaver)
Quin (Don Leaver)
Blockbuster (Jeremy Summers)
A Pocketful Of Posies (Cyril Frankel)
The Insider (Don Leaver)
Wheels (David Tomblin)
Border Line (Charles Crichton)
Bagman (John Hough)
Fighting Fund (Jeremy Summers)
The Last Frontier (Charles Crichton)
Baubles, Bangles And Beads (Jeremy Summers)
Petard (Cyril Frankel)

EMERALD POINT N.A.S.

– Selected Episodes 1983-84

THE A-TEAM

Dishpan Man (Tony Mordente)
Trial By Fire (Les Sheldon)
Firing Line (Michael O'Herlihy)
Quarterback Sneak (Craig R. Baxley)

TELEVISION GUEST APPEARANCES

MEDIC — Black Friday (Jack Gage)
BIG TOWN — Marine Story (Mark Stevens)
GUNSMOKE — Cooter
MATINEE THEATER — The Declaration (Lamont Johnson)
BIG TOWN — Fake SOS (Mark Stevens)
SCREEN DIRECTORS PLAYHOUSE — The Bitter Waters (John Brahm)
THE WEST POINT STORY — The Operator And The Martinet
THE MILLIONAIRE/IF YOU HAD A MILLION — The Story Of Jay Powers
FATHER KNOWS BEST — Betty Goes Steady
ZANE GREY THEATRE — Courage Is A Gun (John English)
TELEPHONE TIME — The Consort
THE STEVE ALLEN SHOW
ZANE GREY THEATRE — A Gun Is For Killing
TALES OF WELLS FARGO — Billy The Kid
GUNSMOKE — Romeo
PLAYHOUSE 90 — The Troublemakers
CLIMAX!
WALTER WINCHELL FILE (Alvin Ganzer)
DRAGNET — The Big Pack Rat
WAGON TRAIN — The John Wilbot Story
JEFFERSON DRUM — Return
RAWHIDE
ZORRO — Spark Of Revenge (William Witney)
THE RIFLEMAN — The Apprentice Sheriff
BRONCO — Borrowed Glory
PLAYHOUSE 90 — Made In Japan
RIVERBOAT — About Roger Mowbray (Felix E. Feist)
THE LINEUP/SAN FRANCISCO BEAT — Prelude To Violence
ALFRED HITCHCOCK PRESENTS — Dry Run
WICHITA TOWN — Passage To The Enemy
LAW OF THE PLAINSMAN — The Dude
LAW OF THE PLAINSMAN — The Innocent
THE ALFRED HITCHCOCK HOUR (John Brahm)
ALCOA THEATRE — The Last Flight Out
THE REBEL — Noblesse Oblige
MEN INTO SPACE
CHECKMATE — Interrupted Honeymoon (Herschel Daugherty)
LARAMIE — The Dark Trail

THE GARLUND TOUCH/MISTER GARLUND — The Awakening (John Brahm)
THE JUNE ALLYSON THEATRE — Emergency
WAGON TRAIN — The Roger Bigelow Story (Jerry Hopper)
STAGECOACH WEST — Object: Patrimony
THRILLER — The Ordeal Of Dr. Cordell (Laslo Benedek)
MALIBU RUN — The Landslide Adventure
THE ASPHALT JUNGLE — The Scott Machine
FOLLOW THE SUN — A Rage For Justice
TALES OF WELLS FARGO — Treasure Coach
TARGET: THE CORRUPTORS — To Wear A Badge
FOLLOW THE SUN — The Far Edge Of Nowhere
87th PRECINCT — The Heckler
CAIN'S HUNDRED — The Debasers
THE DICK POWELL SHOW — The Boston Terrier (Blake Edwards)
DESILU MYSTERY THEATRE/KRAFT MYSTERY THEATRE — Death Of A Dream (Robert Altman)
BONANZA — The Way Station (Lewis Allen)
ELEVENTH HOUR — The Blues My Baby Gave To Me
G.E. TRUE — Defendant: Clarence Darrow (William Conrad)
EMPIRE/BIG G — No Small Wars
THE VIRGINIAN — If You Have Tears (Richard L. Bare)
THE UNTOUCHABLES — The Charlie Argos Story
77 SUNSET STRIP — Your Fortune For A Penny
THE BOSTON TERRIER — Salem Witch Hunt (Blake Edwards)
ELEVENTH HOUR — The Silence Of Good Men
THE DICK VAN DYKE SHOW — It's A Shame She Married Me
JIMMY DURANTE MEETS THE LIVELY ARTS (Alan Handley)
THE DANNY KAYE SHOW (Bill Foster)
PLEASE DON'T EAT THE DAISIES
THE MERV GRIFFIN SHOW — Recipient of Photoplay Gold Medal Award as Most Popular Actor in America
LATE NIGHT LINE-UP (BBC-2, London) — Interview
THE RED SKELTON SHOW
FIRING LINE — Debate on Vietnam War with William F. Buckley
THE GIRL FROM U.N.C.L.E. — The Mother Muffin Affair (Sherman Marks)
THE EAMONN ANDREWS SHOW (ABC TV, London) — Interview by Eamonn Andrews
ROYAL FILM PERFORMANCE 1973 — Lost Horizon (ITV, London) — Interview by Pete Murray
PARKINSON (BBC-1, London) — Interview by Michael Parkinson
A.M. NEW YORK — Host of live tribute to President Kennedy
$10,000 PYRAMID — Celebrity game show
PORTRAIT — The Man From Independence (Jack Smight)
POLICE WOMAN — Blast (Alvin Ganzer)

POLICE WOMAN — Generation Of Evil (Corey Allen)
THE FEATHER AND FATHER GANG — Murder At F-Stop 11 (Jackie Cooper)
GREATEST HEROES OF THE BIBLE — Daniel In The Lion's Den (James L. Conway)
HAWAII FIVE-O — The Spirit Is Willie
THIS IS YOUR LIFE — Nyree Dawn Porter (Paul Stewart Laing and Terry Yarwood, Thames TV, London) — Filmed tribute by Vaughn
TRAPPER JOHN M.D. — Girl Under Glass
CHANNEL 13 NEWS (John Vogt, KCOP TV, Los Angeles) — Interview
THE LOVE BOAT
GOOD MORNING AMERICA — Interview
HOTEL — Charades (Jerome Courtland)
THE MAKING OF SUPERMAN III (Iain Johnstone) — Documentary
THE HITCHHIKER
MURDER SHE WROTE — Murder Digs Deep (Philip Leacock)
THE MAN FROM U.N.C.L.E. MARATHON (Lisa Dimassimo, Channel 61, WTIC TV, Connecticut) — Host of *U.N.C.L.E.* retrospective

MISCELLANEOUS CREDITS

TELEVISION EPISODES DIRECTED BY VAUGHN:

THE PROTECTORS — It Could Be Practically Anywhere On The Island (Vaughn also appeared)
POLICE WOMAN — The Melting Point Of Ice

DOCUMENTARIES PRODUCED BY VAUGHN:

A NATION WITHIN
THE FASTEST MAN ON EARTH (Tony Maylam)

DOCUMENTARIES NARRATED BY VAUGHN:

KENNEDY'S IRELAND
THE FASTEST MAN ON EARTH (Tony Maylam)

STILLS OF VAUGHN HAVE APPEARED IN:

The cinema trailer for THE SHOOTIST (the line-up of *The Magnificent Seven*)
THANKS FOR THE MEMORY (BBC-2 TV compilation — still from *The Man from U.N.C.L.E. — The Yukon Affair*)
FILM 81 (BBC-1 TV — still from *Battle Beyond the Stars*)
FILM 86 (BBC-1 TV — still from *Black Moon Rising*)
The opening credits of PARKINSON (BBC-1 TV chat show — still of Vaughn from his appearance on the show)

FILM CLIPS OF VAUGHN HAVE APPEARED IN:

CINEMA (Granada TV, England) — *The Spy With My Face*
LIFE GOES TO THE MOVIES (Mel Stuart) — *Bullitt*
FILM 86 (BBC-1 TV) — *Black Moon Rising*

Extracts from soundtracks of *U.N.C.L.E.* cinema features were broadcast on BBC Radio shows MOVIETIME and MONDAY AT THE MOVIES.

The poster of *The Magnificent Seven* has been visible in the background of scenes in movies like POSTMAN'S KNOCK. The poster of *Teenage Caveman* was featured in LIFE GOES TO THE MOVIES. The poster of *Bullitt* was visible in LA BALANCE.

UNREALISED TELEVISION PILOT FILM AS PRODUCER:
THE RED CORSAIR

UNREALISED TELEVISION DOCUMENTARY:
THE HAPPY PURSUIT OF STATUS, OR ROBERT VAUGHN LOOKS AT THE WORLD OF ADULT PLAYTHINGS

UNREALISED TELEVISION INTERVIEW:
SIX FIFTY-FIVE (BBC-2, Pebble Mill) — cancelled interview to promote *Superman III*

UNREALISED CINEMA ROLES

CRY TOUGH (Paul Stanley)
THE SWEET SMELL OF SUCCESS (Alexander Mackendrick)
ALL THE FINE YOUNG CANNIBALS (Michael Anderson)
THREE BITES OF THE APPLE (Alvin Ganzer)
CRY HAVOC (unfilmed)
ANYONE WANT TO PLAY ROADHOUSE? (unfilmed)
MAN IN THE WHEATFIELD (unfilmed)
THE ASSASSINATION OF STALIN (unfilmed)
STRAW DOGS (Sam Peckinpah)
THE BIGGER THE LIE (unfilmed)
THE ARDREY PAPERS (unfilmed)
ROBERT F. KENNEDY: CONSPIRACY AND COVER-UP (unfilmed)
THE SWARM (Irwin Allen)

UNREALISED TELEVISION MOVIES

THE MALTHUSIAN AFFAIR (unfilmed) — a 1977 *Man from U.N.C.L.E.* television movie written by series creator Sam Rolfe

UNREALISED TELEVISION EPISODES

THE LIEUTENANT — Measure Of A Man (unfilmed)
THE LIEUTENANT — All About Jessie (unfilmed)
THE LIEUTENANT — Man Burning (unfilmed)
THE LIEUTENANT — A Light Touch On The Panic Button (unfilmed)
THE LIEUTENANT — A Net To Catch Stars (unfilmed)
THE LIEUTENANT — The Little War Of Corporal Meredith (unfilmed)
THE LIEUTENANT — Marta (unfilmed)
THE LIEUTENANT — Twelve Hours Till Sundown (unfilmed)
THE LIEUTENANT — The Aggressor (unfilmed)

Author's Note

This listing of Robert Vaughn's cinema and television credits is not intended to be regarded as definitive. I have not attempted to date the credits due to certain difficulties in being comprehensive and they are not to be regarded as being in chronological order of either production or exhibition, although there is as near a semblance of order of appearance as has been possible to construct. Undoubtedly under-represented are Vaughn's appearances on television chat shows in the U.S. and abroad, and he has told me of his participation in two television films, the titles of which are unknown, which both predate his appearance in *Medic*! Credits have been drawn from a variety of sources, including the U.S. *TV Guide,* which regrettably does not list the directors of episodic television shows, and my own television watching in the U.S. and England.

Aware of the shortcomings of this listing, I did ask Robert Vaughn if he could amplify or correct it but he confirmed that he had kept no record or listing of his work in those early years and explained: "I probably couldn't do it. I think when you start out, you don't necessarily consider that ultimately you're going to have a body of work that's going to be examined by students. You don't think that at the beginning. I mean, I probably started to be aware of that during *The Man from U.N.C.L.E.*"

I also asked if he could recall who directed many of those early television shows and he did contribute the director's credits on *Medic, Big Town* and *Matinee Theater* but again explained: "It's hard to remember so many directors, knowing my attitude toward many directors at that time — since I thought they were hacks, I wouldn't even bother to know their first name! Most directors, I'd say ninety per cent of the directors I worked with in episodic television in that period, never said a word to actors, other than 'Go faster!' or 'More energy!' They usually had been film editors or writers when they came to directing. They had really no knowledge what acting was all about. Therefore they concentrated on the technical aspect of film."

Vaughn is not alone in finding it difficult to remember who directed what. The directors themselves are hazy about the television history they helped create, which unfortunately adds to the difficulty of research. Walter Doniger directed Vaughn in the cinema film *Unwed Mother* and told me: "We have worked together since in television. Don't remember where since I've done about 600-700 films in television." Alvin Ganzer, who directed some fine episodes of *The Man from U.N.C.L.E.* and the excellent *Police Woman — Blast,* could recall that he first directed Vaughn in an episode of *Walter Winchell File* but, when asked for information about the filming of *Blast,* said: "I really don't remember. Bob has always done a good job for me. It would be a pleasure to direct Bob in a *good* movie . . . instead of the crap they hand you today. You must be quite a fan of Bob Vaughn to remember his performances. I can't say the same about any television show. They are a lot of hard work and unrewarding." (A good example of "the crap they hand you today" would be the woeful David McCallum vehicle *Three Bites of the Apple* directed by Ganzer, an obviously talented filmmaker, in which Vaughn was originally going to make a guest appearance — a plan that was thankfully abandoned.)

There remains, then, an enormous job of research to be done before a fully accurate and comprehensive listing of Robert Vaughn's screen credits can be realised. One problem the researcher faces is the lack of co-operation from production companies to which enquiries are addressed. Another is the supply of inaccurate information. The now-defunct periodical *The Monster Times* categorically stated in its issue dated 30th November 1972 that Vaughn had appeared in the science fiction anthology series *The Outer Limits* (a similar claim regarding *The Twilight Zone* appeared in another periodical) but I can find no evidence of this.

I do have strong suspicions about the validity of at least one entry in the list of Vaughn's television guest appearances and apologise for any errors but, in listing an oeuvre as extensive as Vaughn's, this is almost inevitable. The Publishers would be grateful for any amendments or additions that any of Vaughn's professional colleagues or other Vaughn students, especially those resident in the U.S. who have access to constant re-runs of old television shows, can offer for incorporation in future editions of this book. Please write to Thessaly Press, PO Box 130, London E11 1BP, England.